2025

P9-CCV-309

Appointment at the Ends of the World

APPOINTMENT

Memoirs of a

AT THE ENDS

Wildlife Veterinarian

OF THE WORLD

William B. Karesh, D.V.M.

WARNER BOOKS

A Time Warner Company

Warner Books, Inc., 1271 Avenue of the Americas, New York, NY 10020
Visit our Web site at www. warnerbooks.com

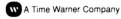 A Time Warner Company

Printed in the United States of America

First Printing: June 1999
10   9   8   7   6   5   4   3   2   1

Library of Congress Cataloging-in-Publication Data

Karesh, William B.
    Appointment at the ends of the world : memoirs of a wildlife veterinarian / William B.
Karesh.
        p.   cm.
    ISBN 0-446-52371-2
    1. Karesh, William B.   2. Wildlife veterinarians—United States—Biography.   I. Title.
SF996.36.K27A3   1999
636.089'092—dc21
    [B]   98-50960
                                                                                         CIP

Dedication

Dedication is the perfect word with which to begin, since it's a theme throughout this book. I don't know how to separate the people I would like to acknowledge from those to whom I would like to dedicate these writings, so I won't. Without the individuals I've written about on the following pages, I would have neither stories nor a rich life. I have to begin by thanking them not only for welcoming me into their lives, but also for their commitment to building a future for our planet.

My mother, Anna, and my sisters, Barbara and Jae, taught me to care, to be creative, and to know few limits; my father taught me how to work hard. My adviser at Clemson University, Sid Gautreau, showed me how to love my work; Bill Conway, the head of the Wildlife Conservation Society, had the vision to create the program I now run and has supported and advised me since its inception; my boss, Bob Cook, has worked tirelessly behind the scenes to keep me up and going and has never avoided a late night phone call when I needed him. For years now a small group of wonderful individuals has generously and graciously provided the financial support necessary for my work to help wildlife, and I have to thank my fellow staff at WCS, the accountants, zookeepers, mechanics, switchboard operators, vets, and everyone else who continually provide me the help I need to accomplish my job.

To transform my activities into the pages of this book, I have to thank Susan Sandler, my editor at Warner Books, for her enthusiasm for this project and for her hard work; my agent, Dorothy

Vincent, for her oversight; Meg Blackstone for her guidance in writing these stories; and Wendy Weisman for helping with all the details, as well as some major concepts.

Finally, I can't thank my closest friends in New York enough: Julie, Diana, Tassie, and Susan, who swathe me in caring between trips and give me the needed emotional support I won't ask for; Stacey, for being amazing; and somewhere out there in Africa, Chloè, who recently reminded me of what a wonderful world we live in.

I had seen a herd of elephant

traveling through dense native forest . . .

pacing along as if they had an

appointment at the end of the world.

Isak Dinesen
Out of Africa

Contents

Part One   *3*
From Blue Jays to Elephants

Part Two   *23*
The Democratic Republic of Congo, aka Zaire
    Deep in the Broken Heart of Africa

Part Three   *101*
Bolivia
    The Center of South America

Part Four   *167*
Cameroon
    The Race Against Entropy

Part Five   *223*
Peru
    Two Sides of the Andes

Part Six   *297*
Borneo
    Hanging Out with Orangutans

Part Seven   *363*
A Quick Trip Around the World

Examining an immobilized African elephant

Part One

From Blue Jays
to Elephants

A quick journey from childhood
in a southern salt marsh
to adulthood in an African swamp.

A Day at Work

I have this recurring image of crawling silently through tall, razor-edged grass in the blistering heat of the African equatorial sun. Loaded with a heavy backpack, I'm holding a rifle in my right hand as I inch forward on the hard, dry ground. Forty yards ahead is a herd of elephants, each animal weighing a few tons or more. A startled, shiny brown seven-foot-long cobra raises up on his forearm-thick body, flares his hood, and looks down at me for a minute before sliding effortlessly through the grass and out of view. The sea of vegetation blurs my vision as I try to figure out how close I am to becoming too close to an elephant. I'm trying to remain focused on my goal—to hit one of the elephants with a tranquilizer dart—rather than reflecting on how I got into this situation or if I'll be able to walk away afterward and see my friends and family again.

The images are not from my dreams; they come from my real world—my job as a wildlife veterinarian. The work takes me to the remotest parts of the planet to encounter rare animals and live with unusual people for most of the year. During the few other months, I live in the Bronx. My office is at the famed Bronx Zoo. To smooth out the highs and lows of this roller-coaster life, I often think that I should buy a motorcycle. Not that I need a motorcycle, or even believe it's a particularly smart idea to have one in New York City. But I think that riding along next to New York taxi drivers would provide some of the excitement and adrenaline rushes to which my job has addicted me. While the addiction is probably real, my joking about the risks could more accurately be described as denial or self-delusion.

You'd think New York City would be exciting and dangerous enough. However, everything is relative: in many ways New York City reminds me of the capital cities of most developing countries—big and crowded, not too clean, and few people who speak English. On the positive side, these qualities definitely help reduce the culture shock when I get back from overseas.

When I'm not in the field, I'm usually in my office at the zoo, headquarters for my employer, the Wildlife Conservation Society (WCS). While I haven't treated any of the animals at the zoo for more than five years, the background I gained handling hundreds of exotic species over the years gave me the broad exposure, flexibility, and hands-on experience essential for the work I do now with wildlife around the world.

Although the job sounds romantic, it's not one that most people would enjoy. It's arduous, uncomfortable, and sometimes dangerous. I don't get to sleep in my own bed nearly as much as I would like to. Most of my patients' homes are remote rain forests or deserts in undeveloped and politically unstable countries around the world. Most of my days are spent exposed to the elements, and many of my nights are spent sleeping on the wet ground in a strange place. There is a lot of risk involved in getting to the locations, living there, working, and leaving. Small planes and boats and long, hot hikes are a normal part of my commute to work.

Some of the animals I handle, like rhinos and buffalo, are quite dangerous. My patients are only one occupational hazard: venomous snakes, deadly tropical diseases like Ebola, and unpredictable humans (including heavily armed soldiers and guerrilla rebels) pose equal threats. In short, I'm grateful for employer-provided health and life insurance. A slightly warped sense of humor also may be essential for survival in my job.

The animals I care for are rare, their habitats are threatened, and extinction for many of the species is an ever-increasing possibility. The work I do is observed carefully by both the wildlife conservation community and government agencies are responsible for the animals. Mistakes with endangered species are not well tolerated, nor should they be. This fact infuses the work with constant performance pressure. Because of the inherent risks, what I do for a living is not fun, at least not while I'm doing it. It is probably enjoyable for those who get to watch, but unfortunately that's not my role.

My professional specialties include determining the health of wildlife populations and the safe handling of wild animals. A foreign government or overseas conservation organization may contact me or WCS and ask for assistance in determining if a wild penguin colony is healthy. Another request for help may require me to dart elephants to fit them with radio collars so park staff can monitor where the animals are spending their time. Private donations to WCS provide the support for this work, unless a government grant is underwriting the cost of the project. A small part of my time has to be devoted to helping in these fund-raising activities, either by speaking to selected groups or by helping to write grant proposals.

THE WILDLIFE CONSERVATION SOCIETY

The Wildlife Conservation Society is one of the best kept secrets in the United States. The organization manages the four zoos and the aquarium in New York City and also supports more than three hundred conservation projects in over fifty countries around the world, more than any other organization. Founded in 1895 as the New York Zoological Society, WCS has been around four times longer than all of the other well-known wildlife conservation organizations. Ironically, they are more widely recognized because they focus their efforts on fund-raising and marketing, referred to as "public education" in their annual reports. Meanwhile WCS has quietly helped to establish more than one hundred parks around the world, including the largest protected areas in the world in Brazil and China.

In the early 1900s the Bronx Zoo sent out the American bison that were used to repopulate the prairies in America's first attempt to save a species from extinction. It supported the first bathysphere construction, and the society's research director at the time, William Beebe, was actually inside the diving bell during its first deepwater explorations of the oceans in the 1930s. The National Geographic Society put some money into the bathysphere research in the final years of the project, publicized it effectively, and reaped the rewards in new subscribers to their magazine. In its behind-the-scenes approach, the New York Zoological Society did not gain a single additional member from the work of Dr. Beebe. His findings were so far ahead of their time and the discoveries he made so incredible that they were not confirmed by other oceanographers until years later. And this scenario has repeated itself for decades with the work my organization does now.

WCS played a key role in establishing the Migratory Bird Treaty Act enacted by the U.S. Congress early in this century, and it was the first group to push for habitat protection in Alaska and the ultimate creation of the vast Arctic National Wildlife Refuge. The first leaders helped to save the California redwoods in the early 1900s, and the "Founders Tree," a massive, towering redwood, was dedicated to them in 1931. The early organizers of WCS were Roosevelts, Grants, Rockefellers, Schiffs, and Carnegies. Some of their grandchildren and great-grandchildren have followed in their footsteps to serve on the board of directors today.

Every conservation organization fills a different niche. WCS's emphasis is on fieldwork and solid scientific research targeted at providing the information necessary to guide conservation planning. That's why I'm in the field most of the time. Projects in the early days often were conducted by dedicated individuals who sacrificed years of their lives in remote parts of the world to enhance our understanding of a species. In more recent times the pressures on wild places have grown more severe and more complicated. Most of our projects are now developed and led by foreign nationals—dedicated people we have found and supported to protect their country's wildlife. The work now demands teams of people from a variety of disciplines such as botany, anthropology, and economics, all working together. This is where I, as a wildlife veterinarian, fit in.

All of our projects focus on wild animals and wild places. We often work in conjunction with indigenous people and local governments looking for ways to protect their futures. The future of wildlife and that of humans does not have to be antithetical. Some people advocate that humans come first and that wildlife should pay its own way to survive. They accuse conservation groups like WCS of caring more about animals than people. I find that ridiculous. We care about wildlife just as we care about people and the quality of life. We may try to protect a vast tract of forest from being destroyed by a lumber concession in a developing country. That same forest is not only home to millions of living organisms, but also the watershed area that provides clean drinking water for hundreds of thousands of people. A few rich and powerful individuals may profit tremendously from logging the area and obtaining the huge construction contract to build a water purification plant to replace the lost clean water, but the true long-term costs to the majority of the people of the country are often ignored in these projects.

I cannot accept the argument that conservation puts animals before people. I'm not sure that distinctions between us are even that relevant. We humans have more in common with other animals than we are often willing to admit, and the differences between us are far fewer than most people think. Many of our needs to survive in the future are similar. To plan for that future, we need to understand as much as we can about species and our interactions with them on this planet we share.

This concept probably led to WCS's decision to develop a medical or health component to its conservation efforts. In 1989 WCS hired me to develop a "Field Veterinary Program"—the first of its kind. The general director, Dr. William Conway, and Dr. Emil Dolensek, who was chief zoo veterinarian at the time, had decided that WCS's vast number of field projects needed the dedicated services of a veterinarian. They wanted someone to provide medical expertise to biologists and wildlife managers working around the world. This novel concept quickly took root within the conservation community.

Now the Field Veterinary Program not only provides health care services to our own projects, but also helps with the conservation efforts of other organizations and government agencies around the world. Most often my services are free because the price is based on the ability to pay. Since we are in the business of conservation, the "bottom line" is our impact, what we call "conservation product," not profit.

Growing Up

Of course, I never realized working with wildlife would be so complicated. From the time I raised my first raccoon, I hoped to grow up and work with wild animals. The one-street neighborhood where I lived was wedged between a lake and the wide saltwater marsh of the Ashley River in Charleston, South Carolina. A fascination with the unknown captured me at an early age, and my childhood days were spent exploring the marsh and the nearby woods. I remember building a "submersible sample collecting vehicle" out of scrap lumber, some broken roller-skate wheels, and plastic test tubes when I was seven years old. It looked remarkably like the *Mars Rover* deployed in 1997 by NASA and had the same problem of getting stuck on rocks. My vehicle, however, had to be pulled along by a rope, and I built it with about $2 worth of materials. I would drag it across the bottom of the lake and pretend to be a scientist obtaining deepwater and sediment samples.

Every spring I brought home orphaned baby blue jays, squirrels, and raccoons to raise and release when they were old enough to take care of themselves. In those days my interest must have been an unusual one. The local newspaper featured me with my first blue jays, Pete and Gypsy, when I was seven years old. My mother, an artist, was exceedingly tolerant of my endeavors and would make sure all my animals were properly fed and cared for every day when I went off on my bicycle to elementary school.

My friends, Pete and Gypsy (photo courtesy of *Charleston Evening Post*)

When they were babies, the animals slept in a laundry basket or cardboard box in my bedroom. As they got a little older they found their own favorite places to sleep. They liked my closet and my bed in particular. Most of them developed mischievous habits: the raccoons opened and climbed through our refrigerator; Pete flew around the house with stolen cigarettes from my father's pack, then landed on the back of the living room sofa, broke the cigarettes into bits, and ate the tobacco.

When the animals were old enough to spend the night outside, I designed and built cages in our backyard that incorporated bushes and trees to simulate their natural habitats. By summertime, the kids were old enough to live on their own. I used the "soft release" approach now used for many wildlife reintroduction programs. My racoons, squirrels, and blue jays were free to leave their cages and pens, but the doors were left open and food was available if they wanted to return. Most stayed close by for a few weeks, then began venturing off for longer periods of time between visits. Eventually most returned to the wilds of the neighborhood, but at least one raccoon returned with a female friend at the onset of the following winters. Ducklings, dogs, and horses filled the intervening days when I didn't have my wild charges.

Our local veterinarian in Charleston, Dr. Horres, was always considerate in helping with my injured and orphaned pets. I admired his way with animals; he handled the baby squirrels so gently. Before examining or treating them, he always explained that he had not been trained in veterinary school to deal with wild animals. I always remembered that: as a result, my childhood dreams to work with wildlife never included becoming a veterinarian.

I was, however, fascinated by Jim Fowler's job on Mutual of Omaha's *Wild Kingdom* television show. I especially liked the episode on which Marlin Perkins says, "Now Jim will jump from the helicopter and catch the twenty-foot-long anaconda." Jim leapt from the hovering chopper into the Venezuelan swamp and disappeared under the churning muddy water a couple of times with the giant snake wrapped around him, finally wrestling the anaconda into submission. I didn't know why he needed to catch the anaconda, but I knew I wanted Jim's job.

Because I was only seven or eight years old at the time, grownups just smiled indulgently whenever I mentioned my career goal. Jobs like that existed only on television, and no one encouraged me to pursue my fantasy. By the time I was in my late teens, family and peer pressure had convinced me to prepare for a "good" job in law or medicine or maybe take over my father's men's clothing store, where I spent my afternoons working from the time I was twelve. The retail trade did teach me three useful skills. The first was how to help people feel good about themselves and make decisions with which they feel comfortable. The second was that quality of service is as important as any material benefits you can offer people. And the third came from a story one of the older salesmen told me.

Old Mr. Taylor was a legendary figure in the local men's clothing business. He commonly hired recent graduates from the nearby College of Charleston to help them get started in life. One day near closing time, Mr. Taylor handed a push broom to one of these graduates and asked him to sweep the sales floor. Aghast, the young man said, "But sir, I'm a college graduate." The elderly gentleman reached for the broom and replied sincerely, "Oh, I'm sorry, let me show you how." His ability to use humor to change someone's behavior was a good lesson. Just as important, I learned that when the time came to get a job done, people trained by the school of life frequently have more to offer than those with brilliant academic credentials.

And how does the men's clothing business fit in with wildlife conservation? As in all veterinary work, the animals are only part of the challenge. Influencing people to make changes that will help the animals is critical if conservationists are going to succeed. Many of my colleagues in veterinary medicine and biology got into their fields because they didn't like working with people. Unfortunately, the reality of helping animals and conserving habitat is as much about working with people as it is about treating animals and protecting wild places. Good science and good medicine by themselves are not enough to effect change. And though they are not usually taught in many academic programs, good social skills with human animals are critical.

Whether I like it or not, no one had a greater influence on me than my father. For years he could not comprehend what I was doing with wild animals. Like many of his generation, he could not see how my concern for wildlife and wild places would give me a comfortable lifestyle or contribute to the good of "normal" people. In his eighties he finally came to understand that I shared his commitment to making the community a better place and recognized that I had defined my community as the planet we all share.

Last year, while I was working with flamingos high in the Andes of Chile, I got a message from my sister Barbara. I had a satellite telephone with me—a gift from a WCS donor who was concerned about my traveling while my father was in the hospital. Over the satellite phone, Barbara told me to get to Charleston as fast as I could. I made it to my father's bedside in a little over twenty-four hours. He had held on patiently to let me know that he was deeply proud of what I was doing in this world. He passed away the next day.

My father was a workaholic (it runs in the family), but the magnitude of his dedication to family, friends, associates, and the Charleston community struck me when I saw the hundreds and hundreds of people who attended his funeral. Everyone there had been somehow touched by his compassion and dedication. I realized that although he'd had little money for most of his life, he was rich in friendships and a sense of purpose. These goals for living were part of my inheritance.

But the road to adulthood was twisted. At age eighteen I knew that my desire to work with animals did not qualify even as an acceptable pipe dream. So I went off to college at the University of South Carolina and majored in business, with the intention of going to law school or running the family business. I switched to engineering, thinking that architecture was the direction for me to go since my artistic mother had given me an added compulsion for creativity, but I didn't like working indoors hunched over a drafting table. By the time I switched majors for the third time in less than two years, and then failed the introductory course in art for elementary education, I was clearly confused, though not very concerned about where I was headed.

When I was twenty and back from college for a weekend, I finally got some good advice. Phyllis Cohen, the mother of one of my best friends, caught us coming home about three o'clock one morning. She sat me down and demanded, "What the hell are you doing?" Clearly she wasn't asking about our staying out late. Her bluntness sobered me up. I admitted that I had no idea. She remembered how happy I was working with animals and wanted to know why I didn't pursue that real interest. I hadn't thought of that type of job since childhood. A light went on.

Coincidentally, two of my college friends, Margaret and Jane, were considering transferring to Clemson University to pursue their own career dreams. It was perfect timing. With a renewed sense of purpose I drove upstate with them to see the university and to meet the faculty in the Department of Zoology.

The department head, Dr. Sid Gautreau, and I hit it off right away. He was a big, enthusiastic Cajun who had used radar to discover that small birds were migrating at night across the Gulf of Mexico by choosing altitudes that provided the strongest tailwinds. Previously, ornithologists believed that birds had to travel along the Mexican coast, stopping to rest every day. Sid is still doing amazing work with bird migrations and has recently been using modern color doppler weather radar to determine their speeds and directions.

Sid told me that he had found a job doing what he loved. I knew then that I had found a mentor. That same summer, Margaret, Jane, and I made the move to Clemson and spent our last years in college getting an education that coincided with our passions. They also cleaned up my life by getting me to quit smoking, take up vegetarianism, hiking, biking, and running, and get serious about yoga. Since then I've really stuck only with the outdoor activities, but we all got on the track to where we wanted to be. With the help of great teachers and a sense of purpose, I managed to get a degree in biology with an emphasis in the study of animal behavior and ecology.

After graduation in 1977, I got a zookeeper job at the National Zoo in Washington, D.C. I still had not considered going to veterinary school; instead I was hoping to work at the zoo while going to graduate school for a Ph.D. in biology or ecology. The zoo provided me with my first exposure (outside of horseback riding) to working with large and dangerous animals. I was trained by a short, skinny keeper named Al who was due for retirement. Or so zoo managers hoped. Al was amazingly good with the animals, but he had no interest at all in rules and policies. Since the National Zoo was a federal institution, Al's attitude did not fit well—he ruffled a lot of feathers.

Al's love was taking care of the elephants. The elephants usually did anything Al asked of them, and he worked with them as if they were huge puppies. They would let him work around their feet or put his hand in their mouths and never tried to hurt him. One afternoon, however, an elephant got out of line and Al casually hit the top of his head with a bottle to get his attention. I'm sure the elephant felt it, but given his massively thick skull, I doubt if the bottle hurt the four-thousand-pound beast. Unfortunately, the bottle broke. A zoo visitor witnessed the incident and filed a complaint. Zoo managers reassigned Al, denying him the chance to ever be close to an elephant again—the main reason he got up every morning and went to work.

When I started a month later, I found myself working with Al in the large hoofstock area. He walked casually into a small pen with a four-hundred-pound scimitar horned oryx that could have gored him with one of his three-foot-long horns. Al slowly and carefully raked out the pen around the animal. Then he turned to me and said, "You do the next one, just don't startle him." Soon Al had me calmly but cautiously going in pens with a variety of animals that could have easily killed me. A mix of naïveté and testosterone poisoning prompted me to believe that Al had shown me most of the tricks of the trade. All was fine until the day a zoo manager spotted me in a wildebeest pen and started screaming at me to get out before I was killed. The yelling made the wildebeest go nuts, and he almost gored me before I managed to escape the little fifteen-foot pen I had been cleaning. I learned that it's much safer to do dangerous things without negative people nearby.

On another afternoon I was raking out a quarter-acre, wooded, sable antelope pen along Connecticut Avenue when the big bull sable decided to charge me. He weighed close to a thousand pounds, stood about seven feet tall, and had ebony four-foot-long horns arching back over his head. Al had told me always to watch out for the male. He warned, "Whatever you do, don't run away."

I grabbed my flimsy leaf rake with two hands and ran straight at the charging bull antelope. He stopped in his tracks, and I went back to raking up the fecal pellets around the feed trough. That afternoon old Al laughed and his eyes sparkled as I told him the story over grilled-cheese sandwiches at the soda fountain across the street from the zoo. Working as a zookeeper, I learned a lot about reading animals and about people.

One day at the zoo I was talking with Dr. John Eisenberg, the head of the research department and a famous mammalian ecologist. John advised me not to waste my time with graduate school because the job market was so poor. He suggested that I go to vet school instead; I could get a Ph.D. later on. With these two degrees I'd have a better chance to get a good job. So I applied to veterinary school and was accepted eight months later at the University of Georgia.

Fifteen years later, with a degree in veterinary medicine and a great job with the Wildlife Conservation Society, I was invited by Dr. Devra Kleiman, John's former wife, to participate on a Smithsonian award selection committee. A well-known animal behaviorist, Devra had been appointed to replace John as head of the zoo's research department when John resigned to take a university position. At lunch Devra asked me why I had gone to vet school; she thought I should have pursued a Ph.D. in ecology or animal behavior. When I told her about my conversation with John, she burst out laughing. She told me that I had just caught him on a cynical day: at that particular time, his graduate students were not finding jobs.

I had invested nine years at three universities and thousands of hours of training because of John's advice. I spent my summers getting practical experience at a variety of government animal disease laboratories and research facilities. I had devoted two more years in a residency program at the San Diego Zoo and Wild Animal Park to acquire experience with hundreds of species of animals, and another five summer solstices honing these skills at the zoo in Seattle. Dumbstruck, I looked across the table at Devra, laughing, and I had to laugh, too. Regardless of the road that brought me here, thirty years after raising Pete and Gypsy, I now had the job of my childhood dreams: caring for endangered wild animals, from the baby macaws of the Amazon to the massive elephants of Central Africa.

There's no shortage of work to be done, either in the office or in the field. A normal day in the office finds me responding to faxes, phone calls, and e-mails requesting information, advice, and assistance from around the world: "Dear Dr. Karesh, could you please send me all the information you have available regarding the use of the new anesthetic alfentanil in wild species?"

I may spend a few hours of the day working out the logistics and applying for permits to conduct a new project, such as a study on the health of gazelles on the steppes of Mongolia or tortoises on the Black Sea coast of Russia. Some of my time must be spent preparing scientific articles and lectures, because the work is meaningless if the results are not shared. I try to make it to professional meetings every year to present findings to colleagues and, even more important, to learn.

Veterinarians must understand every detail of the anatomy, physiology, and behavior of a wide range of animals. We also have to stay constantly abreast of new medical and behavioral findings. To work with wildlife either in a zoo or around the world, a vet has to expand this learning to include hundreds of species. Birds, reptiles, and mammals have similarities and differences, all the way down to the cellular level. Along with knowing the commonalities among them (pigs and humans having similar gastrointestinal systems), we finally must learn the idiosyncrasies and exceptions. Sea lions and elephants do not have lacrimal ducts—the small pore that drains tears from our eyes to our nasal passages. That's why elephants and seals look as though they are weeping.

Most of my time in New York is consumed by paperwork and meetings. On rare occasions I may still help with a medical emergency at the zoo—a late night surgery on a two-thousand-pound walrus, for example. But two-thirds of the year I'm traveling to developing countries to help with conservation projects on wild animals, to train local biologists, veterinarians, and other workers, and to provide advice. The job keeps me busy all the time. The days and nights are long, the pace is fast, and the work is exciting and emotionally rewarding. It's far from comfortable, but as Alfred Kingsley wrote, "We act as though comforts and luxuries are the most important things in life, when all we really need to make us happy is something to be enthusiastic about."

Savanna buffalo

Part Two

The Democratic Republic of Congo, aka Zaire

Deep in the Broken Heart of Africa

In the center of sub-Saharan Africa,
I fly into the forest to help an injured okapi,
stalk buffalo in the grasslands,
and pedal to Uganda.

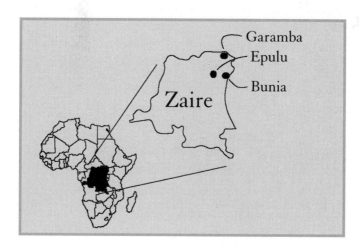

Deep in the Broken
Heart of Africa

In 1995 I was in Nairobi, preparing to head to Garamba National Park in the northeast corner of Zaire (now the Democratic Republic of Congo) to work with buffalo. I got an urgent short-wave radio message from Karl and Rosie Ruf via the Swiss ambassador living in Nairobi. Years ago, while volunteering at the Basel Zoo, Karl, a butcher by training, and his wife, Rosie, a secretary, had fallen in love with okapi and moved to Zaire. They now ran the captive breeding facility in the village of Epulu and had a badly injured okapi that needed my help immediately.

A gentle and rare giraffelike animal, the okapi live deep in the Ituri rain forest of the D.R.C., aka Zaire. Standing seven to eight feet tall, they are less than half the height of giraffe, and their darker, red brown bodies are stockier than those of their distant cousins on the African grasslands. Colonial explorers had found fossils and identified the okapi as an extinct species. In the 1930s, however, okapi were "discovered" by European scientists and announced to the outside world. Of course, the Babuti and Efe Pygmies who have lived in the forest for thousands of years did not realize okapi were extinct, undiscovered, or even rare. They just ate them whenever the opportunity presented itself.

Paradoxically, okapi are simultaneously rare and not so rare. In the Congo basin they are abundant, but they do not exist anywhere else in the wild. The European and American fascination with their unusual beauty has, however, turned them into prized

Young okapi (Courtesy of Dennis DeMello, Wildlife Conservation Society)

collectibles for zoos. The zoo world considers okapi to be among the rarest and most prestigious animals it can possess. Twenty years after the Belgians left Zaire and stopped capturing and exporting okapi to Europe, a private animal dealer tried to restart a capture-and-export operation. Since okapi were worth $250,000 each, he planned to make a good deal of money. The initial attempts failed dismally, and finally a private U.S. foundation took over, which is about when Karl and Rosie came into the picture. Fluency in French and a fascination with okapi led them to become the managers of the captive okapi center. Gradually the goal shifted away from profits. The new program allowed a few okapi to be exported to zoos in exchange for financial support to rebuild the old tourist center and breeding station in Epulu and to supply cash directly to the Zaire Parks and Wildlife Department.

The injured okapi I was on my way to treat was one of the first born in the breeding program. He was slated to be exported as a prime example of the program's success. The early failures in shipping had resulted in a decision not to send out any more wild okapi, only those born and raised in captivity at the station. Karl and Rosie were in a panic, worried this animal might die. Not only was it one of the first born, but for Karl and Rosie it was like their child. They had managed to get some advice on treatment via radio and satellite telephone, but the animal's condition continued to decline. They needed me there yesterday.

They had already radioed Fraser and Kes, another dedicated expatriate couple/field biologist team, who were working in the northeast corner of the country to save the northern white rhino in Garamba National Park, my original destination. Thanks to the "party line," a short-wave radio frequency that everyone there uses, Karl and Rosie knew I was headed for Garamba. Fraser and Kes agreed to postpone my trip to Garamba for a few days. Because there are no commercial flights to northeastern Zaire, they arranged for the Missionary Air Fellowship (MAF) to fly me to a grass airstrip near Epulu. Meanwhile I was sitting in a jumbo jet flying to Africa, completely unaware of events unfolding below.

Miraculously, all of the planning and messaging was achieved over short-wave radio. It takes hours to get a message through using the radio alphabet: "We—w whiskey—e echo, want—w whiskey—a alpha—n . . ." You can go mad sometimes trying to get the simplest message across. I spent the evening and the next morning before dawn in Nairobi reorganizing and repacking my gear for the emergency trip to Epulu. I never go anywhere without my coffee mug and a few other things.

PACKING LIST FOR ZAIRE

Sampling Supplies
Plastic pipettes
Microhematocrit tubes
Microhematocrit clay

Microhematocrit chart
Unopette wbc kits
10-ml serum separator tubes
7-ml heparin royal blue top tubes

3-ml green top tubes
2-ml cryotubes
5-ml cryotubes
Cryotube marking pens
Cryotube rack
Test tube rack
Antioxidant powder (1-g tubes)
Tris/edta buffer (250-ml bottles)
Empty microscope slide boxes
Glassine paper for packing
   slides
Glass microscope slides
   (75/pack)
Pencils or mechanical pencil
Slide fixative (250-ml bottles)
Hemocytometers
Hand tally counter
Alcohol
Squirt bottle for alcohol
3 x 3 gauze
syringes
butterfly catheters
14 g x 5.5″ catheters
18 g x 3″ spinal needles
Syringe needles
Blood collection sets
Microscope
Refractometer
Centrifuge
Liquid nitrogen dewar
Liquid nitrogen dry shipper
Panty hose
Large ice chest
Small ice chest
Metal cans for Plum Island
   samples

Styrofoam shipping
   containers
Exam gloves (large)
Necropsy Kit
8-oz. wide-mouth nalgene
   bottles
Formalin
Fecal formalin kits
2-oz. wide-mouth nalgene
   bottles
K-Y Jelly
Surgical hand towels
White bath towels
Test tube brush
Bleach
Silicon lubricant for syringes

Drugs
Carfentanil
Etorphine
Telazol
Ketamine
Rompun
Acepromazine
Metomidine
Detomidine
Diazepam
Midazolam
Haloperidol
Flumazenil
Naltrexone
Diprenorphine
Narcan
Dopram
Yohimbine
Epinephrine

Atropine

Dexamethasone

50% dextrose

Sterile water

Sterile saline

Sodium bicarb.

2-micron syringe filters

Hyaluronidase

Lidocaine

Heparin

Euthanasia solution

Oxytetracycline

Penicillin intramammary
infusion

Ophthalmic ointment

Eyewash solution

Nolvasan solution

Betadine solution

Betadine scrub brushes

Nexaband

Empty sterile vials

Immobilization/Capture

Soft case for O_2 set-up

Hard case for vaporizer setup

Oxygen tank

Flow valve for O_2 tank

Transfiller valve for O_2 tank

O_2 tubing

Vaporizer

Face masks

Ambu bag

Endotracheal tubes

Laryngoscope set and batteries

Pulse oximeter

Digital thermometer

Stethoscope

Penlights

Ophthalmic lens

Minor surgery pack

Small instrument set

Telinject dart rifle

Telinject pistol

CO_2 adapters for Telinject
pistol

CO_2 cartridges

Foot pump for Telinject

Air couplers for darts

Empty 20-ml syringes

Large paperclips (plungers)

Silicon lubricant

Telinject cleaning kit

WD-40

Telinject darts

Telinject needles

Telinject needle silicon sleeves

Dart protectors

Pliers or Leatherman

CO_2 cap-chur rifle

Powder charged cap-chur rifle

Cap-chur pistol

CO_2 powerlets

Powder charges for rifles

Gun cleaning kit

Cap-chur dart supplies

Lubricant

Pneu-darts

Crossbow

Crossbow bolts

Crossbow string

Crossbow string wax

Dart adapters

Game tracker canister
Game tracker line
Biopsy dart tips
Barbed broaches
#2 flat washers
Sharpening files
Sterile forceps
Cold sterilization box or tray
Pole syringe
12-ml monoject syringes
16 g x 1.5" needles
Medarks anesthesia forms

Animal Handling/Marking
Scales
Hammock
Nets
Leather gloves
Ear tagger and tags
Ear notcher
Superglue
Hemostatic clip appliers and clips
Laminated notch number cards
Tattooer (electric)
Tattooer (manual)
Stocking cap or eye cover
Tape measure
Implantable transponders
Large hemostats

Miscellaneous Items
Silica gel
Dry bags
Ziploc bags
Backpacks
Duffel bags
Gear bags
Gray plastic crates

Field notebooks
Waterproof pens
12-volt to 110-volt inverter
220- to 110-volt converter
220- to 12-volt converter
Electrical plug adapters
Pigtail extension cords
Pigtail socket splitter
Multiple cigarette socket kits
Cigar extension cord
Regular extension cord
Extra cigarette lighter plug
Handheld radios
Radio headsets
Solar panel
Caribiners
35-mm camera
Film and videotape
Videocamera
Video batteries
Battery charger
Tripod
Binoculars
Dictionary
Gift items
Paperwork
Tickets
Money
Passport
Health cert.
Stationery
Envelopes
Address book
Computer
Printer and cable
Diskettes
Business cards
Calendar

Compass
AA batteries
#76 batteries
Epoxy
Superglue
Duct tape

Camping Gear
Flashlights
Batteries
Extra bulbs
Tent
Mosquito net
Hook screws
Mosquito repellent
Sleeping pad
Blanket
Sheet
Pillow
Pillowcase
Hammock
Leatherman
Knife
Butane lighters
Thermos
Coffee filters
Coffee
Coffee mug
Yerba
Bombilla
Water bottle (canteen)

Personal Gear and Supplies
Rain jacket
Work pants
Regular pants
Shorts

Bathing suit
Work vest
Scrub shirts
Long-sleeved shirts
T-shirts
Tank tops
Knit shirts
Sweatshirts
Underwear
Socks
Towels
Hat
Gloves
Boots
Tennis shoes
Walking shoes
Sandals
Soap
Soapbox
Toothbrush
Toothpaste
Dental floss
Shampoo
Condoms
Hairbrush
Razors
Kleenex packs
Watch
Scissors
Sunscreen
Sunglasses (and spare set)
Bandanna or hand towels
Music
Books
Human first-aid kit
Human minor surgery pack

The sun had just risen when I left the little old hotel where I was staying and went to Wilson Field (supposedly the biggest small-plane airport in the world) to check in for the missionary flight to northeastern Zaire. The missionary pilots provide the only air support for medical needs, missionary personnel, and staff of relief agencies or other charitable organizations such as ours. In many remote places in the world, they are the one rapid and reliable link to the outside. I had reserved space for 180 pounds of baggage (normally people are allowed only 40). My luggage weighed in at 220 pounds.

Nonetheless, we got the plane loaded, and after a prayer by Marcos, the pilot, off we went. We always pray at the beginning of a missionary flight; I guess it's the "God is my co-pilot" thing. Different pilots have different prayers. As an ordained minister myself, sometimes I add my own. My clerical career started out somewhat as a joke when friends in Seattle were having difficulty finding someone to conduct their marriage ceremony. Another friend and I became legally ordained (though I ended up being the backup minister). In the process of preparing for the ceremony, we realized how serious and special a privilege being a minister really was. Though the missionary pilots don't know of my ministerial background, they do understand my work and often begin our flight with, "God grant us safe passage today and bless your children who have come to help with all of your wonderful creatures." I'm touched that some of the missionaries recognize we're all on the same team.

In addition to being devout, Marcos is an extremely serious pilot. He's also a very caring person, as are the missionary pilots in general. He's Ethiopian by birth but spent much of his life in Germany and has been flying this part of Africa for years now. I've flown with him several times and appreciate his quiet, calm demeanor.

As always, the flight to Zaire was beautiful. A small plane moves slowly and allows you to take in all the scenery—from the dry grassy plains around Nairobi, to the lush mountains of western Kenya and the shores of Lake Victoria, then up the coast of the lake to stop at Entebbe, Uganda. Flying low over this part of Kenya always leaves me with a particular image seen only from this vantage point. As we cross the grasslands of the national park on the edge of Nairobi, I can see that even the trails beaten down by the animals' hooves mark the surface and change the pattern of things. The earth appears so vast and indestructible on the ground, but the view from the air allows one to see our planet's thin skin. It seems so delicate, so easy to scrape and wound. It's a little chilling, and the image is irreversibly coupled with a sense of responsibility.

After the brief refueling stopover at Entebbe and a quick look at the bullet holes in the airport walls still present from the Israeli hostage rescue in 1976, we took off and headed west again to Lake Albert and into Zaire, finally landing in the border city of Bunia. On the flight we were accompanied by Fraser's family, visiting from South Africa. They were about to witness a completely different Africa from the one they knew so well.

The Customs Game

As soon as we taxied up to the little airport and got the plane open, Alan, Fraser's father, jumped out to videotape his new fiancé, Elaine. Suddenly he was surrounded by screaming Zairoïs, who were quickly joined by two soldiers. Apparently they were upset that he was filming at an international airport. That it's merely a paved airstrip, with a dank, decrepit little building without electricity located at one end of the "runway," did not lower the high security value. If you worked for the Zaire government under President Mobutu, you were lucky to get paid once or twice a year. The salary for civil servants was about $5 a month. The key to surviving was for you and your family to exploit officialdom to collect as much money or as many items of value as possible. Of course, a percentage of the take always had to be shared with your seniors and whoever put you in the post. The men knew the "game," and were touting security as a perfect reason to confiscate the camera.

Twelve men, of whom only three or four actually worked at the airport, went off with the videocamera, Alan, and Lary, one of the MAF pilots stationed in Zaire. The rest of us unloaded our baggage and dealt with immigrations. The airport officials had raised the entry fee to $10 U.S. It had been $5 the year before. No receipt, of course, and nothing posted anywhere in the airport indicating the fees, which were whatever the Zairoïs thought they could get at the moment. The routine was the same every year: about six men passed around the passports, looking at the stamps and talking. Then the one with the most tattered clothing disappeared with the passports for twenty minutes. I have no idea where he goes, but every year I wondered whether he was coming back.

For distraction, the health official, who looked as if he were about to die of a chronic disease, checked everyone's health and vaccination certificates to ensure that none of us were carrying a deadly illness into Zaire, home of the Ebola virus. One year he fined me $10 for using White-out to update my home address on the cover of the certificate.

To clear customs, we had to wait until the "officials" finished searching the departing passengers. They know they can hold up the plane only so long, and it's their last chance either to confiscate nice things they want or to charge some fee for letting people take their personal possessions out of the country. Afterward they have the rest of the afternoon to go through the arriving passengers' belongings. A very clever system. Only four international flights a week land there, and none carries more than ten to sixteen passengers. To make a living, they have to make the most out of the situation.

We began the long process of examining all my luggage. The "authorities" carefully examine one passenger's luggage at a time, so all the guys and their friends get a chance to see what might be confiscated. At least fifteen people gathered around. None of them wanted to miss an opportunity, and none of them trusted that their "colleagues" would share the bounty. I tried to explain what all the items were and why they couldn't have them. "No, that's my hairbrush, you can't have it. No, I have only three shirts, you can't have one. No, those drugs are only for animals, they would be really bad for you." This went on for about thirty minutes. While I was stuck there, Rosie and Karl were waiting for me in Epulu, and the okapi was getting sicker.

Half of these guys had been there for a couple of years and knew me. They also knew I came stocked with gifts for after the "formalities" were over. The newer ones asked lots of questions, trying to figure out whether to grab the gifts I'd brought for this event or go for the cash (duty). The dozens of T-shirts, hats, calendars, pocketknives, and Day-Glo orange sunglasses disappeared in the first fifteen minutes. The following week's arriving passengers would think they'd landed in Miami Beach

The "authorities" took my microscope, computer, dart gun, and videocamera to another room. They wanted me to describe each item for them on a scrap of paper (very official) and assign a dollar value so the items could be "registered." I said that the microscope was worth $250 and the dart gun $150 (10–20 percent of their actual values). They wanted $400 for duty and a onetime fee—next year I could just show the official scrap of paper. I said that it made no sense to me. They said charging a first-time entry fee was a new rule. One more new rule. Another group of men wanted $300 for some other "official" regional fee that I'd never heard of before. We finally settled on $20 for one group and $43 for the other, and everyone seemed happy.

Meanwhile, one man had hurried away with my dart rifle stock. He came back ten minutes later to say that I had to come with him. He'd taken it to the head of immigration, a big fat guy in a shiny silk suit reminiscent of sharkskin. This was a new look at Bunia. Folks told me the upgrade in style was due to the gold and diamonds that were now being taken out of the country through Bunia rather than official channels in the capital. Clearly not everyone was profiting: the other guys at the airport were thin (they can't afford very much food) and wearing slightly ratty clothes (though not as tattered as they used to be, probably because they have become more proficient at their "work"). The guy in the suit wanted me to sit down. Lary, the missionary pilot for the Zaire leg of the trip, went with me because he thought all of this was taking way too long.

The interactions between my interlocutor and me are best portrayed as a game of Ping-Pong. The official kept serving with his best shots, and I kept trying to return the ball. The final amount I would have to pay would be based on how close I kept the score. He wanted me to pay for the gun again. I replied that I had paid twice in customs and did not understand why any further payment should be necessary. He wanted to see the original purchase receipt for the gun; I said it was five years old and I didn't have the purchase slip anymore. He wanted to see my documents from Kenya and the United States authorizing me to carry the gun; I explained that it was gas powered and did not qualify as a weapon. So far the score was still even.

He asked to see my passport again. Nice move. Okay, his serve. He looked through it page by page (it had about sixty stamped pages back then) and finally said, "Your visa is just for visitors, and you are working here." I explained that I assist the Zaïroïs, had come in five times before with that type of visa, and there was a file on me here in his office that he could check. He didn't like my response and asked if I had any official letters about my work. I said that I was there at the direct invitation of the president's delegate general and the letter was also in my file.

Two more heavyset men in shiny suits showed up with an entourage and crowded into the windowless room. Now the immigration official, Lary and I, a thin, sunken-eyed soldier holding an AK-47, and about twelve other men were all squeezed in the small, hot room. Even the open doorway, the only source of light and air, was blocked with bodies. Everyone wanted to see the gun work. I said it wouldn't work without the other parts. They didn't know it had a barrel because the first group never bothered to look inside the PVC pipe I use to protect the rifle barrel during travel. The head of immigration insisted I show him the other parts.

I went out and returned with a carbon dioxide cartridge and the holder for it. I reached out for the gun as if I were going to put it together for him, and he handed it to me. Now that I had the gun, I explained that the parts just screwed on and showing him how it worked would waste the cartridge. He responded by saying that I would have to leave the gun with him and come back tomorrow to get it. We explained that I had to take another flight that day to Epulu to take care of a sick okapi (they all know about the rarity of okapi and rhinos) and I couldn't come back tomorrow.

At that point, he got very agitated and yelled at me. He wanted the gun back. I'd already managed to get my passport and refused to understand that he wanted that also. I handed him the gun because the armed soldier in the room seemed to be getting fidgety with all of the man's yelling. Since they spoke only French and Swahili, I would occasionally say in Spanish, *"No habla francé"* just to remind him that this was not going to be easy to pull off. Lary was serving as my interpreter, allowing me to appear as if I didn't understand the subtle requests for a bribe. The man yelled at me, while Lary translated in his benevolent, missionary way, and I answered in as friendly and calm a tone as possible. He wanted the gun and the two parts to hold until I left the country. He couldn't have cared less about my mission to help with his country's endangered wildlife. He was an excellent thief, skilled in the system in which he was raised. Taking my dart gun would render my trip meaningless. I needed it to conduct all of the work I had described to him. He'd figured out the most valuable bargaining chip—so I acted as though I didn't care. My point.

I told him I'd be happy to sit in his office until tomorrow, or he could keep the gun stock, but not the other pieces. They still didn't know the rifle needed a barrel. Both possibilities upset him. I explained that it was too dangerous to leave the gun assembled and I didn't want him to worry about his staff having an accident with it. Now I'd convinced him he had a worthless piece of equipment I didn't really care about. He shouted at the man who'd given it to him in the first place. The three suits had a heated discussion, then left again. The man who had taken the gun originally slipped me a note that read in English, "Could you please give me twenty dollars to take care of my mother?" He claimed he was intervening on my behalf—if I gave him the money, there would be no problem. I said in French that he should have intervened earlier and then we could have talked money, but now there was a big problem he had helped to create. We went back and forth on that a few times. I let him see I was really pissed, a risky move, and then left the room, ignoring the soldier with his AK-47. The group reassembled outside, where they asked me to write on a piece of paper that I had received the gun back from them. I could now take it, but I would have to leave the country through Bunia and show them the gun.

I think they figured they could get their hands on the gun again when I was leaving the country. Then I'd have to pay, big time, to get the gun back before the plane left without me. By now, so many people were involved in my dilemma that the efforts at extortion were becoming too obvious, even for a place where extortion was par for the course. It was time for the wind-down and the period of cordiality. The game was over—tie score. They wished me the best of luck in my work, and I apologized profusely for not having the proper documents and for wasting so much of their valuable time. All of this negotiating had taken more than three hours. I walked away with my right lumbar muscles in a knot and a severely ill okapi yet to treat.

POSTCARD FROM ZAIRE

The Democratic Republic of Congo, known as Zaire from 1963 to 1997, is one of the richest and poorest countries in Africa. In 1997 the recently deceased President Mobutu's wealth was estimated at $6 billion U.S., while the average per-capita income of a Zairoïs (pronounced zar-wa'h) was $180 U.S., the eighth lowest in the world.

Zaire is from the Kongo word *nzere*, which means "river." The Zaire River is one of the longest rivers in the world, second only to the Amazon in water volume. The D.R.C. is the third largest country in Africa, after Sudan and Algeria, and is about the same size as all of Western Europe. Interestingly, Zaire is seventy-seven times the size of Belgium, the country that colonized it.

In a country built on paradoxes, the capital city should be no different. Kinshasa (long ago called Leopoldville) is huge, hot, muggy, and dangerous. Since the riots that began in 1991, the crime rate has risen steadily and now is one of the highest in all of Africa. The infrastructure is decaying, the chaos is rising, yet Kinshasa is the musical capital of Africa. The Zairoïs bands are great. Congo music has a heavy Latin influence and now tops the Central and West African pop charts. It has also become very influential in the development of the rest of black African music.

A swath of grassland runs across northern Zaire, while the central two-thirds of the country is rain forest. Straddling the equator, the country is tropical. In the eastern rain forests, where I spend much of my time, the dirt roads are almost always muddy and usually impassable. What's considered the most beautiful part of Zaire is also the most inaccessible—just another paradox. What you miss if you can't get here is Virunga National Park, a beautiful lake called Lake Kivu, and the two rarest gorilla subspecies, mountain gorillas and Grauer's lowland gorillas. Garamba National Park is in the northeast corner of the country, bordering on Sudan, and almost equally inaccessible. It's a spectacular grassland wilderness, almost half the size of the country of Rwanda—hard to get to but also worth the trip.

Flying Into the Forest

We loaded everything into Lary's plane and flew from Bunia to a nearby airstrip where Fraser was waiting with the Garamba project's Cessna. He'd made the two-hour flight to help us out with the okapi emergency. It would have been easier if he had been able to fly directly to Bunia, but he won't risk it because he and Kes can never get the "right" paperwork from the capital for the plane even after five years of trying and receiving numerous registration and authorization documents. The officials in Bunia can always find a lucrative inconsistency in his paperwork.

We split up my baggage, repacking the things I needed for Epulu and leaving the rest for him to take to Garamba later. It was good to see Fraser again. I had missed his smile and his wry sense of humor. Since we are both five-feet-eight and fair (he has strawberry blond hair and mine is blondish brown), locals often take us for brothers—or at least from the same tribe. Living with him and his wife, Kes, every March and April for the previous four years had actually brought us close to being brothers. Like siblings, we developed a greeting ritual that was the same every year. It goes like this:

I show up with a couple of hundred pounds of equipment and supplies for the work. After a quick hug we immediately begin our argument about baggage and weights. The plane will carry only a thousand pounds, including the fuel and passengers. We don't want to waste even a pound of space, and something usually has to be left behind. It always comes down to the few treats we want to have at camp. Do we leave my Starbucks coffee or the bottle of single-malt Scotch? Fraser always wants his childhood favorite, Ultramilk custard from South Africa, but each pint weighs a pound. Of course, if one of us weighed less, we could bring both the custard for him and the coffee for me. We're the same height and roughly the same build, but he never believes that I weigh 160 pounds while he tips in at 175. At this point, a small crowd of Zaïroïs usually has gathered to watch an animated argument, which always ends with me on the cargo scale. And every year I have to gracefully conclude the debate with a public proclamation that his extra weight must be tucked away where we can't see it. Then we can pack the plane and leave.

This time was no different. Once the greeting ritual was completed, we took off in his black-and-white zebra-striped plane and flew west about eighty miles to Mandima, a missionary airstrip near the town of Mambasa. During the flight we left the grasslands of the eastern border of Zaire and Uganda and crossed into the Ituri forest. It was nice to be over the forest again. This piece stretches for hundreds of miles across Zaire and up into the neighboring Central African Republic. Karl Ruf had sent two vehicles from Epulu to meet us at the airstrip. As soon as we landed, we loaded up the trucks, said our good-byes, watched to make sure Fraser took off safely, and then headed down the road.

From the airstrip it's another forty miles to Epulu, about a three-hour drive. The road is the trans-African highway, going from East Africa (Kenya) to the Atlantic Ocean. In Zaire it's less a road than a continuous, rutted mud hole. It hadn't been graded in more than eight months and was impassable in the rains. We were lucky that day. Since the rainy season hadn't begun, the road was fairly dry. Jean Nlamba, who had picked us up and who worked for the okapi breeding project, said it was the best stretch of road anywhere at the time. The quality of the roads in this area, of

Garamba project's Cessna

course, is relative. Deep ravines ran down the middle of the road from the previous rains, and the mud-filled potholes were merely the width of the road, fifteen feet long and three feet deep.

On the positive side, these impossible travel conditions had slowed down the immigration of people into the reserve area over the previous year. The "highway" cut right across the middle of the recently declared 1.25-million-acre okapi reserve, which slowly was being settled by new immigrants who cleared the forest. When the road was better, trucks would come through on the main road with goods from other areas and pick up items of trade to sell farther down the road. Epulu was a small village in the middle of the reserve that had grown to about three thousand people during the previous five years. Because of its placement on the trans-African highway, it had taken on the character of a truck stop. The horrible road condition had also discouraged use of the trade route, so the town had shrunk recently and become fairly deserted.

View of village along trans-African highway

Items that once came to Epulu from the eastern edge of the country were now being trucked south to sell to the international aid organizations. At the time, the United Nations was helping the hundreds of thousands of Rwandan refugees who had fled across the border into eastern Zaire. Canny merchants could charge outrageous prices down there. As a result, staples such as rice and beans often didn't make it to Epulu anymore, and they'd become very expensive.

In addition, no one was bringing cattle up the road from the grasslands anymore. People used to walk the road with cows and slaughter them along the way, selling all the meat in the small towns. Now they could send the cows south and get much more money from the refugee workers and the camps. Because people in Epulu had to depend more and more on eating what they raised, there was less to sell locally. A chicken cost 32,000 Z's ($6—about one month's wage). The unfortunate irony was that the humanitarian aid for the Rwandan refugees was impoverishing the Zairoïs. The resulting resentment probably helped to destabilize this part of Zaire and aided in the Kabila takeover.

Mud and politics aside, the drive was beautiful. About halfway from Mandima to Epulu, you enter the Okapi Reserve: the forest along the road is usually denser here because it has not been cleared so dramatically. We were passing through in March, however, and February and March mark the end of the dry season and are the months when the forest is cut and burned. The forest burns better and the coming rains help the newly planted gardens, or *shambas,* grow. Flying in earlier that day, we'd seen fires burning everywhere in the forests to the east of the reserve.

TWO WAYS TO GARDEN

The immigration of non-Pygmies into previously sparsely inhabited forests has caused dramatic changes. The new immigrants clear away primary forest near any road and plant heavily for commercial production (rather than creating mixed gardens with a wide variety of a few plants of each type). The newcomers' corn and other cash crops tax the soil heavily and leave the normally rich earth depleted after only a few years. Then new areas of forest must be cleared, and the depletion of the soil continues.

Pygmies, on the other hand, have used a different approach to growing food for centuries. Being more comfortable in the forest, they cut gardens a few miles away from a road. They use patches of secondary forest (forest regenerated from previously cut areas) that they have been rotating for centuries. Their mixed gardens of vegetables, coffee, bananas, manioc, and other local plants mature over the years. New plants are added in and around the older ones as they finish their productive stages, and forest trees are allowed to become established again. This traditional system prevents the soil from being depleted rapidly, and over a decade or two of use the area is well on the way to becoming secondary forest, which will be left fallow while an adjacent area is cleared again in this continuing cycle.

As we got deeper into the reserve, we moved away from the heat of the cleared areas to the moist cool of the thick rain forest. Branches and vines arched over the road in a dense canopy, creating what seemed to be a never-ending tunnel of many shades of green. Lining the sides of the tunnel were the thick, wide, glossy leaves of wild ginger plants. Above them hung the branches of young emergent trees. Occasionally, clumps of massive bamboo pushed aside the other vegetation and squeezed up to the edge of the road. In the evening you might see a troop of olive baboons crossing the dirt road after a day spent foraging.

When we got to Epulu, Karl and Rosie had dinner waiting at the station. Even after years in Zaire, they keep to a schedule with Swiss precision. As a part of their work, they had restored the old Belgian colonial buildings built of the smooth stones of the Epulu River on whose banks the station sits. Karl and Rosie chose to live in a large house set back the farthest from the road. They had an electric generator and a freezer, both extremely rare in the region, so they could maintain a good supply of food. Even better, Karl is a great cook.

Since it was already dark when we arrived, I couldn't accurately or safely examine the okapi that evening. I didn't want to scare the animals with lights at night, particularly because a female with her ten-day-old calf was in a pen adjoining that of the injured young male. Tired from the three-day journey and relieved to be finally in Epulu, sleep came quickly after a great dinner.

The Patient

I got up early the next morning to check on the wounded okapi. He was living in a pen about fifty yards behind Karl and Rosie's house. At one year of age he was close to full adult size, standing over seven feet tall and weighing about 450 pounds. He already had the striking markings of the okapi—a burgundy velvet coat and black-and-white rings striping his legs up to his rump. During a big storm a few nights earlier something had re-

Okapi with broken horns at Epulu

ally scared him. Unluckily he'd run straight into the fence at the only place where there was a metal crossbeam and broken off both his horn knobs. Like giraffe, okapi don't have true horns. The males, however, have three-inch fur-covered horn buds. Having been born and raised at the center, he was very calm and used to people, but his injuries were making him nervous. He walked cautiously over to the fence with his giraffelike gait, allowing me to get a close look at him.

The top of his head was swollen where the horn pedicels had been broken. The wounded area was flyblown (infested with maggots). The skin of the okapi is so thick that rather than increasing the size of the original wounds, the maggots were forced to mine under the skin, spreading farther and farther. Because of the infection, the okapi had stopped eating and drinking. He was already losing weight, and his eyes were sunken from dehydration. The swarm of flies circling his head was making him restless and uneasy. He was continually sticking out his tongue and wiping it across his brow and under his ears. He was one sad puppy.

TONGUE COLOR

The foot-long tongues of okapi are black, while those of their grassland cousins, the giraffe, are dark blue.

Within the next day or two this okapi would have sloughed his face off like a mask—literally shedding the damaged skin and muscle—and died from the infection. It was maddening to know I could have treated him the day before instead of dealing with pirates at the Bunia airport who don't have enough to do because only thirty people a week come into this spectacular country. I gave my assessment of the situation to Karl and Rosie. We discussed the various treatment options, such as injectable antibiotics and topical solutions or surgical intervention. They agreed with me that we needed to pursue an aggressive course of action, which meant accepting the risk of general anesthesia.

Okapi, like cows, are ruminants. The first section of their stomach, the rumen, contains about twenty to thirty gallons of fermenting green-leaf puree. When they're awake, the muscles of their esophagus and stomach control the flow of this mixture, and, like cows, they're capable of expelling some into their mouth and chewing their cud. Under anesthesia they lose control of these muscles. If their head goes lower than their stomach, this thick soup will run back up their throat and block the trachea. With their next breath they can inhale it and choke to death. The trick during anesthesia is always to support their head and neck, keeping them above the level of the rumen.

We walked back over to the house to get my equipment. Most of what I needed I had brought with me, but I borrowed a large brace and bit, in case I had to bore holes through his skull to access the sinuses. While I was getting my equipment ready, one of the staff, a Mbuti Pygmy, had gone over to the Harts' *parcelle* (a parcel of land) to retrieve a few male okapi skulls so I could review the exact bone structure. Another expatriate family, the Harts have extensively studied the ecology of wild okapi. They are the people who brought me to Zaire the first time and since have become part of my extended family.

The night before, in an ongoing file I keep on my laptop computer, I had reviewed all the anesthesia records from the other okapi I had immobilized previously. I'd worked both with the station's animals and with free-ranging ones in the forest, helping the

Harts put radio collars on wild okapi for their research. After considering the options, I'd decided to use straight carfentanil, a synthetic opiate several thousand times as potent as morphine. This drug has the advantage of being reversible. An antidote or antagonist drug counteracts the effects of the carfentanil and wakes up the animal. Sometimes vets who work with okapi premedicate them with a mild tranquilizer and then, ten to fifteen minutes later, dart them a second time with a low dose of carfentanil or etorphine (another, slightly less potent synthetic opiate). This is a good approach for minor procedures in a safe, controlled setting. In this situation, however, we had a nervous animal who might run into the fence again during the induction of anesthesia and who had a severe infection that might necessitate extensive debridement (surgical removal of dead or infected tissue). A single high dose of carfentanil—enough to kill about fifty people— would provide a very rapid induction and a deep plane of anesthesia, allowing me to work without the animal feeling any pain.

When everything was ready, we walked quietly over to the pen where the okapi lived. I used a small air pistol and plastic dart to inject him with the anesthetic. He went down in two minutes— perfect. He was anesthetized beautifully but had already dropped his head to the ground. Jean Nlamba, who had a bodybuilder's physique, stood on one side, holding the okapi's seventy-pound head and neck up high to reduce the risk of regurgitation. I did a very quick physical, listened to his lungs and heartbeat with a stethoscope, and took his body temperature. He had a slight fever. Unlike people, most animals have a wide-ranging normal temperature. Normal for ruminants like the okapi is from 100 to 102.5 degrees Fahrenheit.

I went to work on his head. The open areas were packed solid with maggots. There wasn't even room for them to wiggle around.

They reminded me of cigarettes, packed tight with just their little butts sticking up. Layers of maggots were embedded within the connective tissue around the skull at the area of the wound. They had already begun to dissect under the skin along the sides and front of his face from the base of the horn pedicels.

I cleaned out all the maggots I could with my hands, curetted and cut out the necrotic tissue, fragments of bone, and sharp points that were left on the skull from the loss of the horn knobs. If not completely removed, these tiny pieces of bone and dead tissue would provide point sources (nidi) for further infection. The bones of the pedicels had been broken off at the base when the animal had originally run into the crossbeam of the fence. I packed the wounds with ivermectin. This is a drug normally given orally to eliminate parasites and is extremely effective for killing parasite larvae. Since maggots are the larval form of flies, this drug would also effectively kill them. Given orally, the drug would require a day or two to take effect, but putting it directly into the wounds would allow it to make contact with any larvae still present. It would also kill the ones due to hatch from their tiny egg cases later in the day. Last, I placed a concentrated fly wipe on the adjacent areas to discourage flies from laying more eggs in the wound.

I gave him an intramuscular shot of antibiotics and injected the reversal drug for the anesthesia into his jugular vein. He was standing again within a minute or two. By the end of the day he had begun to eat again. I, on the other hand, wasn't very hungry for the rest of the day. Maggots really disgust me.

The Harts of Africa

When I had landed at the airstrip at Mandima, Jean Nlamba had handed me a letter from Terese Hart. She'd heard through the local grapevine that I was arriving and wanted me to come to a party at their home to celebrate the second anniversary of the crocodile attack on their daughters' tutor, Sandi. A strange occasion for a celebration. By a weird coincidence, upon landing I'd just changed into my favorite cut-off T-shirt, the one with a crocodile on the front. I was definitely dressed for the party.

John and Terese Hart are both biologists working for the Wildlife Conservation Society, studying the ecology of the region. They've been living and working with the Pygmies in Epulu for almost two decades. Over the years I've helped them radio-collar okapi in the wild and conduct health studies on duikers, small forest antelopes from which the Zaïroïs derive close to 20 percent of their dietary protein.

The Harts gave up the conveniences of the modern world to adopt a life not unlike that of the local villagers to study okapi, other animals of the rain forest, and the ecosystem in general. Their work had been invaluable, not only in the establishment of the 1.25-million-acre Okapi Forest Reserve, but also in understanding the wildlife and the plants of the rain forest.

The Harts have a beautiful home by the river. The local villagers gave them the *parcelle* to use as long as they wanted. Their simple mud-wall house and half a dozen thatched-roof huts stand on a tree-shaded bluff overlooking a long stretch of the Epulu

Terese and John at a forest elephant rubbing tree

River. A calm eddy of water in a curve of the river under the bluff makes a perfect swimming hole. They've raised their three daughters there and have committed themselves to helping Zaire become a better place, both for its wildlife and its citizens. Not only are they top-notch biologists, over the years they've become dear friends. Their two field camps deep in the forest and the *parcelle* in

Epulu have become part of my concept of home. We even keep apartments in the same complex back in New York, where our schedules overlap occasionally.

After a beautiful sunset on the river and two baths to remove the smell of rotting flesh and the creepy feel of maggots, I left for the Harts'. I stopped by one more time to check on my patient's recovery as I headed across town to their *parcelle* a half mile away from the okapi station, on the other side of the village, where the Epulu River curves and heads north eventually to meet the Congo (Zaire) River.

Since arriving the day before, I had been thinking about Sandi's croc attack two years previously and now the party. Those of us working in remote areas all too often experience life unfolding in such bizarre ways. After the attack, Sandi had been rushed away, first to the missionary clinic in Mambasa, then to Nairobi, and finally to the United States. Months later she told the Harts she wanted to come back to Zaire to see the kids and say her good-byes to Africa in her own way.

My arrival in Epulu coincided with her recent return. That night at the Harts', Sandi entered the house with a cake they had baked over the fire. We didn't sing "Happy Birthday," but when we all gathered around, Sandi blew out the two candles she had lit. She told us she was happy that she had lived another two years, the time was a gift to her, and she was pleased we could all be with her to celebrate. Now the bizarre festivities all made sense. Sandi had found a way to mark the occasion in the most positive light. I was touched and impressed with her strength.

I'd been up at Garamba working with Fraser and Kes when the attack had happened. The Harts had gotten the message to me over the short-wave radio. One of those "Charlie, Romeo, Oprah, Charlie" conversations. At the time, I was scheduled to fly down from Garamba to Epulu for our Africa regional meeting. Every two years WCS staff on each continent meet to share information and make plans. Because of the crocodile attack, I ended up staying with the Harts rather than at the new training center with the rest of our staff. The Harts wanted the company; they put me in the bedroom Sandi had not come back to the night before. It was a traumatic event for the entire family. Sandi had come over as a tutor for the children, and the Harts were crazy about her.

At dusk about six-thirty in the evening, she'd been down at the river, bathing with eight-year-old Bekka, three-year-old Jo Jo, and Ken, an American college student doing volunteer fieldwork for the Harts. Sandi was only waist deep in the water when a croc grabbed her arm and pulled her down. She managed to stand up for a second and shout, "A croc's got my arm!"

"Don't joke about that," Ken replied. He thought she was kidding. Then she went down again, and he realized she was deadly serious. The croc was flipping her over and over in the water. While Ken reached for her and shouted for help, Bekka grabbed little Jo Jo and ran to find someone. When they returned with one of the guards, Ken was holding tightly to Sandi's free arm. The croc was still attached to the other. The guard helped him drag Sandi and the croc to shore—the crocodile thrashing, Sandi's arm crushed between his jaws. The guard tickled the croc under its arms to distract it while Ken pried its mouth open. Sandi's arm was mangled and bloody. Bekka, thinking quickly, provided a T-shirt to wrap the wounded area. Children grow up fast in Zaire.

Ken and the guard got her to Lazo, the Zaroïs nurse in town who had been trained at the missionary hospital. He tied off the bleeders, started an IV drip, and pushed in antibiotics. His skill helped save Sandi's life. Then they drove her to the missionary hospital at Mandima, where several hours later the doctor amputated her arm below the elbow. First thing the next morning, a missionary pilot flew her seven hundred miles to Nairobi. Alan Root, a wildlife documentary-film maker who has worked with the Harts and made several films in Zaire, met her at Wilson Field and took her to a trauma specialist at the Nairobi Hospital whom he had already alerted. All the arrangements had been made over the short-wave radio during the night.

The Harts had been out in the forest with the WCS group at the time of the accident. They got a radio message at seven P.M. and hiked the fourteen miles through the jungle to town in the dark. John drove on to Mandima to see Sandi, while Terry went and got the kids at Karl and Rosie's house in Epulu. Through the entire ordeal Sandi had stayed clearheaded enough to remember to ask Karl to go get the kids and take care of them and to remind him not to forget to feed their baby antelope.

When I arrived the next morning, the family was extremely traumatized. The WCS meeting was under way, but neither John nor Terry could manage all of the sessions. We took turns going to meetings and hanging around the house with the kids. I remember asking Terry if it was okay to swim in the river. I hadn't had a bath in a while, and I really needed one. "Sure, just be careful," she told me. I bathed without swimming, diving into the river to rinse off but getting right back out. Delightful as they were, I knew there would be no more sunset or night swims in Epulu.

Sandi's attacker was only five or six feet long, not one of the huge Nile crocs that hang out around the river bend by the okapi station. A few months later a little boy was killed by one. Some locals subsequently caught and killed two fifteen-foot-long Nile crocodiles, more for vengeance and food than anything else. Humans have a strange, misplaced compulsion to punish the relatives of a wrongdoer. Certainly bathing wouldn't be any safer because two crocodiles were gone.

"Sure, just be careful." Terry's answer and the context in which it was given sum up what it's like to live and work in Zaire.

I spent my last day in Epulu hanging around the okapi station and the Harts' *parcelle*. The okapi was doing well: his behavior and appetite had continued to improve dramatically. That was great to see, and Karl and Rosie were delighted. It always feels good to help an animal, or, in more general terms, I guess, to make a difference. Sometimes I'm amazed that I can spend up to a week going through an unbelievable amount of hassle to spend thirty minutes working on an animal. But that is the reality of this work—rare and endangered species seldom are conveniently located.

I would guess that 5 percent of my time is actually spent with my hands on the animals. Veterinarians in private practice recognize this phenomenon—they call it treating the client, not the patient. As the director of the Atlanta zoo, Dr. Terry Maple, once remarked, "There are very few true animal problems, just people problems." Much of my energy is spent either convincing or helping people to improve conditions and the safety of wildlife, or simply getting in and out of each country. Just because a country is underdeveloped doesn't mean it lacks an intricate bureaucracy.

Much of the impact of my work is indirect. For centuries local people in Epulu did not consider the okapi something special. The fascination of the Belgians during colonial times, the long-term presence of scientists like the Harts, the financial investment in restoring the old station, tourists visiting, and my flying in to help, all have a significant impact on the local community and the surrounding region. In a country with no newspapers, no regional radio, and no mail service, the news and stories are all passed by word of mouth along the roads, as they have been for centuries. Their mode of communication is very effective, however: within a few days most people within a hundred kilometers knew about my work with the okapi, for example. The idea that an animal living only in their area can make a *mzungu* (white person) fly around the world and endure the grilling and badgering by officials registers with them. The attention makes the animals seem special and worth protecting and gives local people something to be proud about.

For my last night in Epulu, Karl and Rosie hosted a party outside by the river at the okapi station. Karl roasted a goat leg and did a beautiful job with it. The Harts came over with manioc leaves stewed in palm oil and banana bread made in the tin oven they use at home. We had a wonderful nice time celebrating the okapi's recovery. A big thunderstorm passed by at very close range, but we didn't get rained out. The wind blew through and cooled things off a bit, and from our place on the wide river we could watch the lightning and hear the rain in the forest not far away. The moon came out around midnight. It was almost full, and the night air was so clear that you could see its craters as if you were looking through a telescope. Finally I felt the muscles in my lower back, tied firmly in a knot since Bunia, start to relax.

Ahh, Garamba

Early the next morning, Jean Nlamba drove me back to the grass airstrip at Mandima to meet Fraser. He flew in a little after noon, and then we hopped over to pick up Alan, his father, back at the missionary airstrip in Nyankunde, where we had left him a few days before. Alan had spent the time visiting the missionary hospital in Nyankunde and said there were tons of AIDS cases. He's a research doctor in South Africa, and the HIV epidemic is his area of interest. The rise in AIDS cases at the hospital in Nyankunde was fairly new. In just a few years AIDS had become the most common disease in the area after malaria. Very sad. Alan estimated that 50 percent of the people between ten and forty years old were HIV-positive. The hospital was also admitting a lot of paraplegic HIV-positive patients, a condition not seen in other places. The high percentage of HIV-positive tests (not necessarily AIDS) may have made the paraplegia look HIV related, or perhaps the fact that patients were immune suppressed allowed another etiologic agent to cause the spinal lesion signs. Research in remote areas of the world continually reveals new diseases as well as new manifestations of old ones. Further work may solve this mystery.

After picking up Alan, we took off to the north, crossing over the forest until it started to fade at its northern edge. The change is gradual, first with rocky hilltops sticking out of the forest. From a distance, the islands of rock look like kopjes (the rocky outcroppings found on the grasslands of east Africa), but as you get closer you see that they're surrounded by thick forest instead of grass savanna. Fraser took us down low over the trees. The pilots call it broccoli hopping—the forest canopy does look like the vegetable from above. Along the small rivers we saw groups of forest elephants and forest buffalo emerging from under the trees to drink and eat the tender vegetation along the banks.

As the terrain flattens out, the little rises become grass covered and the trees are confined to the valleys. From the air, the whole region looks like a beautiful paisley patchwork of forests winding around grassy clearings. This growth pattern has not been well explained, but it's probably caused by a combination of soil types and moisture and maybe some human activity, although no roads go into this area. No documentation exists of explorers or scientists ever working here. There are no villages, but you can see little brown mounds in a lot of the clearings. When you fly really low, you suddenly realize that the little mounds are Pygmy huts. Their small size and domed shape distinguish them from the huts of other African tribal groups. They're built with thin branches curved and lashed together with strips of liana bark and thatched with broad leaves. They actually look like small brown igloos. Since very few had anything planted around them and no old, felled tree trunks littered the clearings, we knew they weren't active communities, just temporary hunting camps. The Pygmies probably just burn the grass, keeping the areas clear over the decades.

As you fly farther north, the clearings get larger and the forested areas change to more typical riverine woods. Then the land gets flat and changes to scrubby mixed woodland stretching as far as you can see in every direction, until you reach the Dunghu River marking the boundary of Garamba National Park. Across the river in the park, pure grasslands reach to the horizon.

The rains had not started yet when I arrived at Garamba that

PYGMIES

Though Pygmy groups such as the *Efe, Bambuti, Batwa,* and *Bayaka* live in the forests across the entire forest belt of Central Africa, they have no common language or tribal affiliations. Most find the term *pygmy,* derived from the Greek unit of distance measuring from the elbow to the first knuckle, to be derogatory and prefer to be called by their specific tribal group. They have always lived in symbiotic relationships with villages or communities of Bantu or non-Pygmy tribal groups who fear the forest. The Pygmies provide forest products such as plants, honey, and game in exchange for salt, soap, and other trade items. Needing only a carved spear, bow and arrow, or hand-woven net, they can easily spend months to years in the jungle, hunting and fishing. Pygmies know all the plants and animals of the dark African forests. Unfortunately, while they are complete masters of their jungle universe, in villages and towns other Africans regard them as second-class citizens at best and servants or slaves at worst. Pygmies have virtually no political voice in any country. Sadly, lack of health care and education coupled with low birth and child survival rates make Pygmies one of the few declining races of people on the African continent.

Mbuti pygmy with his handmade hunting net

March, so everything was still brown. That would all change over the next four weeks. The grass grows over nine feet tall before it blossoms, dies, and dries out. If it burns in the dry season, the fires are incredibly hot and kill almost all the young trees. The elephants and buffalo eat any little seedlings that manage to survive. From a distance the park appears to be a typical dry grassland savanna, although it lies on a vast aquifer, which produces hundreds of spring-fed streams. The streams form shallow valleys and in some places have kept alive a few of the old trees that covered the land before the rain forests receded, five hundred to a thousand years ago.

The park is two thousand square miles—roughly the size of Delaware. When the Belgians established it in the 1930s, an additional three thousand square miles surrounding the park were set aside as *Domaines de Chasse,* or hunting zones. Now these areas fall under the jurisdiction of the park authorities, and no hunting is allowed. This makes the total management area about half the size of the entire country of Rwanda.

Garamba was one of the first parks established in Africa and now is home to the only northern white rhinos (*Ceratotherium simum cottoni*) left in the wild. In the early 1970s over a thousand rhinos lived in the park and another two thousand or so in neighboring Sudan and Uganda. Rampant poaching later in the decade, much of which is thought to have been internally sanctioned, resulted in only eleven animals remaining inside the park in Zaire and possibly a few others scattered in Sudan and Uganda. Garamba received worldwide attention because of this slaughter, and international organizations formed an alliance to rebuild the park's operations. Kes and Fraser Smith went to help with the park restoration project in the early 1980s and have been working and living there ever since. Kes, a small lithe woman with dark brown hair highlighted by the intense sun, had been studying rhinos in East Africa for years and had exchanged her British citizenship for Kenyan. Fraser, born and raised in South Africa and Zimbabwe, had been working with the Natal Parks Board. Kes and Fraser met in South Africa and married later on the shores of the Dunghu River just around the bend from park headquarters in Garamba.

They are another couple who have given up the comforts of civilization, living at least three hundred miles away from the nearest telephone, raising their two children among the local village kids, and dedicating their lives to protecting a special place. I began working at Garamba because Kes and Fraser wanted help in determining whether the small population size of the remaining rhinos was leading to inbreeding or loss of genetic variation. They had heard of the biopsy dart I had developed to study orangutans. It's a modified drug dart that takes a tiny piece of skin for genetic studies, avoiding the necessity to anesthetize and capture the animal. The concept is so simple, no one had thought of it before.

For the Garamba rhinos, the risks of anesthesia and capture outweighed the benefits of knowing the relatedness of individuals. The biopsy dart enabled us to answer such questions without risking the life of an animal. Over the years I came to serve as the veterinary adviser for the park. While I'd like to think that I was offered the position because of my skills, it probably had as much to do with the lack of trained Zairoïs wildlife vets. Moreover, few foreigners were willing to work in or even go to remote areas of Zaire.

In my experience, the risks have been well worth it. I've helped with the care of the elephants that have been domesticated at the park for tourism purposes, have assisted in putting radio transmitters in the horns of some of the rhinos to aid antipoaching patrols, have immobilized wild elephants for radio collaring so their use of the park and surrounding lands could be mapped, and have conducted health evaluations on other species living there.

Fraser made his usual low pass over park head-quarters to announce our arrival, banked tightly along the main curve of the Dunghu River behind their house, and headed for the airstrip. Thirty or so hippos were wallowing in the river as we flew over. We skimmed down the airstrip thirty feet above the grass to chase off any animals that could be hit when we landed. Hitting a medium-size bird could break the plane's windshield, bend a wing, or damage the propeller or engine enough to prevent us from taking off again. Fraser lifted the nose near the end of the strip, made a climbing hairpin turn, and brought the plane back down to earth.

Kes drove over in her old Land Cruiser, Kafaru (Swahili for "rhino"), and helped us unload and tie down the plane. Her little Supercub, called Echo Zulu from its registration number in Kenya (KEZ), was also at the strip. She'd gotten the fabric-covered plane when she'd first started flying in Kenya years ago. Unlike the Cessna, which can squeeze in six people or two people plus some cargo, Echo Zulu seats only two people, is very light, and uses little fuel. It can fly low and slowly without stalling, so it's perfect for doing reconnaissance flights to monitor the animals in the park.

We got everything unloaded from the plane, and I got at least partially settled in at headquarters that afternoon. It was hot in the park: the equatorial sun was intense and the humidity smothering while it built to rain. At that time of year the weather might be miserably hot and muggy for two or three days and then rain, briefly cooling the air just a bit before beginning the cycle again the next day.

Dr. Mbayma, me, and Kes working on an immobilized elephant at Garamba

Dr. Mbayma, a veterinarian in charge of rhino conservation for the park, was not there when I arrived. He had gone to the capital of Zaire, Kinshasa, for a stay of a month or two. Veterinary training in Zaire is similar to that for an animal husbandry degree. Animal husbandry involves feeding, housing, and breeding animals, as opposed to the more technical aspects of delivering medical care to animals and monitoring the health of wildlife populations. Despite his lack of formal training with wildlife, Dr. Mbayma is second in command at the park. Coincidentally he is married to the conservator's daughter.

Muhindu, the conservator, or chief park warden, was also gone. He had driven one of the park trucks to the closest big town to get supplies. We got word on the radio that the truck had broken down about a hundred miles away. This was a major problem because he was bringing back the guards' salaries and the beer. The guards got paid only two or three times a year, and beer was even harder to come by.

Since Muhindu and Mbayma were gone, I didn't have to undergo many formalities, just unpack my equipment and reorganize it to begin work, visit with Kes and Fraser and the kids, and then go see some of the guards. Actually, a few of the guards already had come over to the house to say hello since we had not seen each other in a year, or more relevantly, since the end of the last dry season.

After a nice dinner I headed over to Kes and Fraser's old house to spend the night. When they'd first come to Garamba eight years earlier, they had built a great house on the river about a mile from headquarters. Constructed of locally made brick, red from the laterite soils, and a grass thatch roof, it stood alone on the river in a little grove of trees. The house curved in the middle to fit the river. The wall on the river side was only a meter high—leaving an open gap to the thatched eaves, which provided beautiful views of the river and beyond. The back side had solid walls in some areas and half walls in the kitchen and bedrooms. The openness of the house made it one of the most pleasant places I have ever lived in.

When they built it, Fraser had inserted a fifty-five-gallon drum in the brickwork of the oven and run a water line from the stack of drums they used for water storage. Because the brick oven design held so much heat, hot running water was available almost all the time. I took my first hot shower in a week and enjoyed every minute of it.

Of course, beauty and serenity do not guarantee security. In 1994 the Zaire army took to looting in the neighboring towns, but it seemed they were reluctant to come up to the park. They knew that the park guards were probably better equipped than they were. Apparently every time the Sudanese Army attacked the rebels who lived across the northern boundary of the park, the rebels surrounded and chased them south into Zaire. The last time the Sudanese ran through the park they dropped their weapons so the Zaïroïs army would not attack them when they showed up in nearby towns. The park guards went out and filled two trucks with automatic weapons, ammo, grenade launchers, and machine guns.

Consequently the park armory was packed full. Such an arsenal was unusual in Zaire. Guards in other parks carried ancient rifles whose moist, twenty-year-old ammo made them completely unpredictable. Another unusual situation at Garamba was that Fraser had arranged with President Mobutu's elite force, the Beret Rouge, to come and give special training to the park guards. Knowing all this, the regular Zaïroïs army had yet to wander up the road from town to loot park headquarters.

But since nothing is ever certain, Kes and Fraser took the added precaution of giving up the beautiful house they had built on the river and moving their family to park headquarters. They were now living in one of the old Belgian colonial houses at the guard station. Also on the river, it was old and mildewed, with so many bats living in the roof that the whole place reeked of bat guano. It was not a lovely place, but they had made the right decision to live close to the guards. In 1997, when the Zaïroïs army, famous for its looting, was fleeing from Kabila's advancing rebel troops, French and Belgian mercenaries took over the park and offered protection in addition to their normal wartime "liberation" privileges.

I Yearn for Buffalo

The next day we headed into the park proper to begin work. On previous visits I'd worked with the northern white rhinos, the rarest subspecies of white rhinoceros, which actually are not white at all. Unlike black rhinos, which have a pointed upper lip used for stripping leaves from woody plants, white rhinos have a wide square upper lip used for grazing on grass. The Dutch-influenced Afrikaans of South Africa named the species "wide-lip" rhino. Later it was mistranslated to "white" rhino in English. On this trip, however, I was planning to work on savanna buffalo, the massive animal that the South Africans named Cape buffalo.

With the dedication of the park staff and the help of people like Kes and Fraser, Garamba had become a safe haven for wildlife once again, but the challenges to keep the park running and continue to protect its wildlife inhabitants was constant. Political and economic realities affect the region. Poverty and civil disturbances have resulted in the extinction of any remaining northern white rhinos in neighboring Sudan and Uganda. Protecting this precarious enclave of progress was and still is a formidable task.

If I were developing a human health program for a country, I would need to know what diseases were present. Likewise, to adequately monitor the health of the park's wildlife community, we needed to understand the disease risks. African buffalo are notorious carriers of a large number of diseases, including Foot and Mouth Disease, that can have devastating effects on wildlife as well

INFECTIOUS DISEASES

A healthy immune system produces antibodies to fight off infectious viruses and bacteria. We can test for the presence of these protective proteins in a blood sample to determine an animal's history of infection. The high prevalence of disease exposure in healthy-appearing buffalo at Garamba reflects their hardiness and also indicates the diseases that may affect other species sharing the park.

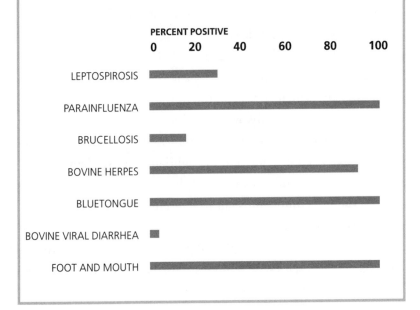

as on domestic animals. Because Garamba forms the international boundary between Zaire and Sudan, it is a potential entry point for many diseases that can threaten the equilibrium that has been achieved in the park. Periodic health examinations of antelopes, African buffalo, and elephants provide information vital to protecting all the wildlife in case of any disease crisis.

Beginning our study in Garamba with buffalo would give us a good overall picture of the general status of wildlife health. In veterinary terms, they make a good sentinel species. Their tough nature manifests itself as disease resistance. When buffalo encounter viral and bacterial diseases, they generally suffer little. Their immune systems beat back these pathogens and at the same time provide me with their personal biographies. A blood sample contains the antibodies they produced to fight these disease agents over the years, and laboratory analysis will chart the record of this exposure. The analyses will fill in the gaps that even my close examination of the animal for subtle clues won't reveal. The lab report will give me the history the buffalo can't verbalize.

The downside to this is that I have to obtain a blood sample. Unlike shaggy brown "home on the range" bison, savanna buffalo are huge, black, and really dangerous. Their natural predators are lions and hyenas, and even they are reluctant to attack a big adult. Buffalo have keen hearing and eyesight and an excellent sense of smell. They are continually aware of the situation around them. If they detect something unusual at a distance, they will generally move away. When startled, however, their most effective defense is to use their size, power, and plowlike horns to drive away any potential attacker. That's why buffalo are so dangerous. If you happen upon them suddenly, you will very likely be trampled or gored.

After driving for about two hours, we arrived at a small campsite we use every year in the central part of the park. Most of the afternoon was devoted to setting up camp and preparing equipment. The evening was spent around the campfire, discussing plans and recent events and catching up on everybody's personal life. I usually bring recent issues of *Time,* the *Economist, Interview,* and *Cosmo.* These always provide a wealth of topics for late night discussions.

Early the next morning we set off in search of buffalo. By eight o'clock we had found a good-size herd. Kes stayed back with three of the guards. We didn't want to risk alerting the buffalo to our presence by having too many people close by. One of the park guards, Gingingayo, and I hiked away from the vehicle to sneak up on them. Gingingayo knows animals well and, unlike most of the guys, isn't scared of them. He and I had already been partners in these endeavors for several years. He's slightly graying at the temples, lean, and muscular and has a gentle face. Gingingayo had been a schoolteacher for many years before joining the guards.

Unlike many of the guards, Gingingayo takes very good care of his rifle, breaking it down and cleaning it every night, so I feel comfortable that it will work if we need it—at least most of the time. More important, he's very quiet and coolheaded, so I don't have to worry about him freaking out and firing a whole clip of ammunition at an animal while I'm standing in front of him. Stalking and darting an animal requires concentration and being mentally prepared for anything—like accidently crawling up to a cobra or lion in the long grass. The work is dangerous enough without being distracted by the threat of friendly fire.

As we got close, the main herd moved up the other side of the valley, but a small group of animals stayed down in the bottom. We crawled up to them through the grass, trying not to be seen or heard, taking about thirty minutes to advance fifty yards. Before we could get close enough for me to shoot, they either saw or heard us and moved off. We followed two of them for another half hour, but they ran before I could get into a good enough position to take a shot. On level ground the dart gun is accurate for forty or maybe fifty yards. Shooting even slightly uphill decreases the range. We spotted another two males about a mile away and tried unsuccessfully to approach them. Now it was ten A.M. and getting hot in the grass under the baking sun with no clouds and little wind for relief.

Gingingayo spotted three more males only another mile away. They were in a great position, standing right next to a good-size mound from an old termite nest (termiterium), which would allow us to sneak up from the other side and shoot over it from a distance of about twenty yards. Unfortunately, when we reached the back of the mound, the occasional breezes shifted direction and blew from behind us and toward them. They caught our scent and thundered off.

It is said that more people are killed in Africa by buffalo than any other animal, usually after someone surprises the buffalo. A woman was killed by one in Kenya just a couple of weeks earlier while waiting for a bus. The animal must have wandered out of the bush and responded to her justified shock by killing her. Would sneaking up on a buffalo in the grass and then jumping up and shooting it with a dart qualify as a surprise? I wondered. More specifically, when does surprise cause them to run away and when does it prompt them to kill you?

Meanwhile, Gingingayo didn't seem too worried. Of course, he might have been under the impression that I knew what I was doing, whereas I was assuming the converse. We hiked back to the original area and saw a group of five females and a huge bull. An hour later we'd managed to sneak up to within thirty yards of the bull. He realized something was wrong and turned to face us. He continued staring in our direction for about twenty minutes, trying to see us through the grass or smell or hear us. We lay motionless. Finally the bull turned sideways. I jumped up, took aim, and pulled the trigger.

Nothing happened. I pulled the trigger a few more times— still nothing. This had happened during target practice the day before, but the dart gun had behaved itself later on. Frustration wasn't a strong enough word for what I was feeling. Gingingayo was glaring at me—so much for thinking I knew what I was doing—and the 1,300-pound bull now had me in full view. Luckily the females ran away, and after a moment's hesitation, he followed them. That decision must have been a very testosterone-charged dilemma for him.

They all stopped a hundred yards away on a dry grassy slope. I let the gas out of my gun, recharged it, and fired it without a dart: it seemed okay. I put the dart back in, inserted another gas cartridge, and was ready to try again. We moved down a ravine and crawled up to the back of another termiterium with the bull standing on the opposite side. It was a perfect setup—the bull was about twenty-five yards away, its head down, eating grass, and the females were behind him, so they wouldn't get spooked by our presence. I stood to dart the bull, and again the gun wouldn't fire. The rifle was an expensive piece of German engineering. You pay for reliability. I'd never hit anyone in my adult life, but if the manufacturer had been next to me at that moment, I would have smacked him with his high-quality rifle butt.

I dropped back down to the ground, let the air out of the gun, and recharged it, keeping the pressure low this time, hoping that would help the trigger release. At a lower pressure I would have to aim high and let the dart "drop" into place. The bull hadn't noticed my last feeble attempt and was still grazing in the same position. I stood, took aim, and pulled the trigger. My adrenaline-enhanced alertness and lower air pressure of the gun made it seem as if the whole event were taking place in slow motion. I saw the dart leave the rifle and arch toward the buffalo. The dart hit his shoulder and bounced off as if it had hit a brick wall. The bull looked around and stared in our direction. He didn't even take one step. I was impressed. We hid and waited to see what would happen.

Twenty minutes later the bull seemed completely unaffected

by the contents of the dart, although his ears did look a little droopy. Just as I was deciding to dart him again, the whole group began to graze away up the slope. I couldn't shoot him. He'd wandered out of range. As quietly as we could, we crawled through the grass toward the bull again. Before we could get close enough to get a shot, he spotted us. This time, instead of running away, he circled and ran directly at us.

We were sitting out in the middle of two-foot-tall grassland, the closest tree half a mile away. Nowhere to go. Gingingayo signaled for me to come to his side. He leveled his weapon at the bull's head as he charged with his head down, horn tips and crown leading the way. I had maybe three seconds to act. The pressure gauge on my gun indicated I had very little gas left, so I wouldn't be able to shoot very far, and I wouldn't get a second shot. Maybe never make another shot again, actually.

I turned to face the bull squarely, raised my dart rifle, and aimed for an imaginary spot in the air two feet above his shoulder as he thundered toward us. The distance shrank rapidly: at fifteen yards I fired. The dart made a smooth arc, dropping swiftly but managing to find its way into his front leg halfway between his shoulder and his elbow.

He froze in his tracks, staring and snorting at us from a little over ten yards away. It was a standoff. Suddenly he turned and ran off after the females. Gingingayo radioed the guys in the truck to drive in the direction the animal was headed, and we followed him as fast as we could on foot.

The bull went down in four minutes, pretty well immobilized. He tried to throw his head occasionally, but he couldn't get up on his feet. What an impressive animal. Unlike most hoofstock, the bases of a buffalo's horns spread out and connect to form a thick, virtually indestructible yokelike structure called a bosque.

His body was massive, built of solid muscle. He was breathing hard and snorting.

When the rest of the team arrived a few minutes later, we began the procedures that were the purpose of this entire grueling exercise. We determined his age by the amount of tooth wear: he was about ten years old, a male in prime condition. I did a complete physical exam, took body measurements, collected blood samples and ticks (each buffalo has a couple of hundred), and ear-tagged him so we wouldn't accidentally dart him again. Working at top speed, we finished in twenty minutes. I woke him up by giving him an intravenous injection of the reversal drug. Two minutes later he jumped to his feet, paused to check us out, and then took off across the valley.

It was now one P.M. I was crispy from the intensity of the sun and the intensity of the work. The temperature had been in the high nineties for the last three hours. We were all glad to head back to camp for lunch and a break in the shade. While the guys ate the beans and rice left over from the night before, I centrifuged and stored the morning's samples, wrote up my anesthesia and examination notes, and drank two liters of water.

A DARTING PRIMER

Long before veterinarians were darting wild animals, indigenous peoples around the world had developed remote drugging systems to catch wildlife. Most of these involved coating the tip of an arrow or wooden dart with paralyzing compounds extracted from plants or animals. Poison arrow frogs from the genus *Dendrobates* received their name because they were a source of potent chemical that would immobilize or kill animals. In the 1950s the development of purified paralyzing agents and modern darts to inject them began to make live capture possible.

Over the last few decades darting systems and drugs have improved tremendously. The original paralyzing agents immobilized the animals but could also paralyze the chest and heart muscles. They also provided no analgesia (pain relief)—the animals were completely conscious but unable to move. This is inhumane: using paralytic agents without the addition of other drugs to block pain and consciousness is now considered unethical in wildlife work. Newer agents are much more effective and allow for humane handling. Some of these modern drugs are very potent and extremely dangerous to humans. Great care must be taken when preparing the darts or cleaning them after use.

Modern darts, whether metal or plastic, all operate in a similar fashion. A chamber in front containing the drug is separated by a rubber plunger from a second chamber in back that either is pressurized with air or contains a gunpowder charge or spring device. When the dart strikes the animal, the pressure in the rear chamber pushes the plunger forward, injecting the drug. Dart failures are common. They can break, leak, lose pressure, or bounce out of the animal before injecting their load. Normally you have to wait to see whether the animal becomes immobilized before knowing the system worked.

Many systems are available for shooting the darts. Your choice is determined by the physical and behavioral characteristics of the animal to be darted. Pistols and rifles using compressed air are quiet and relatively safe, but most have a limited range (five to fifty yards). Powder-charged rifles typically use a .22-caliber blank to provide the power to shoot the dart. These rifles are accurate at forty or more yards with a larger dart but tend to be louder and hit the animal harder.

Dart guns do not perform like hunting rifles. With a good hunting rifle and scope, you can hit an animal hundreds of meters away. Darts are heavy and slow. Their trajectory is more like a rock shot from a slingshot or a cannonball. The weight of the dart varies with the drug dose inside, and the speed of travel varies with the pressure in the gun. Darting uphill or into a tree is completely different from darting downhill. A tremendous amount of practice is necessary to become accurate in a range of settings.

While television and movies give the impression that the dart takes effect almost immediately, this is completely false. It usually takes five to ten minutes, a long period of time in which the animal can run off and get into trouble. Darted animals can injure themselves while running away or can be attacked by another animal who has noticed the unusual behavior. Keeping track of the animal and preventing it from getting into trouble is as challenging as successful darting. If all goes well, we finally get to worry about anesthesia.

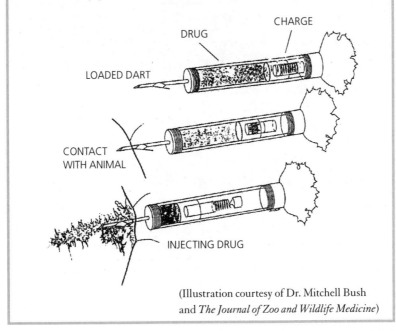

(Illustration courtesy of Dr. Mitchell Bush and *The Journal of Zoo and Wildlife Medicine*)

The next morning Gingingayo and I spotted a small group of male buffalo near a stream. Our luck was improving. We could see a hippo down there also but lost sight of it as we hiked along the stream in the tall grass. Because the buffalo kept moving farther away from us, it took about half an hour of sneaking through the grass to get close. I tried quietly to remind Gingingayo about the

Preparing an anesthesia dart with Fraser

hippo, but he pretended not to understand me. I think he under-stands about thirty words of English, and I have about ten words of Swahili in my repertoire, mostly "good morning," "good after-noon," "good night," and "thank you." We made a great team.

Finally, three buffalo stood right in front of us, slightly to our left. They heard a stalk of grass break, realized we were there, and ran off. You have to realize how hard it is to walk silently through a sea of dead grass. We thought they were gone, then heard the sound of an animal wallowing in the mud just to our left in the swampy streambed. I was sure it was the hippo because it was so loud, but Gingingayo said it was buffalo. They say that more peo-ple are killed in Africa every year by hippos than by any other ani-mal. I know, earlier I said, "They say buffalo kill more people in Africa than any other animal." Take your pick. I'm just repeating what "they" say. One thing's for certain, never get between a hippo and its water.

HIPPO SUNBLOCK

While the skin of a hippopotamus is over an inch thick, its surface layer is quite sensitive. To protect themselves from burning in the intense African sun, hippos stay in the water most of the day and come out to feed on land at night. They also have what is called *blood sweat,* a red-tinged fluid produced by their sweat glands that protects them from ultraviolet radiation.

Luckily Gingingayo was right—there were three buffalo wallowing in the little stream. I don't know how he could tell the difference. There might be a subtle difference in the sounds, or maybe it's more intuitive. This was not the right time to ask, however, and I wouldn't have been able to articulate my question anyway. When we crept over, one of them saw me. Startled, the whole group jumped right up out of the mud and charged by us about twenty yards away. I took a shot at the biggest one and hit him in the shoulder.

He stopped briefly, ran for about another fifty yards, then turned and charged toward us, stopping near the spot where he had been darted. He repeated this somewhat unnerving maneuver two more times before the drug took effect. Finally he got a dazed look in his eyes, trotted in a wide circle around us, and turned to lope toward us.

It was a great scene: a drug-crazed, 1,400 pound buffalo bull coming at us while we were standing in a field, four hundred yards from the nearest tree.

Gingingayo signaled me to run. "Sure, where to?" I muttered. I charged up my dart gun and shot it at the buffalo with no dart.

Gingingayo and me taking a blood sample

The hollow sound scared him, and he turned away for a few moments. Then he ran at us again. I shot the gun in his direction, and once again he turned away. I was beginning to wonder whether I would rather take my chances with a hippo when the drug finally started to work. The bull was prancing toward us. At this stage I knew we would probably be able to dive out of harm's way if necessary. The prancing gait was the classic sign of narcotic effects in hoofed animals. The buffalo stopped a few yards from us and stood frozen like a statue for a few minutes. He would not lie down. Thinking the bull could still kill us if he wanted to, Gingin-gayo ran—a good instinctive move.

The bull was in trouble. The muscle tremors and rigidity were causing him to overheat. I had to help him. I snuck up on the buffalo and slipped an injection of Valium into a vein on the back of his ear: in less than a minute he relaxed and lay down. The guys found the dart. He had gotten only about a quarter of the dose— enough to kill a dozen or so people, but for a buffalo equivalent to a couple of beers with dinner. No wonder he'd taken so long to stop. He was barely drugged. Incredible.

No two buffalo immobilizations are alike. Each presents a different challenge. The most difficult part of the job is keeping it safe for the animals and for all of us. To date we've been lucky on both accounts. We were out there day in and day out. The work was grueling and repetitive, but I had to get samples from a statistically significant number of animals to develop a meaningful picture of the population's health. This number varies with the size of the population in question and the degree of variation among the individuals. The work had to be done, but the end of the workday was always welcome.

Sunset that day was spectacular, brilliant oranges and violets lighting up the end-of-the-day clouds. The open grassland of Garamba made it look like a picture without edges. The fading intensity of the sun gave us much needed relief from the heat of the day. On the way back to camp, we came across a small family of elephants crossing the road with a one- or two-day-old calf. Even at 150 pounds, the newborns look tiny compared with the adults. Their trunks are proportionally shorter than those of the adults and make their faces look a little like those of newborn puppies. Although they are still wobbly on their feet, they're completely aware and alert to their surroundings.

The whole family halted just off the road and let us watch them for ten minutes. A few of the adults were feeding on the grass, using their trunks to tear off the young green shoots that mark the start of the rainy season. Some of the younger elephants investigated the newborn calf, smelling him and exploring him with their trunks. The little calf would stand for this for a minute or so and then run between his mother's legs. They ended our viewing session by sauntering off quietly. Just another day in the bush.

Life at Camp—Or Just When I Think It's Safe to Fall Asleep at Night

Each year we use a quiet little campsite in the middle of the park with freshwater springs and a small stream that's usually free of crocs. It's generally safe to bathe in, even at night. Eight or ten huge old ficus and other broad-leaved trees along the stream provide shelter from the sun. Five hundred or so years ago Garamba was at the edge of the great Ituri forest and consisted of forested valleys and grassy or thinly wooded knolls. Environmental changes over the last millennium caused the forest to recede, and now the old rain forest trees are found only along the streams and rivers of the area, forming tiny patches of gallery forest.

From camp we had a panoramic view of the surrounding grassland. On some evenings we could see a light show on the northeastern horizon: the Sudanese army bombing the Sudanese rebels and the rebels firing shoulder-mounted missiles in response. The rebels control southern Sudan, which borders the park about fifteen miles from camp. Every spring for the past twenty years, the Sudanese government makes its last attempt to route the rebels before the rains set in and make further maneuvers impossible.

Everyone on the team sleeps in tents along the stream. Two shelters, or *barazas,* have been built with meter-high mud walls and grass-thatched roofs. One serves as a storage shelter and rainy-day classroom for Kes and Fraser's two children, and the other serves as a kitchen area. Camp life is pretty simple. A local man, Ngela, has worked for Kes and Fraser since they came to the park. He works at their house at headquarters but likes to accompany us for the three or four weeks of camping. He helps around camp and cooks while we're out working all day.

One of the Belgians who used to be at Garamba taught Ngela how to make bread. He's adapted the method to making wonderful bread and cakes by putting the bread pan in a cast-iron pot and burying it in the campfire. Besides my Starbucks coffee and Fraser's precious custard from South Africa, it's really the only luxury we have. Hot fresh bread is not a bad choice if you have only one. Ngela's presence at camp is also a huge help, since cooking dried beans (the regional staple) takes hours and we rarely make it back to camp before dark. When we do get back, we're exhausted, dehydrated, and filthy. No one is in the mood to start cooking. Most of all, I want to fall in the stream for a while to cool off and bathe and then drink as much water as I can from one of the springs flowing from the clay streambank.

Almost every night I have to deal with the blood samples, doing blood cell counts under the microscope, centrifuging samples, freezing them in liquid nitrogen, writing up records on all of the data collected, then cleaning the equipment and getting it ready for the next day. By nine or ten o'clock, we're all clean, fed, and caught up on work. That's the time to sit around the fire, make coffee or tea, and talk about the day's events or catch up on what's been happening in each other's lives since we've last been together. Someone usually has a little short-wave radio, and we'll try to catch a BBC news broadcast to see what's happening in the rest of the world. By eleven or twelve everyone wanders off to their tents for some quiet time, reading or writing. By dawn the next morning we're all up and packing for the day's work. It's a simple life—hard work, basic food, and good friends teaming up to try to make a difference.

Buffalo, hippos, elephants, hyenas, and lions occasionally wander around camp at night, attracted either by the smell of food or just out of curiosity. One night I was awakened by the sound of elephants near my tent. They were eating branches that an afternoon storm had torn off a massive fig tree. Almost every night I hear lions roaring or hyenas "laughing" nearby. Hippos plod up the streambed and around camp on their nightly foraging forays into the grassy pastures. The animals here haven't been habituated to humans as they have in eastern Africa from decades of tourism. Hunting and poaching over the decades have left Garamba's animals with a mix of wariness and aggression toward humans.

DON'T SNORE NEAR HYENAS

East African folklore claims that hyenas only attack people at night if they are snoring. I have a Swedish friend who, while sleeping outside one night in Kenya, awoke to the sound of her girlfriend screaming in the nearby woodland. She found her friend still tucked in her sleeping bag, babbling about being dragged from camp by a hyena. Next morning they found the hyenas' footprints. I would not recommend camping without a tent in hyena territory.

More daring than the larger wildlife, safari ants had come into camp several nights, hunting for anything that moved. When they'd invaded my tent the previous year, I was asleep. I dreamed that an insect bit me on the neck, and I wiped it away. Another one bit me on the shoulder; I wiped that one off also. I remember wondering in my dream why there were insects in my tent and also why I could hear the sound of them being crushed.

Suddenly I woke up and saw thousands and thousands of ants streaming into my tent. Some fell from the holes they had cut in the roof and landed on me. Others flowed in like brown water from the holes they had cut in the floor. In the ensuing battle they broke formation; the larger guard ants with huge pincers bit anything that moved—in other words, me. The smaller workers injected their dose of formic acid and held on until it was time to carry the carcass back to the nest. I'm a little big for that, but clearly outnumbered, I abandoned ship. Luckily they left at dawn, and the following day I patched the tent holes with duct tape.

On this trip they thoughtfully arrived before I fell asleep. I spent a couple of nights on the roof of the Land Cruiser while they ate hundreds of holes in my tent and covered everything inside in search of food. A more exciting way to get rid of them is to grab bundles of dried grass, light them, and beat the ground around your tent until 1) the surrounding grass is on fire, 2) you can't hold the blazing fireball of grass stalks any longer, and 3) you've made even more holes in the nylon fabric from the flying sparks. Ostensibly, this fiery drama drives away most of the ants. More important, you get revenge for all the bites you've just sustained and wake up everyone else in camp so they can't get a good night's sleep, either.

Pedaling to Uganda

After a couple of weeks, the rainstorms turned the rolling hills of the park green again. Much of the tall grass had burned back or fallen over during the last few months, leaving only occasional hundred-acre patches of dead grass stalks. Otherwise, the southern portion of the park was covered with short, lush green grass. During those weeks we were able to examine a couple of dozen buffalo. We'd collected hundreds of tick specimens and stored them in alcohol for laboratory identification, and I'd banked a large number of blood samples. At camp, some of the blood was used to prepare microscope slides for evaluation and the rest had been spun down in a centrifuge to separate the red blood cells from the serum. Each had been put in special plastic tubes that could withstand the low temperature of liquid nitrogen without cracking.

To maximize the holding capacity of the liquid nitrogen tank, I bundled the tubes in panty hose to suspend in the tank instead of using the bulky metal holding canisters we use when space is not an issue. Few people realize that panty hose does not get brittle even at 270 degrees below zero. With the samples collected and safely ready for transport, it was time to make arrangements to get out of the country.

The Zaire government had closed the borders to air traffic shortly after my arrival. The missionary flights between Bunia and Nairobi had been rerouted: folks were being flown by the missionary plane service up to Aru, a little village in northern Zaire with a grass airstrip at a mission school, and taken by truck to the border, where they crossed to the little town of Arua in Uganda. From there, a missionary plane from Nairobi picked them up. The flights were reduced from two or three times a week to once a week. It was a real hassle for everyone.

Since this was Zaire, we'd heard several explanations for the closed borders: no one had access to real information. One rumor was that President Mobutu's government was restricting all flights to keep tabs on opposition leaders and rebels. Another story was that the government was concerned with people smuggling out diamonds, gold, or money without properly paying off government officials in Kinshasa; they closed the borders assuming that all smugglers use airplanes. One more theory—the most plausible—was that they were allowing only Air Zaire, the airline owned, at the time, by Mobutu and his cronies, to fly commercial international flights. Since they serviced only the capital, it was not much of a problem for the decision makers.

No wonder helping the Zaroïs is almost impossible. But day-to-day life still goes on. Most people are so removed from the capital city that life there has little impact on them, except when the army loots and pillages. The chaos that had trickled down from Mobutu's "throne" was one of the major reasons the Zaroïs welcomed Laurent Kabila's 1998 military takeover. People were fed up with government abuses, but not so fed up they wanted to rebel themselves. After all, you could still stick a seed in the fertile soil, wait for the rains, and watch it grow.

I decided that I didn't want to wait for the following week's flight and talked Fraser into flying me over to Aru on Friday. I would see if I could cross the border to Uganda, get a ride to Kampala and then either a flight or a bus to Nairobi. The bus was more dangerous because Ugandan rebels were holding the roads near Zaire. A fellow coming to Garamba a couple of weeks earlier had been riding in a truck in Uganda that was attacked and wrecked by rebels. They also attacked and burned a convoy of trucks and public buses with the passengers still inside. Sheila, the tutor for Kes and Fraser's two kids, wanted to go back with me overland to Nairobi, but because of the danger, Fraser and Kes wouldn't allow it. On the other hand, they agreed that it would be an interesting adventure for me.

Fraser flew me to Aru early the next morning to give it a try. When we couldn't find a missionary to give us a ride from the airstrip to town, a man at the Aru airstrip got us a taxi (actually two, because I had so much equipment). These were *vélo-taxis,* which to someone with my poor grasp of language suggested a fast taxi.

Of course *vélo-taxi* is French and means "bicycle taxi." I had never seen them in Zaire before, bicycles being extremely rare. In Uganda, however, they are plentiful, and many had slipped across the border into the little town of Aru. My taxi turned out to be a one-speed bicycle with a metal cargo rack over the back wheel, much like a book rack. The driver sat on the seat and the passenger sat on the rack. I needed two bicycles, and Fraser borrowed another bike from the guy at the airstrip so he could ride with me on the two-mile trek through Aru and help with the immigrations and customs procedures at the border station. This is the only international crossing in northeast Zaire. I had hoped to catch a ride on a truck going to Uganda, but naturally, no one was driving across the border.

A car was actually available—a local man was shuttling the missionaries across the border to the airstrip in Arua, Uganda, for the Nairobi flights. He was charging $80 U.S. for the trip because the missionaries had no choice. My taxi drivers, two ten- or eleven-year-old boys, volunteered to take me to Uganda on their bicycles for $6. Ever sensitive to my organization's fiscal conservatism, I

Pedaling to Uganda

opted for the scenic route, and off we went for the three-hour bike ride to Uganda.

I thought Aru was at the border, but the town is some distance from Uganda and simply serves as the official immigration point in Zaire. Clearing Zaïroïs customs and immigration in Aru was nothing like the shark-feeding frenzy in Bunia. In Aru they had almost no foreigners coming through—I was the only one crossing that morning. Another difference, due perhaps to the absence of institutionalized corruption, was that they were really friendly. Since Fraser flew this route to Nairobi to avoid Bunia, he had managed to work out a nice relationship with the officials: he always brought them requested items from Nairobi that were unavailable in Zaire.

The customs and immigrations folks admired the color brochure that describes my field program; I gave them each copies I had brought along for just such situations. They were amazed at the photos of people working with jaguars, anacondas, and fur seals and were very impressed that okapi, elephants, and white rhinos from Zaire were featured. So we all got along fine, and they didn't want to look through my bags. I forced a bear hug on Fraser just to spite his proper heritage, and the boys and I took off on the bicycles.

It's actually not far to Arua, a little more than fifteen miles from the checkpoint at Aru. Of course, nothing is ever that simple in Zaire. For one thing, the terrain was hilly and the boys could not pedal the bikes up the steep hills. We walked those stretches or double pedaled with my feet on the pedals and the boy's feet on top of mine. The road was made of loose dirt and sand, difficult to ride a bike on, and the wind was blowing against us for much of the way. When the boys took a shortcut through the woods, I wondered where they were really taking me. Eventually we always came back out on the road.

One checkpoint is never enough for Zaire: I had to stop two more times to show my passport to young AK-47-bearing Zaïroïs soldiers and log into their books before actually reaching the Uganda border. Luckily they didn't hassle me or want to look through my stuff—I wasn't sure how they would react to my dart rifle. Apparently the sight of me and my duffel bags on two bicycles traveling down a dirt road in the middle of nowhere was bizarre enough for them.

Except for the checkpoints, we saw few signs of people along the way. The hilly land was lightly wooded with an occasional open grassy area. Other than passing someone walking to Uganda, we had the dusty road to ourselves.

We finally made it to the Uganda border and cleared immigrations, which was straightforward except for one tiny detail. The boys needed visas to take me into Uganda. No one had told me this before, probably because they wouldn't have needed visas had they not been with a "rich"-looking *mzungu*. By now they were like fellow staff, so I agreed to pay the $4 charge. I had only three ones and twenties, which they didn't have change for. They took the $3 and gave the kids the necessary papers. U.S. citizens don't have to pay for a visa: I liked this country immediately. Then I had to take my stuff over for police inspection.

A couple of military policemen with automatic weapons were waiting for me. Before they had a chance to ask me to open my bags, I launched into an account of my mission in Zaire and pulled out a brochure to show them the pictures. They too were impressed and wanted to know if it was dangerous work. They were referring to handling the animals. I was thinking more of riding a bicycle through the middle of rebel-infested nowhere and mediating my fate with teenage soldiers equipped with better weapons than educations.

My honest answer, "Sometimes, just a little," seemed appropriate. They laughed and said there surely was no reason for them to inspect my bags. With a smile and my best southern accent, I said, "Yes siree, just mostly my dirty clothes and some old veterinary equipment, thanks." We loaded up the bikes and took off again.

In less than an hour we neared Arua and merged with the road from Kampala. Suddenly there were people walking everywhere, bikes carrying supplies, and vehicles roaring by at sixty miles per hour on the dirt road, covering everyone in dust clouds. In striking contrast with the almost complete lack of commerce in Zaire, Uganda was alive and bustling. Arua even had a paved road, as well as busy shops, lots of people and lots of United Nations and foreign development agency Land Rovers and Land Cruisers. Nothing like big international relief money to stimulate a local economy. I stopped a CARE truck to ask where Logiserv was, and the Ugandan driver said, "Jump in, I'll take you up there." I paid the *vélo-taxi* kids, who took off happily with a handful of money and a booming city to spend it in.

I didn't have the vaguest idea what I was getting into. Fraser had told me to find a company called Logiserv in Uganda and ask them for advice. Logiserv was a logistics service run by ex-pats for the relief missions (mostly United Nations) supplying food and medicine for the Sudanese refugees in Uganda. The CARE driver left me at the Logiserv guest house. The abundance of religious decorations indicated a missionary connection. The Ugandan manager said I could stay there for $10, which included breakfast and afternoon tea (Uganda had been a British colony), but told me MAF flights in Uganda were restricted to missionaries and aid workers. Saving my reverend degree as an ace up the sleeve, I told him I worked for a conservation organization that did projects with the U.S. Agency for International Development. This turned out to be fine as long as I paid with cash.

I would make it back to Nairobi within a day or two, depending on how things went with air travel. Getting shot down had become a real possibility over the last few days: the presidents of Rwanda and Burundi had been shot down the week before. I read in the local newspaper that the first big Ebola virus outbreak in Zaire in decades had occurred in the past month while I was there. Communications in Zaire were so bad that we hadn't heard about any of this. Another big news item in the Uganda newspaper was that Madonna had been on *The David Letterman Show* and chewed him out for his comments about her. Ahh, back to "civilization."

Back Home

After more than a month of fieldwork, I made the long flight back to New York. The plane ride provides personal time to reflect on what I have accomplished and the tasks ahead. I'm alone. I can relax. For the next twelve to twenty-four hours no one can add to my list of things to do. Time to think and time to sleep. By the end of a month in the field, I'm usually exhausted. The work is rewarding, but also grueling. I'm beat up physically and emotionally—I've just spent a month with people I've grown attached to and don't want to leave. Saying good-bye is always hard. The flight home gives me a temporary refuge to regain some sort of emotional and physical equilibrium. By the time we land, I'm ready for action again. I've rested, have begun writing reports on the trip, and am already anxious about reentry. My New York persona has begun to take hold.

When I arrive in New York, I frequently head directly from the airport to the office. It may sound crazy, but it's often easier that way. Since I usually take a night flight, it's morning when I arrive, and I want to get on with the day. Sometimes a trip to the zoo is a necessity, because I have hundreds of precious frozen blood samples to put in the special freezers at work. Sometimes I just want to see everyone at the office and get reoriented.

There is always a lot of work to be done: unpacking, briefing other staff members, catching up on a month's worth of correspondence and phone messages, and, of course, getting ready for the next trip. More important, seeing my colleagues and friends provides the "nutritional" supplement of familiarity and warmth that fills the hole created by the people and places left behind. I call the city Vitamin NY.

I've yet to come up with the correct word to describe my relationship with New York. I can't imagine a future without New York. I sometimes feel myself starting to use the word "home," then catch myself before the word escapes my lips. I have an apartment in New York—an extremely nice place by city standards. It's on City Island in the Bronx, a well-kept secret and nearly idyllic haven. Only a couple of blocks wide and less than a mile long, the island has been spared from development over the last few decades.

The island has no high-rise buildings, is virtually crime-free, and has that great small-town atmosphere. Everyone recognizes each other as "locals." The community is an old one by U.S. standards. It was founded in the late 1600s as a port that would rival New Amsterdam, an obviously unfulfilled aspiration. The island flourished in other ways, however. In this century City Island became the birthplace of America's World Cup racing sloops and is still ringed by marinas, boatyards, and seafood restaurants. For me, the smell of the sea and salt marsh at low tide bring back soothing memories of growing up on the Ashley River in Charleston.

My theory on the human animal is that, like birds, we imprint on places at an early age. Birds return every year from their migrations to nest at the same spot. When I'm reminded of the marshlands, rivers, and ocean I grew up with in Charleston, a comfortable sigh wells up from within me. It's a completely unconscious response. Deeply imbedded memories of days spent exploring the marsh on imaginary adventures, fishing and crabbing on the creeks formed at low tide, swimming, skiing, and sailing almost year-round have given me a lasting attachment to the sea. Every night as I drive back from the office and cross the little drawbridge onto the island, my body relaxes as I catch the first glimpse of the moored sailboats offshore and breathe in the salty air.

My apartment contains the few possessions I own, souvenirs, handicrafts, and gifts from my travels, no pets, but some huge plants that allow me to come home to something green and alive. A computer and an Internet connection give me a technological link to the rest of the world. My craving for the apartment is based on two simple luxuries. Dry, clean sheets on my own bed and hot showers are two of the most delightful pleasures in the world.

My office at the Bronx Zoo hospital is also a highly desirable place. It's neither big nor very fancy, but the windows along one side overlook a lush pasture where a herd of tawny Mongolian wild horses graze. Now extinct in the wild, these representatives of the only truly wild species of horse are now found exclusively in zoos and captive animal facilities. They have lost their fear of humans, but they're still wild—both are traits I admire. Having evolved in the harsh Mongolian steppes, the horses outside my window gallop around the pasture regardless of the weather in New York, and the foals mimic their parents in play.

The Bronx Zoo is the headquarters and the hundred-year-old home of the Wildlife Conservation Society. It's home base for me and all of my colleagues—the other vets who take care of the nine thousand animals in New York's four zoos and one aquarium, my immediate boss, Bob Cook, and our CEO, Bill Conway. Vets, Ph.D.'s, and visiting M.D.'s pepper the hallways of the Wildlife Health Center, where my office is. I like my colleagues, another reason to call myself lucky. Like family, my colleagues always take the time to welcome me back. I recognize how much I've missed them and feel a sense of homecoming. Our discussion about recent political and conservation events, medical developments, and upcoming projects are always refreshing.

I spend most of my waking hours in New York at the office, at least ten to twelve hours a day. I'll walk over to the Italian neighborhood around the block from the Bronx Zoo a few days a week to get the best fresh mozzarella in New York from Joe's Deli or the best pizza in New York from Joe and Maria's Pizza. In New York I've learned to feel comfortable saying who makes the best pizza in town. The shop owners also make me feel at home. Dom, both Joes, and their wives named Maria always ask with their thick New York/Italian accents how my last trip went: "Whud ja do, Doc?" I tell them about elephants and crocodiles, and they, in turn, update me on the neighborhood. "A gang from the South Bronx has been hanging around, don't wear red, yellow, or black. It'll be taken care of soon, though." I love it when crime gets organized. I want to call this city home.

When I'm not in the office, I try to be down in Manhattan with my closest friends, my New York family. Since childhood, most of my best friends have been women. Maybe it's from growing up with two older sisters. I had close male friends, of course—they were my partners in misadventure. But the girls were the ones with whom I could discuss serious subjects. Now, rarely a day or night passes without talking to my adopted New York sisters. They always check in to see if I'm okay, and their happiness has become an important aspect of my emotional well-being. For most of their waking hours, my friends are involved in the worlds of fashion, movies, music, construction, and social work. Discussing their interests and vocations provides me the balance I need to keep from falling too deeply into the world of animals. Beside being supportive and flattering each other with attention, we offer each other different perspectives.

I have had the good fortune to fall in love with some remarkable women and had the honor of having the feeling returned. Most of them I met while working overseas, making departure even harder and further confusing the issue of where I belong. Distance is tough on relationships, but it's also a convenient excuse for their failure. In my experience, there has always been a more substantial reason. When our egos haven't gotten in the way, I've managed to maintain friendships based on love and respect. It's not a bad way to go through life.

I don't believe I've sacrificed having a relationship or a family to my work. I hear field biologists bragging about the sacrifices they have made for their professional commitment—living in developing countries, not owning their own home, forsaking a more lucrative career, or surviving their failed relationships. I find it peculiar that people try to praise me by identifying my sacrifices, the things they have that I don't.

Who cares? We all make choices for personal reasons about which path to take. Renaming something I chose not to do "a sacrifice" would only be self-aggrandizing. Circumstances also dictate where we end up. Although I don't have everything I want, I feel my life is full. Whether or not I want to be in a loving relationship or married, I do have people in my life whom I love dearly. My attachment to my friends in New York makes me want to return from each trip more than anything else. I should call New York home.

Yet I still can't quite manage that word. Last year I was talking with Rick Linnehan, a colleague who used to be the vet for the Baltimore Aquarium but now pilots space shuttles for NASA. I realized he might be the only other vet in the world who would answer the question "Where are you from?" in the same way I do: "Earth."

Baby white-lipped peccaries

Part Three

Bolivia

The Center of South America

Where I spend years looking for wild peccaries and come face-to-face with a jaguar.

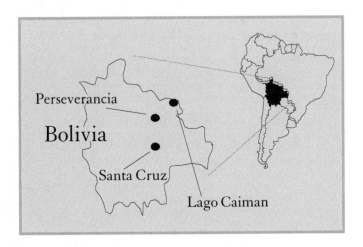

The Center of South America

When I'm planning a trip, I call my travel agent, Judy, whom I've worked with for years. She knows it will be a complicated booking, which will change three or four times before I actually go to the airport. She's amazingly patient; I could never have a travel agent who wasn't. I'm a lot of work, and we both know it. Judy knows my preferences—aisle seat to the left of the aisle so when I cross my right leg it doesn't get hit by the cart, and nonsmoking. I'll visit the smoking section for a cigarette several times, but I don't want to sit back there. Secondhand smoke is bad for you, and it stinks.

In 1995 I was headed to the rain forests of Bolivia to look for white-lipped peccaries. For many years biologists in the Amazon had been trying to study these distant relatives of pigs. Their habit of traveling vast distances in the forest makes them nearly impossible to locate. So many of the studies were based on indirect evidence, such as footprints or feeding damage, or carcasses collected by native hunters.

Peccaries are important animals. They are a major source of protein for the indigenous Guarayo Indians as well as for subsistence hunters throughout Latin America. Biologists suspected that peccaries also played an important role in maintaining the natural architecture of the forests through seed predation and eating or uprooting seedlings. One of the purposes of our study was to confirm this role. My role was to capture and examine them in order to initiate long-term studies on their population dynamics, feeding ecology, and health. Over the course of several years, I made five trips to Bolivia in search of the elusive peccary. Four of them were in vain.

Although Bolivia is the second poorest country in South America, after tiny Guyana, it is also one of the richest in biodiversity, making it a regular part of my itinerary. As with the other places to which I travel routinely, I've amassed a stock of medical and camping supplies in Bolivia. To prepare for another trip, all I need to do is review the inventory I keep on my laptop computer and make a list of items to add for the particular project at hand. The more valuable or perishable items, such as microscopes, darting equipment, liquid nitrogen tanks, and medicines, I keep in New York. "Packing light" requires three or four duffel bags or crates. I get a good laugh seeing the advertisements in the airline magazines for the garment bag that holds everything you need for business trips.

Most of the time I take night flights out of New York's John F. Kennedy Airport. At dawn I'm in another country. On the flight to Bolivia, the sun rises just as we land in the capital city of La Paz. At an altitude of approximately fourteen thousand feet, La Paz has one of the highest airports in the world. You feel light-headed just picking up your carry-on bag and walking down the aisle of the plane. The plane stops for forty-five minutes and then heads to my usual destination, the lowland city of Santa Cruz.

Santa Cruz de la Sierra is the center of the southeastern portion of the country and is now the country's second largest city, with a population of just under one million. A small, dusty cattle town in the 1950s, Santa Cruz has metamorphosed into a boom town. It is the fastest-growing urban center in Latin America. Often associated with drug traffickers, Santa Cruz has recently made its economic mark in tropical agriculture. The city is also the capital of the department (state), which goes by the same name. Santa Cruz Department is larger than Italy.

The old central district reflects its colonial history. The typical Spanish colonial plaza is surrounded by the obligatory old cathedral and government buildings. Close to a million people live and work there, and like Los Angeles, the city has spread out instead of rising upward. The result is a mix of narrow streets paved with white, diamond-shaped stones, lined by small shops, Spanish-colonial style homes, and wide, tree-shaded boulevards. Though Santa Cruz boasts an international airport and the city is busy all day long, three-toed forest sloths—a little smaller than racoons—still hang peacefully upside down from the trees in the central plaza. The local people are warm and friendly, making the city feel comfortable and relatively safe, unlike many cities I have to pass through.

I usually spend a day or two in Santa Cruz reorganizing the supplies I left there the year before and shopping for food, cigarettes, coca leaves, and liquid nitrogen to take into the field. To get to the field site, I charter a flight with missionaries or the Fundación de Amigos de la Naturaleza, a local conservation organization that has two Cessnas. Then all I have to do is wait for clear weather, load up the plane, and take off to the wilds of Bolivia.

POSTCARD FROM BOLIVIA

Bolivia encompasses more than 1 million square kilometers, making it almost the size of Alaska, and has a population of approximately 7.5 million. It has five geographical regions—the highland valleys, the Altiplano, the Yungas, the eastern lowlands, and the Chaco.

The *highland valleys,* also called the Cordillera Central, boast the most temperate climate in the country and fertile soil. Grapes, olives, nuts, maize, and wheat are grown here, and wine is produced in the city of Tarija. Many well-to-do Bolivians have homes in this region—mostly in the major cities, Cochabamba, Sucre, Tarija, and Potosi. The latter three cities were once centers of wealth due to their proximity to the legendary silver mines.

Altiplano means "high plateau," and some of the highest mountains in the Western Hemisphere surround these plains in Bolivia. The open grasslands run from the Peruvian border north of Lake Titicaca all the way to the southern Argentinean border. Altitudes range from fifteen thousand to over twenty-one thousand feet, and the snow-covered peaks of the Cordillera Real and other mountain ranges are much higher.

Toward the south of the Altiplano, where the land is dry and sparsely populated, there are two salt deserts—vast, eerie expanses of white shimmer and reflect light in near mirages, making the horizon seem to disappear. The Altiplano is a desolate, haunting area. Lonely mountain peaks and windswept plains form a surreal landscape and overwhelming sense of solitude. Those who live here are hardy souls, contending constantly with drought, wind, and freezing temperatures. Alpaca herders and farmers eke a living from this harsh land. The Altiplano used to feed a population of six million people using a complex system of raised field agriculture and intricate stone-lined irrigation channels. The system was destroyed by the arrival of the Spanish.

The *Yungas*—an area of misty, cloud-forest valleys—constitute the area between the southwestern highlands and the eastern lowlands. The Yungas form a natural division between the veritable wasteland of the Altiplano and the fecund lowlands of the Amazon rain forests. Coffee, bananas, citrus fruits, and sugar are produced in great enough quantities here to supply residents of the barren Altiplano.

The *eastern lowlands* of Bolivia constitute approximately 60 percent of the country's total land area. Two great river systems drain this area, and the many rivers of the region flow north to Brazil and into the tributaries of the Amazon. A vast portion of this region is marshland.

The *Chaco* covers the southeast corner of Bolivia, western Paraguay, and a small part of Argentina. It is an almost uninhabited, flat, rough scrubland. The human population consists of isolated indigenous Indian groups and a few ranchers, military posts, and a handful of resilient Mennonite colonists. The Chaco has become a refuge for rare species, such as the jaguar and the giant Chacoan peccary, where they are relatively free from contact with humans. Freezing nights and scorching days produce thorny scrub interspersed with some beautiful flowering bushes and trees.

Bolivia's vast size and small population have given it the mystique of being a great place to vanish, especially if the need arises. Butch Cassidy and the Sundance Kid disappeared into its wilds.

A wild relative of pigs, white-lipped peccaries travel in herds of hundreds. Weighing from sixty to a hundred pounds with a gray to light brown bristly hair and thick, chisel-like tusks, peccaries scour the forest floor in search of fallen fruits and nuts and turn the thick layer of fallen decomposing leaves while rooting up tubers and grubs. Their ability to crush larger nuts plays a role in reducing overgrowth of some tree species. On the other hand, small nuts and seeds pass through their digestive system unharmed, helping to reseed other areas of the forest with different plants. Peccaries have an excellent sense of smell, good hearing, and terrible eyesight. Peccary herds roam hundreds of miles through the jungle, operating much like a brigade of natural vacuum cleaners, snorting and grunting as they go.

While with the herd, peccaries are fierce and are known to scare off jaguars. Their tusks, powerful jaws, and tough hide make them formidable. The Indians give them the honored distinction of being the most dangerous animals in the forest. When peccaries feel threatened, they charge through the brush, opening and closing their jaws to clack their tusks. The sound scares away predators and stimulates their herd mates to join the frenzy. I find it an extremely intimidating experience.

A WCS field biologist, Andrew Taber, began to study the ecology of peccaries in Bolivia in 1990. Andrew grew up living in many places around the world, as his father was in the U.S. Diplomatic Corps. After training as a zoologist in England, he began to work in Argentina, where he met his artist wife, Dolores, then moved to Paraguay, where he was the first biologist to extensively study the largest of the three species of peccary—the giant or Chacoan peccary. Thought to be extinct for decades, the giant peccary was discovered by biologists in 1972, living in small populations in the harsh, dry Chaco environment of Paraguay. After completing his studies in Paraguay, Andrew and Dolores moved north, to Bolivia, to explore its wilds. That's when I met them. In 1992 Andrew sported an untamed look himself; lean from fieldwork, he had unkempt, sandy brown hair, and a short untrimmed beard. He turned out to be one of the kindest and most genuine people I've ever met.

My role was to help Andrew safely capture the animals for examination. To check the animals for diseases that might affect birthrates and infant survival, I would give each peccary a thorough physical examination and collect blood samples for infectious disease testing back in the United States. My "little black bag" included a portable ultrasound machine to determine whether the females were pregnant, an important piece of information in determining reproductive success and therefore population growth or decline.

Peccaries range over a vast area of the jungle in search of enough food to satisfy the whole herd, so they're not easy to find. Field biologists had yet to define the size of the "home range" of a

Andrew Taber, radio tracking

white-lipped peccary herd in the Amazon. Often I've found my-self spending week after fruitless week hiking through the forest looking for them. On one of our forays we ended up at a private ranch owned by an American named Ronald Larson.

After graduating college in the late 1960s, Ron drove through South America in a Volkswagen bus and decided to spend the rest of his life in Bolivia. Eventually he came to own two hundred-thousand-acre ranches, one where we would be looking for pecca-ries and the other in the south. Within ten minutes of talking with this tall, lanky Montanan, you realize that he's a hardworking, eth-ical man, committed to people and the land. Ron had done well with his two ranches, introducing commercial popping corn pro-duction to Bolivia and becoming the popcorn king of the country. His bags of kernels, found in stores throughout the country, bear the silhouette of his great dane, Tracker.

Ron also ranches cattle and, like most ranchers in the tropical parts of South America, must cope routinely with having his calves killed by jaguars. Most ranchers kill the endangered jaguars to protect their cattle. Thus, dealing with these so-called problem jaguars has become one of the most critical issues for the conserva-tion of this species today. Ron chose to take two unorthodox ap-proaches: First, he managed his herds, bringing cows out of the forest and into smaller fenced areas when they were ready to give birth; jaguars typically attack only young calves and are not com-fortable going too far from the forest. Second, he forbade his staff from hunting wildlife for food on his ranches, providing meat from his own cattle as an alternative. Most ranchers don't "waste" their cows on staff, letting them fend for themselves for meat to feed their families. As a result, the workers hunt the same deer, peccaries, and large rodents the jaguars eat. By leaving the wildlife prey for the jaguars, Ron dramatically reduced the number of calves attacked on his ranch. He was rightfully proud of what he had accomplished and excited about getting us out to his place to see the wildlife.

Andrew and our team set up camp at a new clearing in the forest that Ron had made, partly for us and partly to establish a new staff camp to maintain a presence on that part of his property. Neighboring Bolivian landowners had been clearing roads onto his property to claim the land for themselves. Bolivian law gives land rights to people working the land: if you don't use it actively, you lose it easily. The measures were adopted during the popularist land reform movement to encourage development and prevent a small number of land barons from owning, but not using, the land. Unfortunately this policy is not conducive to conservation.

The site Ron selected was at the junction of two small rivers, a beautiful place surrounded by dry tropical forest. It was August: with the onset of the austral winter, many of the trees had lost their leaves. The season brought cold southerly winds, the equivalent of northerly winter winds in North America.

It was also pepper tick season. Wherever we went, we picked up dozens of the little suckers. They are the first instar, or stage, of the tick life cycle. When ticks hatch, they are miniature versions of their parents, and they're hungry to feed. After their first blood meal, they drop back to the ground to molt their exoskeleton and grow to the next larger size. They will do this three times before becoming adults and finally reproducing. In their first instar, they are so minute that they look like splotches of ground pepper on your clothing or skin. The best way to get them off is to use adhesive tape on a whole patch before they spread out and settle in for dinner. We always carried tape with us.

Lunching with Peccaries

Unfortunately, the beautiful campsite that Ron had selected was on the opposite side of the river from where the peccaries were supposed to be. Two ranch hands served as our guides and stripped down to their underwear to cross the river. I decided to go shirtless and barefoot. All of our gear went into waterproof bags, which we pushed ahead of us as we swam. The deep water was extremely cold, but it felt good. When we got to the other side, the guides announced that we had to find a place to wash off the mud and plant material, or we would be itching all day. They unknowingly were referring to avian schistosomiasis, the larval form of a parasite specific to birds that will accidentally burrow into the skin of humans, crawl around for a few days, then die because we are not its proper host.

The guides found a gap in the floating water hyacinth bed lining the riverbank that we could use to rinse off. The blossom of the water hyacinth is truly beautiful, but it lasts only a single day and wilts just after sunset. Regardless of its ephemeral glory, the water hyacinth is considered a major pest because it clogs up waterways—it's the river weed of the tropical world. For wildlife it provides shelter, a floating platform on which to stand or walk, a favorite hiding place for caiman (a South American version of crocodiles that can grow to be up to eighteen feet long), and, for species such as manatees, a significant source of food.

Flailing through the tangled plants when we first swam ashore had stirred up the sediments and made the water filthy. And of course, we sank a foot or two into the mud bottom in the process of trying to rinse off the "contaminated" water. It was pretty ridiculous. Then the men told us we should have brought soap and that I shouldn't keep wearing the same pants. I resigned myself to itching. What was a little schistosomiasis among friends? Besides, we had been using the same water for washing, cooking, and drinking.

After an hour of hiking we heard a troop of peccaries clacking their tusks and grumbling in the distance. We approached slowly. When I was about ten yards from one big adult, I took a shot, which fell short. The lightweight darts I was using were aerodynamically sensitive, hardly a match for any jungle foliage—even a leaf could dramatically alter their trajectory. My intended target was not close to any of the other animals when I shot at him, and the air pistol I was using made hardly any noise when fired. Although it seemed as if we had not upset the rest of the herd too much, they disappeared into the swamp. We decided to take a break and try again later in the day.

We were having a leisurely lunch, eating crackers and sardines and chatting in a mix of Spanish and English, when two peccaries wandered up to see what we were doing. Maybe they smelled the sardines. They were literally ten feet away. My mouth dropped open. But in the minute or so that it took me to get the darts out of my backpack and assemble the gun, they caught our scent and, clacking their tusks and snorting in the classic peccary defense tactic, alerted the rest of the herd. Suddenly peccaries were running through the undergrowth all around us. They were moving so quickly and erratically that I couldn't get a decent shot at one.

Finally they calmed down, the tusk clacking subsided, and I caught a glimpse of a big female and two kids about fifteen feet away, too far to get a clear shot through the undergrowth. I went crawling on my belly after them, but they could walk much more quickly than I could crawl through the thicket of brush and vines. The pathways they used through the dense brush were only a foot and a half high. I crawled through long tunnels with no regard to where I was heading until it was clear the peccaries were long gone. I had started the day concerned about getting my clothes wet, at midday I was pushing everyone to wade through swamps, in the afternoon I was crawling through peccary wallows, and at the end of the day I was jumping into the hyacinth-lined, parasite-filled river for a refreshing swim.

We spent another week searching the woods but found no more peccaries at Ron's ranch. We decided to try a new location about three hundred miles away. Using a short-wave radio, we made arrangements to be picked up by a small plane. The next day a missionary pilot flew in from Santa Cruz and landed his little Cessna at the dirt airstrip Ron had built near his ranch house. We loaded up his plane, thanked Ron, and took to the skies.

HOW PECCARIES CAME TO BE

Like all peoples, including those in modern civilizations, the Indians of the Amazon basin developed and shared knowledge that explained the world around them. Key animals, plants, and landmarks highlight these histories. Peccaries have long been one of the most important species for subsistence hunters throughout Amazonia. Because they are unique in appearance and extremely dangerous, it's not surprising that they are ever-present in indigenous folklore and legend. Many of the legends are shared by native groups that live in vastly separated areas. One of these stories uses the exquisite knowledge of peccary nature to explain how they came to be and provides an object lesson about greed and sustainable hunting practices:

In the time of the Old Ones, several families had gone deep into the forest on a hunting trip. They had set up a *pascana,* or hunting camp, next to a stream and were having a very successful trip. The place they had chosen was rich in trees with ripening fruit and nuts. Many deer and agouti (a large South American rodent that looks a bit like a rabbit) and large fruit-eating birds such as piping guans had traveled into the area to feed on the falling fruit. In only a few days the hunters had caught many animals with their handmade wooden bows and arrows and snares made with cord fashioned from strips of vine bark. They dried and smoked the meat over their campfires and collected as much as they could possibly carry home.

However, they were greedy and decided to continue the hunt even though it would lead to waste. A strong wind began to blow, and the *Dueño*—the spirit owner of all the plants and animals of the forest— appeared and told them to stop hunting. The spirit had allowed them to collect their fill but now wanted them to go home. Unable to resist the tempting abundance of animals, the hunters waited for the *Dueño* to leave and then resumed hunting in a low-lying, swampy area full of Chonta palm trees. The tall Chonta palms are found in clusters and have straight, six- to eight-inch-thick trunks encircled with razor-thin, painfully sharp black spines. At certain times of year, they produce thousands of oil-rich, flesh-covered nuts that fall to the ground when they are ripe.

The *Dueño* was infuriated and blinded the hunters. Unable to see, they began stumbling in the swamp and falling against the spiny-trunked palms. Soon their bodies were bristled with the two-inch-long Chonta spines. In agonizing pain and sightless, they crawled around in the mud, grunting and moaning to each other. The small brown palm nuts got stuck in their eye sockets, giving them a beady-eyed look. They managed to survive like this in the forest by staying together and rooting for food. Today we know them as peccaries, and this story explains why peccaries have very poor eyesight and bristly coats and are found in family groups around palm trees with ripening fruits.

From Ron's ranch we flew two hours north to a recently established forest reserve. As in the United States, Bolivian law allows logging in forest reserves. In theory, wildlife is protected because hunting is not legal. Nobody would protect fish by banning fishing and then draining the lake; but many agencies around the world behave as if forest animals can survive without the trees. In the Bolivian lowlands, the number of trees extracted from a given area of land is actually very low. If the hundreds of logging operation workers weren't forced to hunt to feed themselves and their families, there would be minimal impact on wildlife populations.

Our destination was a region of the country that had been heavily populated after the rubber boom at the turn of the century. A few thousand people were tapping or processing rubber by the 1930s and through the 1940s. A British company owned the rubber operation at the site called Perseverancia, Spanish for "perseverance." At that time, when you bought land in Bolivia, it included the workers, who were slaves in everything but name. In 1954 indentured service and ownership of workers was banned. When the rubber market dropped after World War II, rubber tapping stopped and the area was abandoned until the sixties and seventies, when fur and skin trappers moved in. The fur trade targeted exotic cats such as jaguar and ocelots; their skins were sent to Paraguay or Argentina for export to the United States and Europe. Other game animals were shot or trapped for food. Black caiman skins and live macaws for the overseas pet market were possibly the most important trade items. By the time the demand for wild skins waned, most of the large vertebrates in the area had already been hunted out of existence.

In the 1980s activity in the area picked up again because of cocaine-processing labs. Coca leaves were brought in from the highlands, processed into cocaine, and reshipped to other countries. Most of the access to these remote labs was through the airstrips that dotted the forest. Perseverancia was said to have been used as one of these cocaine-producing centers until the late 1980s, when drug enforcement action moved the activity elsewhere. In the past fifteen years hunting in the area has been almost nonexistent. Happily, wildlife populations have rebounded dramatically.

Except for not catching any peccaries the week before, I thought everything seemed to be going smoothly until the missionary pilot got lost. The trees all looked the same, and our maps were not very helpful. When the pilot turned to me and asked if I recognized anything, I realized we had a serious problem. A minute or two later the plane engine died. After a brief moment of panic, I remembered that this pilot liked to let one fuel tank run completely dry before switching to the other one and restarting in midair. His passengers' reactions also amused him. I have such a strange commute to work.

Twenty minutes later we recognized the Rio Negro and used it as a landmark to find our way to Perseverancia. A couple of years earlier some transplanted Italians had built a lodge and renovated the airstrip at Perseverancia to encourage ecotourism. They'd cut trails through the forest for wildlife viewing and maintained a clearing on the river around the lodge. The wildlife is fairly tame and approachable because of the lack of hunting. Sitting on the lodge porch, you can watch giant river otters swim by during the day. In the evenings you can see the huge caiman that have finally repopulated the river.

When they first arrived, the lodge staff had found and raised a baby collared peccary. Pancho had grown into a beautiful young adult with a thick grizzled charcoal gray hair coat and two-inch-

Pancho and his cat

wide white neckband. Weighing thirty to forty pounds, collared peccaries are half the size of the white-lipped peccaries we were searching for. Collared peccaries live in family groups of eight to ten and do not travel very far from their home territory. They do have sharp tusks like their larger cousins and, like small breeds of dogs, compensate for their pint size with a snappier attitude. Pancho acted a little like a terrier. He ran out excitedly to greet us at the airstrip, and he waited near the lodge for anyone to come outside and take him for a walk. He loved having his neck and back scratched until he almost fell over in ecstasy. Like a house cat, however, he got excited by the petting and then attacked, trying to bite my hand or leg. To avoid serious injury, I found myself being chased around the lodge frequently. Like most wild animals kept as pets, little Pancho could be charming or vicious. Unpredictability makes this perfectly natural schizophrenia dangerous.

Night Work

Once again we began our daily search for peccaries, although the staff at the lodge had not seen any sign of them in weeks. Peccaries are active only during the day, which left our nights free to look for nocturnal species on which we could conduct health evaluations. After sunset we searched for tapirs, the squat, five-hundred-pound prehistoric cousin of the domestic horse. Tapirs have a big neck and head with a long, narrow face that ends with an extended muscular nose that works like a miniature elephant's trunk. The shape and size of a rubber traffic cone, the front end of a tapir is designed perfectly as a wedge to penetrate the forest understory.

I wanted to collect blood samples to establish normal or baseline test values for organ health, such as liver and kidney function, and natural vitamin and mineral levels, and to determine to which infectious diseases wild tapirs had been exposed. None of this information had ever been collected before.

Late one afternoon, Pipi, a mestizo who worked at the lodge, Andrew, and I traveled upriver to a site to look for tapirs. They suggested that I wait in the bushy crown of a fallen tree. Pipi was adamant about two things: first, the tapirs would not come once the moon had risen; and second, the tapirs wouldn't come to the area if many people were around. We decided that I should wait alone in the clearing. Andrew would wait near the river, and Pipi would go back downriver to wait.

As the sun set, I climbed into the branches of the tree, made a little seat by wrapping a hammock between two branches, and set up the darting equipment. Right below me a blue-crowned motmot was trying to catch a frog in the little water-filled tapir tracks in the mud. Motmots are magnificent birds with striking turquoise plumage. They nest in long tunnels that they dig underground in streambanks. I whistled to him, and he flew up to a branch at eye level. I couldn't resist taking a couple of pictures of him.

As night fell, the mosquitoes came out in the expected droves. Luckily I don't get a skin reaction from their bites; I usually don't even feel them biting. But the incessant hum around your head is definitely distracting. Opting for a short but relatively sane life, I spray a tremendous amount of the sure-to-be-toxic chemical repellent directly on my skin. The hot flush I get after rubbing it on lets me know it's working. I can easily use half a dozen bottles during a short stay in the jungle.

By evening the afternoon stormclouds had cleared and the stars blazed spectacularly. The Milky Way was so bright that at first I thought it was a band of thin white clouds. The moon was not due to rise for a few hours. The time was perfect for tapir darting.

I couldn't see anything, but I could hear the sounds of the forest, which was quite active and noisy in the early evening. The nearby river complicated things, because the splashing of fish in the water sounded like tapirs stepping in mud puddles. In addition, lots of leaves and fruit were crashing through the understory, also simulating the steps of an animal. These sounds combined with the intermittent buzzing of mosquitoes and other insects around my head, the bats and night hawks flying through the clearing, their wing tips tapping the leaves at the edge of the clearing, and gusts of wind rustling through the forest. I had to ignore these background noises while listening for my target species. I wanted to turn on my flashlight when it was time to shoot—but not a moment sooner, or I'd scare off the animal before it came into the clearing. So I sat in the dark, and listened, and waited, and listened—a zenlike experience.

Around eight P.M. leaves or fruit started falling more regularly from a tree right beyond the clearing, and I heard some quiet leaf crunching to my right in the undergrowth. The crunching sounds became less random and seemed to be getting closer. I picked up my dart gun carefully from its resting place in the branches in front of me and popped the rubber top off the trailer line reel. The line felt as if it were tangled around the attachment of the rubber stopper, but in the blackness I couldn't be sure. It was so dark, I couldn't see anything.

As quickly and silently as possible, I tried to make sure the line wasn't caught on anything. The 1,700-foot spool of line was as thin as dental floss, but it was coiled safely inside a plastic container I had duct-taped to the handle of the dart gun. The nuisance was the five feet of line attached to the dart that ran out the end of the barrel and looped back to the reel. Even in daylight the line is difficult to untangle. This system is a huge hassle but essential for safety. The darted animal runs off into the forest, spooling out the line. When the line stops playing out, I can then follow the trail of string through the thick undergrowth to find the anesthetized animal. Without the line attached to the dart, it could take much longer to find the animal sleeping in the dark forest, and time is critical to ensure the animal's safety. If I were under anesthesia, I wouldn't want the doctor wandering around the hospital looking for me.

Something was definitely nearby, but I doubted it was a tapir. For a while I'd had the uncomfortable sensation of being watched. When I turned on my headlamp, two huge shining eyes stared back at me from no more than fifteen or twenty feet away. As I shifted the light, I saw that the eyes belonged to a crouching jaguar. A jaguar that was stalking me. He was a beautiful animal—big wide head, golden yellow coat with sharp black-spotted markings. I thought it was a male because his head was huge, larger than a female's. I was awestruck, but only briefly.

Here I was, sitting in a bush, in easy reach. In most places jaguars don't attack humans because they are afraid of them. But because people don't hunt the cats here, they don't fear humans. I wasn't in a position to do a whole lot. I didn't want to yell at him and risk scaring away any tapirs in the area. I thought it would be nice to get a photograph. I also thought the flash might scare him away. Quietly I reached back to fish my camera out of my backpack without moving my head, thus keeping my headlamp focused on his eyes.

I took a picture, waited for the flash to recharge, took another one, waited for the flash to recharge, and shot a third one. No reaction from the cat. Since the dart I'd prepared for a tapir contained enough drug to kill a jaguar (or a human), I couldn't dart him. I was wedged into a thicket of brush, pinned down by a loaded dart gun with two yards of line acting like a seat belt. If he wished, the jaguar could get me within two or three seconds. His powerful jaws could snap my neck as if I were a gingerbread man.

I needed to be calm, or at least act calm. Both the jaguar and I were watching my behavior. Nonchalant seemed as good an approach as any. My next strategy was to get my Streamlight out of my backpack and turn it on. I thought the intensely bright (15,000 candlepower) flashlight might annoy the jaguar enough to make him retreat; or if he attacked, at least I could wedge it in his mouth like a speculum. I couldn't reach the light without moving my head, however. I twisted to get it out. When I turned it on, the jaguar was gone. A brief (milliseconds) sense of relief was followed immediately by a serious concern about his new location. With the Streamlight I found his eye shine again and lit up his whole body. He was closer now, having used the opportunity to advance. He crouched twelve feet away from me.

The big cat sat there, essentially blinded by my flashlight. I reviewed my options. If he jumped, I could reach behind me and pull out my machete, grab the blade about halfway up, and jab it into his chest as he landed on top of me. However, the tip wasn't sharp enough to stick into anything tougher than cardboard. Contrary to popular opinion, a machete is not a great weapon at close quarters—you can't use it to hack at something on top of you while wrestling in a bush. Option number two was my Leatherman pocket tool, the handy-dandy pliers-file-knife-screwdriver-leather-punch-can opener that every in-the-know field person carries.

I feared that in the intensity of the moment, I would first open the file rather than the little knife blade, although it wouldn't matter because both would be equally useless. My best fantasy plan involved using the three-inch knife blade to incise between two ribs, deflate a lung, then reach in and grab his heart.

Now that I had thought through my options, I was ready for him to leave. I had enjoyed his good looks, tried a few things to get him to move on, and reviewed all the reasons he was still there but had not attacked me. The novelty of the situation had long worn off. His refusal to leave was making me nervous.

If I had smelled like a human, which I should have, the cat should have gone away. When darting elephants in Africa, the guys rub fresh elephant dung on my clothes and under my armpits to mask my human scent. Andrew is more high-tech; he insisted on spraying me with Scent-Off before we left so I wouldn't scare the tapirs. He was excited about trying this new product because the label on the can guaranteed to eliminate all human scent or your money back. He had sprayed me down thoroughly—now I was wondering what, instead of human, I smelled like. Hmmmm, the spray was made for deer hunters and fur trappers—maybe I smell like a fawn. Nice. I wondered how the guarantee would apply here. If the cat smells me, realizes I'm human, and runs away, I get the $4 refund and my life; if not, the spray worked and I get no refund . . . for obvious reasons.

Later, Andrew said the cat was just curious. Now come on, I can get only so anthropomorphic. A cat wouldn't take that long to figure out that some human was sitting in a bush. What else could he be curious about? *Can I really take a human? What does human flesh taste like? Why does this guy not smell completely like a human? Must be using the new deodorant for deer hunters.* Maybe he was curious about the latest in darting equipment, or maybe he was just checking to see what I was waiting for. Sure, lots of perfectly logical reasons for him to be sitting there.

Finally, I decided tapirs be damned and yelled over to Andrew, who was waiting near the river outside the current danger zone, "Hey, Andrew!"

"Yeah."

"There's a beautiful jaguar over here."

"Oh, I was wondering what you were looking at for so long. Where is it?"

"Right here."

"Right by you?" His voice rose an octave.

"Yeah, right here."

A pause. "Is it still there?"

"Yep, about three or four yards away. Staring right at me."

"What's it doing?"

I thought I had just told him. Maybe he wanted me to be more descriptive: "He's doing that ready-to-pounce, tense trembling cat thing," or, "He's just reading the *Time* magazine I threw at him." I kept it simple and answered, "Not much. He's crouched down, looking at me."

Another pause. I think Andrew got the message.

"He's really a spectacular cat, huge head!" I yelled.

"Are you scared?" Okay, I think we were really communicating then.

"Well . . . there's really not a whole lot I can do. I already took some pictures."

"Yeah, I saw the flashes and wondered what you saw."

"I think I got some good shots, at least of eye shine. The bushes are kinda hiding most of his body."

Meanwhile, the jaguar was still crouched down. He yawned, showing his huge curved canine teeth. I realized that the Streamlight was the wrong size and shape to use as a speculum. It was too long to fit in his mouth lengthwise, and the diameter was far too small to hold his mouth significantly open. Damn. A few more minutes passed. I thought about how nice a cigarette would be at the moment.

The jaguar yawned again. He had nice teeth, none broken. As a vet, I'm supposed to notice. Was he nervous and acting nonchalant like me? The yawn was not a reflection of boredom—animals frequently yawn in a threatening situation. It's a casual display of their weapons. Finally, to my immense relief, he stood up, turned away, and slunk off into the bushes.

We never did manage to catch peccaries, or tapirs, on that trip. But we were not easily discouraged and continued our planning to tackle the wild peccary health question as well as develop other projects for endangered species in Bolivia. Coming fairly close to being a jaguar's dinner didn't make this the best trip on record, either. Then again, very few people have the opportunity to observe this magnificent cat at such close range. I was already looking forward to my next trip to the jungles of Bolivia.

AMAZONIA

The Amazon River is the largest river in the world and contributes at least one-fifth of all the earth's fresh water. The Amazon water flow is five times that of the Congo River and twelve times that of the "mighty" Mississippi. In one day the Amazon discharges as much water into the Atlantic Ocean as the Thames River carries past London in one year.

In 1953 the true source of this great river was discovered: a small spring less than a foot wide that feeds a stream called the Huarco, located high in the Andes Mountains in Peru. While the Amazon technically does not run through Bolivia, tributaries of the Amazon do, and a large portion of the country's rain forest is considered part of the Amazon basin. Referred to as Amazonia, this vast, lowland basin surrounding the Amazon and its tributaries covers an area about half the size of the entire United States.

Most experts agree that the protection Amazonia enjoys from drought and extreme cold and frost helps to explain its tremendous variety of flora and fauna. The annual rainfall is approximately three times that of most areas of Europe and North America. The greatest diversity of plant and animal species in the world have evolved in the area. Amazonia is one of the most immense uninterrupted tracts of nature left on earth and the only large, tropical one.

At the end of the twentieth century there is more than a little trouble in this natural paradise. Although 80 percent of the rain forests remains intact, heavy localized destruction, particularly in the Brazilian forests, justifies legitimate concern for the future of the area. Despite all the attention the rain forests of the Amazon have received worldwide, the area is still in real jeopardy. Between 1970 and 1989 the

burning of the forests and the damming of rivers destroyed approximately 10 percent, or 150,000 square miles.

You might say, as goes the Amazon, so goes the world. The Amazon ecosystem contains approximately one-tenth of the total number
of plant and animal species on the earth. Most scientists agree that the
forest canopy is still basically intact. However, the same experts agree
that some irreversible damage has been done to the region, particularly in Brazil. Efforts are now being made to conserve Amazonia, with
the understanding that the preservation of all species is impossible.

What is interesting about the stretch of the Amazon basin found in
Bolivia is that, though tiny in comparison with the Amazon rain forests
of Brazil, it has not been plundered to the same degree. Therefore it's
more truly what the Amazon once was. Rare species of monkeys, wild
cats, birds, and reptiles still flourish here, and the vegetation is lush in
many places. There's a chance that with the appropriate conservation
programs and an increased awareness of what a precious resource this
area is, it could be salvaged from its neighbors' fate.

The following year, 1996, I was back in Bolivia helping two of
Andrew's former students, Rob Wallace and Lilian Painter, dart
and radio-collar black spider monkeys. Rob had decided to study
them for his Ph.D. project, while Lil had followed Andrew's lead
and taken on the challenge of studying peccaries for hers. Lilian's
mother is from the Bolivian highlands, descended from the traditional aristocracy, and her father is a Brit working for the United
Nations Development Program. Because her father was assigned
to different posts around the world, Lilian grew up in many countries, much like Andrew.

She was educated in England but always wanted to return to
her "homeland" to work. Lilian met her husband, Rob, during college in England. After he was bitten by the Bolivia bug—the

Rob, student, and Lil collecting data

warmth of the people, the spectacular wilds, and of course, malaria, hepatitis, bot flies, and parasites—he adopted the country as his home. They've been together ever since, living and working in the jungle. Some of the longest-lasting relationships I know are rooted in the jungle.

Rob and Lil both began fieldwork under Andrew before developing projects of their own. For her Ph.D. research, Lilian decided to thoroughly explore the reproductive dynamics of peccaries and elucidate their precise role in seed predation and seedling disturbance and how these activities help to maintain forest diversity.

Late one night during our spider monkey work, we were reminiscing about our fruitless searching for peccaries. I mentioned that it would be great to catch a whole herd at once in a huge corral that would act like a trap. Lil looked over at me and smiled. It dawned on us all at the same time. We could build a huge capture pen at a salt lick, wait for them to come, and shut the door behind them. The plan would work only during the rainy season, when peccaries visit the salt lick almost every week. Such a strategy had never been tried before, but we convinced ourselves we could pull it off.

Six months later it was February and the peak of the rainy season. Rob and Lil met me at the grass airstrip at Noel Kempff Mercado National Park. They had come down the Itenez River from camp the night before my arrival. The river runs along one side of the relatively new park and forms the international border with Brazil. A local conservation group purchased the land a few years earlier from a cattle rancher and gave it to the Bolivian government to establish the park.

Noel Kempff Mercado, for whom the park was named, was one of the fathers of conservation in Bolivia. He was shot and killed along with the pilot of the small plane they were in after landing at a remote airstrip in what is now the park. They had noticed grass airstrips throughout the area that were doubtless being used by cocaine-processing plants. Some people say that Kempf knew where he was going and what he would find there, but he might have believed the area had been abandoned. Others say that aerial photos exist indicating the U.S. government was involved in the cocaine operation. Rumor has it that the photos show a minitractor towing a trailer with Porta Potties, and according to the story, the operation was connected with the CIA's support of Noriega's anti-Contra efforts in Central America. Although this isn't absolute proof, it's also true that neither drug lords nor ranch owners would fly in portable toilets for Indian workers.

OF COCA AND THE COUNTRY

Cocaine is illegal in Bolivia. So are hashish and marijuana. Not so the coca leaf. The coca leaf is the good friend of many Bolivians, though you won't hear it spoken of in any upper-class social circles. Coca leaves grow on bushes at altitudes of three thousand to six thousand feet. The bushes are most prevalent in the Upper Chapare and Yungas regions. Traditionally used only by the highland Indians, coca leaves are now sold throughout the country.

Though the country uses the metric system, coca leaves are sold by the pound in most Bolivian markets—probably American or British influence. At the market, you also have to buy legia, an alkaloid made of potato ash that draws the drug from the leaf while it is being chewed. If you have a tiny bit more money, you can purchase bicarbonate of soda, or bico, which also frees the cocaine from the leaf.

Many indigenous people consider Mama Coca to be the daughter of the earth mother, Pachamama, and coca is a gift to the people. They believe coca is able to banish evil both from the fields and from homes, in planting or mining ensure good luck, heal illnesses, and exorcise demons. Chewing coca does not induce a high. The amount of cocaine alkaloids in a handful of leaves is very low. It takes one or two grocery bags of leaves to make a gram of cocaine. A bolo, or ball of coca leaves, has an effect more like a cup of coffee. It wakes you up, staves off hunger and thirst. A cup of tea made with coca leaves is commonly used to cure altitude sickness and stomach upsets. The alkaloid is simply a mild stimulant and anesthetic similar to Novocain.

When the Spanish came, saw, and "conquered" Bolivia, they too were impressed with the magic of the coca leaf. They observed that laborers who chewed the leaves were more dedicated to the task at hand, so they encouraged chewing coca leaves. Nowadays Bolivians chew coca leaves socially in much the same way Europeans might share a cup of coffee.

Until the 1980s, the export of cocaine accounted for one-third of the Bolivian economy, making cocaine a hard habit to eradicate. Foreign development money, especially from the United States, is highly contingent on the suppression of the cocaine industry in Bolivia. Huge sums of money back up both sides of this battle.

At the local level, it's a very touchy issue. A peasant farmer can grow coca and make barely enough money to support a family, or the same farmer can grow potatoes and make one-fourth as much money—not nearly enough to support the family. It's difficult for a Bolivian who views coca as we view coffee to understand the restrictions imposed by developed countries.

Rob and Lil had my limo waiting for me—a fourteen-foot aluminum boat with a little fifteen-horsepower outboard motor. We loaded all my gear, including a sixty-pound tank of liquid nitrogen, and headed up the Itenez. The rapidly flowing river is at least a hundred yards wide during the rainy season. The closest settlement in Bolivia is four hours away by boat. The Brazilian side is more developed, and an old abandoned rice plantation is nearby. Downriver about thirty minutes is the town of Pimenteras. It is a thousand-mile drive to the little river town from Rio de Janeiro. The trip is not uncommon, because the Itenez is known by the Brazilian urbanites for its sportfishing. The wide, flat river is lined with thick rain forest along the Bolivian side and long stretches of forest interrupted by clearings for fishing huts and agriculture along the Brazilian bank.

Nonetheless, the area is still fairly wild, and it's not unusual to see pink river dolphins swimming by. These remarkable animals live completely in fresh water, thousands of miles from the sea and cut off from the Amazon by impassable waterfalls. True to their name, they are pink, or at least the younger animals are. The adults tend to turn grayish as they age. Like most dolphins, they feel smooth and firm. Their squeaky clean skin covers a swimmer's well-muscled, 250-pound body. They're about six feet long and have beady little eyes that could be considered vestigial. Because the water is so darkly stained with tannins from the jungle trees, good eyesight is irrelevant. Instead they have highly developed echolocation, or sonar, capabilities, which allow them to catch fish easily and even navigate through the forest when the rivers overflow their banks in the rainy season.

Their dorsal fins have shrunk to a three-inch-tall ridge, which enables them to swim more easily through submerged vines, bushes, and tree roots. While other dolphins leap from the water in play or for television cameras, the pink river dolphins barely arch over the surface when they come up to take a breath. This is not to say that they are not playful or curious. A group of three or four will frequently race alongside a boat until, after a minute or two, they lose interest. As a species, we're really not as fascinating as we think.

The trip along the river provides wonderful wildlife viewing. The birding is great—we spot a wide assortment of ducks, herons, egrets, and other waterfowl, as well as hawks and falcons. Even eagles are not uncommon. Red howler monkeys sit in the trees along the riverbanks, and in the evenings or early mornings we listen to their mournful calls as though to a far-off choir.

In the forest patches on the Brazilian side of the river, we often see a subspecies of squirrel monkey not found on the Bolivian side. This type of observation is critical for conservation planning. While most organizations practice their conservation business in capital cities and depend on expensive high technology like satellite photos and computer-generated mapping, we at WCS feel strongly that there is still no substitute for having someone in the field. Call it a reality check. If Rob and Lil had not been working here with little more technology than a pair of binoculars, no one would have realized that some animals are found on only one side of the river. A little blue line indicating a river on a map may signify an uncrossable barrier to the animals living there.

Three Rooms, Lake View

After an hour or so of motoring upriver on the Itenez, we needed to cross into the oxbow lake that was once the major river course. In the dry season we have to portage the boat and all the gear across land. In the rainy season it's possible to go through the flooded sections of the forest, ducking under branches and lianas to make your way into the lake. Another half hour and we arrived at camp—home.

Rob and Lil had been living there for ten months by then, spending every day in the forest. Rob had been following the spider monkeys that I had helped him radio-collar on my previous trip. Lil was out every day studying peccaries in the forest. Like most field biologists working in the jungle, she saw her animals very rarely. But they left a lot of evidence—footprints, rooted-up earth, and droppings—for her to study. She documented her work in field notebooks filled with data and photographs of dung samples with seedlings sprouting from them.

Camp was much the same as on my previous trips—a mud-walled hut with a dirt floor and a plastic tarp for a roof served as a storage room, dining area, lab, and office space. Another plastic tarp strung between some trees created an open-air kitchen. Rob and Lil lived in a small tent. Their field assistants, Jose and Yate, lived in a large, houselike tent. Additional tents housed the Bolivian college students who came to work with Rob and Lil for six to eight weeks on senior thesis projects. I set up my tent a little way from camp, down the trail, where a jaguar sometimes wandered by at night. I like being a bit out in the jungle, and being awakened at night by animals always compensates for the less than comfortable sleeping arrangements.

The camp is located on the edge of a typical Amazonian oxbow lake, named Lago Caiman because a local pilot flying over the area once looked down to see the largest caiman he'd ever spotted in his life. The lake provides water for cooking, dishwashing, doing laundry, and bathing and also fresh fish for dinner. We act as if it's perfectly clean water and drink it without sterilizing it.

Bathing is accomplished by squatting at the edge of the lake and using a plastic bucket to scoop up water and pour it over yourself. In the dry season there are too many piranha in the lake to allow for comfortable swimming.

The lake rises seven or eight feet during the rainy season and overflows its banks into the surrounding forest. The piranha are no longer forced to congregate in the deeper part of the lake near camp. It's still not completely safe to swim, but when it gets hot, you're driven to jumping in and jumping out very quickly. Night swimming is out of the question—besides the piranha, twelve-foot-long black caiman are out patrolling. Piranha, however, are good to eat—a bit bony, but very tasty. They probably think the same about us.

Fieldwork in the rainy season has its advantages and disadvantages. The rains in January and February coincide with the austral summer, making it hot (close to 100 degrees Fahrenheit) and humid (close to 100 percent). The daily rains keep tent, bedding, and clothing wet, while the heat causes them to mildew within a day or so—but the mildew stains provide natural camouflaging and enable you to blend into the environment. The warm evenings feel cool compared to the sweltering days, but the mosquitoes are so bad that it's not comfortable to be outside. Although the muddy trails and

THE EVOLUTION
OF AN OXBOW LAKE

Throughout the Amazon basin, rivers flow from the Andes mountains through the jungle on their way to the sea. They carry with them the silt and soils washed away by the rains. At each bend in the river, the water flows more slowly on the inside of the curve than it does on the outside. On this inner edge, where the water slows, the silt settles on the river bottom. On the outside edge, where the current is strong, the water slowly erodes the mudbanks. Over decades, each curve becomes more and more exaggerated as the outer edge is carved away and the inner is built up with the silty soils. Eventually two curves come back to back and the soil between them washes away, leaving the large bend in the river that once connected them out of the loop, so to speak. As the ends become silted and overgrown, the section in between becomes isolated and forms a lake in the shape of the curved horns of an oxen—an oxbow lake.

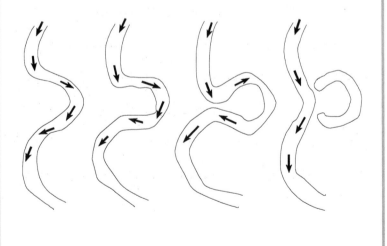

swampy forests are easily dealt with by wearing rubber boots, I believe these helpful accessories are the original source of foot fungus on this planet.

The highlight of the rainy season at Lago Caiman is the return of the peccaries. The rains saturate the forest and, in some way we do not understand, change the nature of the soil in certain spots. These areas are called *salitrales* in Spanish because they are thought to be salt or mineral licks. They have been used for centuries as hunting spots. Tapirs, deer, birds, and peccaries come to these areas and eat the soil on a regular basis. At Lago Caiman, white-lipped peccaries visit one of the *salitrales* about a half mile from camp almost every week during the rainy season. In the dry season they may visit only once every month or two. We don't know why.

Lil had obtained a small grant from the Dutch embassy in Bolivia. The Dutch government is extremely active and supportive of conservation and environmental efforts all over the world. Lil's grant covered the costs of building our experimental capture pen around one of the *salitrales*. She had bought four hundred yards of chain-link fencing and couple of thousand yards of heavy-gauge wire in Santa Cruz and trucked and boated it all the way to camp.

Lil chose a *salitral* that was wet enough to consistently attract the peccaries but would not get so inundated after a few weeks of rain that an animal might drown while under anesthesia. Lil, Yate, Jose, and a couple of extra local guys she hired stretched the chain link through the bushes and trees to encircle a half acre of forest. With saplings and chain link, they built two thirty-foot-wide doors held aloft with ropes strung over nearby tree limbs. Near each trap door they hung hammocks about fifteen feet off the ground, where they tied off the door release ropes. At one side of the *saliltral* they built a funnel-shaped chute leading into a small round pen. Drop doors separated the pen from the large forest corral. The whole area was left alone for a few weeks before my arrival, allowing the rains to wash away the scent of humans.

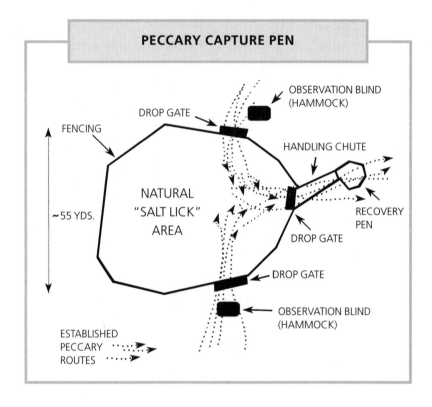

PECCARY CAPTURE PEN

OBSERVATION BLIND (HAMMOCK)

DROP GATE

FENCING

HANDLING CHUTE

NATURAL "SALT LICK" AREA

~55 YDS.

RECOVERY PEN

DROP GATE

DROP GATE

OBSERVATION BLIND (HAMMOCK)

ESTABLISHED PECCARY ROUTES

Now all we had to do was wait for a herd of peccaries. The animals had been coming to these *salitrales* for many years. The paths they used were well trodden, and their cloven hooves had left marks that clearly indicated their direction of travel. We hoped that aligning the trap design with their habitual movements would make it less alarming when we shut the big pen doors behind them. Once trapped, they would follow their normal exit route, which would lead them to the funnel chute and small pen for the darting and anesthesia. Since no one had ever attempted such a large-scale entrapment before, we hoped our theory would work in practice.

We took turns spending hours in the hammocks, suspended fifteen feet up in the trees, waiting for the peccaries to come. Walkie-talkies allowed us contact with the team waiting back at camp. We anticipated a wild scene when the peccaries arrived; we would need at least eight people to help manage all of the animals. But it didn't make sense for the whole group to spend every day at the trap site.

Spending a day in a hammock sounds great. Had it been one day and had we selected a comfortable spot, it might have been delightful. But this was the peak of the rainy season and the hottest time of year. When the sun was out, we baked. During the daily rains we got drenched and chilled, since our bodies had adjusted to the heat. We could wear shorts and a T-shirt as long as we wore enough mosquito repellent to keep from being sucked dry. The repellent doesn't discourage the biting flies and sweat bees that play an important role: not letting us sleep on the job.

All we had to do was wait patiently. Between downpours I managed to read the five issues of the *Economist* I had brought along, as well as *Time, Newsweek, U.S. News & World Report, Smilla's Sense of Snow,* and *Les Misérables.* Reading *Les Miz* allowed me to lose track of the slow-moving days, and Smilla's arctic adventures provided an enviable contrast to my heat stress.

Listening to music on my Walkman was unacceptable because I needed to hear the peccaries approaching. They are easy to hear while they are traveling in the forest. Once you are familiar with the sound, you can recognize their approach from two hundred yards away. Their constant grumbling and snorting may contribute to group cohesiveness (or it may just be to get the dirt out of their noses). Given the dense undergrowth, visual contact with one another would be impossible even if they had good eyesight. So the sounds they make most likely help to keep them from becoming separated as they roam the forest.

A hundred peccaries grumbling and snorting in harmony punctuated with the occasional squeal of a youngster is hard to miss. The deeper tones blend into a continuous rumble and reach down toward the infrasonic range. This is the frequency at which it becomes difficult to distinguish between hearing and feeling a sound. After experiencing the peccary rumble a couple of times, you can close your eyes and get a sense of a herd far off in the forest. First you feel it in your guts, than within another minute or so you hear the distinct rumbling sound, almost like a distant thunderstorm. It's similar to the deep, subsonic rumble used by elephants that you can feel sometimes when you are close. When you hear the first little peccary squeal, then you know the herd is nearby and your heart rate goes up.

A group of peccaries showed up near the end of the first week of our vigil. There were at least sixty animals. I heard them coming and radioed the others. The peccaries were headed toward the gate over which I was suspended. Quietly I changed into long pants, a workshirt, and the fishing vest stocked with my emergency drugs and slipped on my rubber boots. I felt like a fireman.

A few herd leaders stopped under my hammock. They acted suspicious, looking around, snorting, and sniffing the bushes. Peccary eyesight is notoriously poor—as long as I stayed fairly motionless in my hammock, they could not see me. The point animals needed to lead in the others, but they were taking their role as responsible guides seriously. My heart pounded as the grumbling and squeals of the approaching herd surrounded me. It had taken years to get this close to success.

I knew that Rob and Lil and the backup team would be arriving soon. They would have to wait on the trail about two hundred yards away until I let them know the peccaries were safely trapped in the pen. We had brought along a collection of four-foot-long poles made from saplings. These poles, which we'd left at the waiting point, were our protection in case of peccary attack. We never carry guns or even keep them at camp. We were there to protect the animals, not shoot them. The subsequent risk is one we assume without discussion.

Peccaries were everywhere in the bushes below me, but they were hesitant to go through the pen door. Four or five minutes elapsed before the first few went in. Another dozen or so followed quickly, trotting into the thickly forested capture pen. I needed to decide when to drop the trap door. Should I wait to get more animals inside and risk losing the ones already there, or should I close the door on what I had? Twelve animals would not be enough for our study, but those twelve were far more than I or anyone else had ever worked on. I had to come to terms with biogreed—the biologist's insatiable appetite for more data, higher numbers, and better results. I found myself thinking about what happened to the ancient hunters when they got too greedy.

It was time to act. As slowly and quietly as possible, I loosened the three ropes holding open the trap door and threw them free. The huge trap door swung down. The commotion startled the peccaries that had remained beneath me outside the trap, but they didn't run away. This was good because we wanted the captured animals to remain calm so that I could dart them safely. But it was also bad because I needed to climb down from the tree outside the pen and secure the trap door.

Without causing too much of a disturbance, I needed to chase off the peccaries standing under my tree and around the outside of the pen door. I didn't want them to signal the ones inside, and I didn't want them to attack me when I climbed down to the ground. Projecting my voice so the penned peccaries forty yards away wouldn't hear me, I shooed off the loose ones. Despite my efforts, they clacked and grunted, warning the peccaries inside the pen that something was amiss.

It was now or never. I jumped to the ground and waded through the mud to wire one end of the drop door shut. The flexing of the thirty-foot-long wooden frame had left a six-inch gap between the post frames. If the trapped peccaries pushed against the gaps, they would be able to escape.

Before I could wade to the other end of the door to secure it, the captured peccaries charged back to where I was standing. When I huffed at them they stampeded back out of sight. That bought me enough time to secure the far end of the trap door.

We were all set. Rob and Lil arrived with the rest of the team, carrying bags of equipment and supplies and the loaded drug darts. The drug I was using, Telazol, was a combination anesthetic composed of a tranquilizer agent that provided good muscle relaxation and a dissociative anesthetic that disconnects the circuits in the cerebral cortex, the part of the brain responsible for conscious sensing and control from the rest of the brain. Imagine pulling out the wires from an old telephone switchboard: the separate parts still work, but they cannot communicate with each other.

Telazol is one of the few good immobilizing drugs for piglike animals. When selecting an effective tranquilizer, you must understand its properties, and every agent has some negative characteristics. Once reconstituted from its crystalline form, Telazol is stable only for a few days at room temperature and then becomes ineffective. But mixing ten bottles with sterile water and then carefully measuring the drug into thirty or so darts would waste too much time once the peccaries were captured.

To avoid delay, which would increase the stress to the captured peccaries, I had prepared the drug darts ahead of time and then frozen them in liquid nitrogen. Frozen at minus 270 degrees, the reconstituted Telazol was extremely stable. I bundled the darts in panty hose like a chain of sausages and suspended them in the tank at camp. Of course, when removed, the darts were so cold that they would rip your skin off on contact. When Lil and Rob ran up through the jungle, they were carrying a plastic pitcher of water containing the thawing darts. The sweat-drenched, suited-up jungle team, with backpacks, machetes, and wooden poles in hand, arrived with a bright orange plastic pitcher full of smoking water. We were ready, and excited.

Whispering, I quickly briefed the team on the situation. We had about twenty peccaries inside the capture pen and another forty or so wandering around in the forest nearby. We still needed to be careful about threatening either group and causing them to attack. There was no real safety on either side of the fence now.

While I was busy with the darts and equipment, the peccaries began charging around inside the forested pen. Although we couldn't see them, we could hear the little stampede. We heard them splash through a stream, and then suddenly it got disturbingly quiet. Rob and Yate started yelling to each other across the capture area. Something had gone wrong. They couldn't figure out where the peccaries had gone. They had escaped. I felt sick. All the hard work, the preparation, and day after day of waiting had resulted in nothing.

The peccaries had managed to find a gap at the bottom of the fence. The heavy rains the previous days had flooded a stream and eroded the bank on one side. When the water level dropped again, it had left an eight-inch gap under the fencing. Once the lead peccary found the space, the rest of the group followed right behind him, escaping into the forest.

We all plopped down on the muddy ground to wallow in self-pity, at least for a few minutes. Rob and I were moaning, Lil had slumped over, her face buried in her dirt-covered hands. Yate was smiling and saying something like "aye yai aye yai aye." Soon we were all laughing at ourselves. Jose set to work repairing the gap in the fencing. We were not to be dissuaded; we knew they would return eventually. We took turns convincing each other that our plot to pen peccaries would succeed.

Night Ops

During the long days waiting for peccaries, we once again needed to feel productive. When Lil was not on duty at the capture pen, she worked at camp entering ecological data on her laptop computer. She had spent the year collecting and processing the samples of plants and seeds that peccaries eat. She laid out plant specimens between sheets of newspaper, then pressed them in a wooden frame hung high over the cooking fire, to allow them to dry slowly. She needed a complete inventory of the peccaries' diets throughout the year.

On some days Rob hiked the two miles into the forest where his radio-collared spider monkeys lived. With their long arms and legs and long prehensile tail, spider monkeys are the tallest primates in South America. The subspecies Rob studied were jet black. On his monkey days he would take one of my walkie-talkies with him just in case the peccaries came and we needed his help. Meanwhile Rob's studies were progressing nicely. His work was the first to show large communities of spider monkeys sharing the same area. He discovered how the spider monkeys utilize their resources throughout the different seasons and how, like peccaries, their feeding and travel habits play a role in maintaining the architecture of the forest by affecting the seed distribution of plants and trees.

We all felt the need for more contact with animals. The unpredictability of working with wildlife has taught us all that to be successful in this field, you have to be not only patient, but also innovative and opportunistic. So on moonless nights we went out in search of caiman.

The lake at camp contained three species of caiman. The most endangered, the black caiman, were relatively abundant because hunting them in the lake, their preferred habitat, had been prohibited for many years. The yacare caiman are more common but still endangered. We occasionally found the third species, the dwarf caiman, but it prefers small forest streams.

Few studies have been conducted on wild caiman in South America. I was interested in comparing the health of the population with that of the animals living at Perseverancia. We could use both populations to develop baseline data to contrast with data from animals living in areas more disturbed by humans.

We focused on caiman health for two reasons. First, we hoped to gain a better understanding of their overall status and to learn what diseases may threaten them in the wild; no one had ever studied the health of wild caiman. Second, since they are long-lived (thirty to forty years) and at the top of the food chain (eating fish, birds, and small mammals), they accumulate evidence of environmental disturbance such as pesticides and other pollutants that affect wildlife. Therefore they serve as bioindicators of the health of the aquatic environment in which they live.

Catching a caiman is pretty straightforward. Some people put out traps baited with a carcass, but we preferred a different approach. All you need is a small boat, preferably with a very shallow draft so you can get close to shore when you need to, a number of flashlights or headlamps of varying intensity, and a noose on the end of a long pole. Some people use a wire snare made for leg trapping fur-bearing mammals, and others use a homemade rope snare. Both are essentially just a lasso with a slipknot. I prefer a rope snare because it's gentler and safer for the animals. Finally and most important, you need help from people who won't become paralyzed by fear. Unless they're veteran caiman or crocodile catchers, I've learned that there's no telling how they will react. Unfortunately I have to wait until we snare the first big one before I can see how the team will cope. Losing control of the caiman after you pull it into the boat can be a really bad scene.

To find them, you motor along the lake's edge while shining a bright flashlight onto the surface of the water and the floating vegetation. The retinas of caiman, like those of most nocturnal species, have a highly reflective surface called the tapidum lucidum. This lies just behind the light receptors of the eye and improves night vision by reflecting light back to the cells responsible for creating the images we all see. Because the reflective qualities of the tapidum lucidum of different species vary, different colors are reflected. Humans have a little bit of reflectivity that can be seen with an extremely intense and focused light—the "red eye" seen in flash photography. Caiman "eyeshine" is a bright orange red, the color of the tip of a burning cigarette.

At a distance of fifteen feet or so, I switch to a less intense light. The bright flashlights tend to illuminate a big area and wash out the contrast of the eyeshine, allowing the caiman to blend in with the surrounding aquatic grasses and water hyacinth as they do in the daytime. A small headlamp frees your hands, allows the eyeshine to reflect directly back to your eyes, and does not produce an overwhelming amount of light. Because the headlamp is not blindingly bright, it has to be kept directly on the caiman's eyes so it can't see you. You can't turn your head away. If the moon is up and bright, the headlamp can't compete with the ambient light. The caiman see you and quickly disappear into the depths of the river.

We spotted a caiman in the dark water and drifted toward it as silently as possible. I tried to slip the snare over the animal's head and neck without touching it or disturbing the water or surrounding vegetation. The challenge was increased by the fact that the boat was moving and I had only a few seconds to assess the best approach and follow through before the boat bumped into the caiman. Steady hands and a very good boat driver are key.

I managed to slip the snare around the animal's neck and immediately pulled the rope taut. The caiman responded instantly, flipping its tail violently, paddling with all four limbs, and snapping its jaws. While I pulled the caiman's head toward the side of the boat, somebody grabbed its thrashing tail. With both ends in hand, we heaved the animal into the boat.

I quickly got the caiman's head under control by holding the back of its jaws where the neck begins. By pressing down on the top of the snout, you can hold a caiman's mouth shut. It's actually a bit safer to tape its jaws shut, just in case the caiman breaks loose in the boat. Not only are their teeth extremely sharp, they stick out around the sides of their closed mouths. Even with their mouths taped securely, you are holding a flat paddle rimmed with needle-sharp points. If the animal spins, the teeth will slice open your hand. It's important not to become complacent while holding one.

If everything goes like clockwork, caiman catching can be simple. However, it's not uncommon for someone accidentally to let go of one end or the other, which generally causes quite a stir in a tiny boat containing four or five people and a large caiman. Also, after the second or third animal, everything is wet and slippery. I remember working with another biologist, Steve Platt, in Belize. We had just caught a huge crocodile when Steve fell. Luckily he maintained his hold on the animal's neck. Then I slipped and landed backward on top of the croc, managing to control his tail with my legs and pin his upper body with my elbows behind my back. The two of us were laughing hysterically. Everyone else in

Rob with yacare caiman

the boat, however, was paralyzed. As long as two people know
what they are doing, subduing crocodiles and caiman is relatively
safe. One person controls the head, and the other sits astride the
hips and tail. All but the really big caiman (nine to sixteen feet) can
be managed this way. The huge ones require soft "shackles" to
hold their front and rear legs—another great use for duct tape.

We wanted to measure the animals at Lago Caiman, mark
them, and collect blood samples for future analysis. I examined
each one thoroughly, checking their long, flat snouts for signs of
injuries or malformations. In areas with pesticide or chemical contamination, we sometimes find animals with deformities. Since
this was a pristine area, I didn't find any abnormalities. After in-
specting their eyes, we taped them shut with paper masking tape to
calm the caiman. Caiman eyes pop up from the top of their skull
like twin periscopes. When you close their eyelids—unlike snakes,
they do have eyelids—their eyes sink down into the bony orbits of

the skull for protection. Putting a piece of tape over the top of their head holds their eyes closed and safely tucked away.

The top surface of their bodies is covered with hard, bony plates, or scutes, hinged together by a thin line of tough but flexible skin. Green and black algae usually grow on the scutes along their back, making them a bit slippery but providing perfect camouflage. Their undersides are smooth and clean, with the square scales that characterize crocodile or alligator skin products such as shoes and purses—the reason caiman have come so close to extinction. Their bellies are kind of pudgy—you can push them in like the Pillsbury Doughboy. Their feet, toes, and tail tips are vulnerable to injury from larger caiman and big carnivorous fish, so I always make notes of any healed injuries or missing extremities.

Caiman legs are small relative to their bodies, but they have massively powerful tails that propel them through the water. The beginning of the tail is almost as big as the abdomen but is pure muscle and bone. It is said that a caiman can break your leg with a flick of its tail. This is a myth, and a particularly irksome one when you are trying to catch caiman with inexperienced assistants. Their fear and hesitation can result in a caiman loose in the boat. While it hurts to get hit with the tail, the blow won't break your leg.

The sex of a caiman is not easily identifiable. Inside their vent, or cloaca, you can discern the difference in genitalia. The vent is the common name for the slit that opens into the vestibule on their lower belly. As in all birds and reptiles, this vestibule (also part of the cloaca) serves as the common terminal for the urinary, reproductive, and intestinal tracts. Inside a male's cloaca is a penislike organ called the hemipene. It is not connected to the urinary tract as in mammals, but it does inseminate females during copulation. By slipping your finger into the vent of a caiman, you can feel the hemipene and determine that the animal is a male. If you can't feel a hemipene, it's a female. Both sexes usually wiggle a bit when you do this.

CHOOSING YOUR BABY'S GENDER

The sex of crocodilian and some other reptile hatchlings depends on the temperature at which the eggs were incubated (temperature-dependent sex determination). Females are produced at cooler temperatures, while males predominate at warmer temperatures. In a natural caiman nest, males hatch near the top, where the previous two to three months sun has had the most effect, and females emerge from deeper in the pile, where it was a bit cooler.

Using measuring tapes I'd bought at a little fabric store in the Bronx, we determined the length of their bodies from the snout to the vent and the vent to the tail tip. Then we weighed them. Growth rates for different populations of caiman have yet to be determined. We marked them by cutting a small notch in one of the hard scutes on their tails, each one receiving a different notch corresponding to a standard number system used by biologists who study crocodiles. When these animals are recaptured in the future, we or others will be able to determine survivorship and growth rates. Marking them was also important to prevent multiple sampling from the same animal.

Finally I collected a blood sample. The old-fashioned way, practiced by biologists for decades, was to stick a needle into the caiman's heart: this is an easy method and produces a lot of blood. On the downside, it's possible to lacerate the caiman's beating heart, in which case the animal may die after you throw it back into the water. Nowadays vets draw blood from either the caudal vein that runs underneath the length of the tail or a venous sinus at the back of the head. I prefer the latter method because with a bit of practice, I can obtain a syringeful of blood quickly with little risk to the animal.

With one person holding the head securely and another controlling the body, I first used alcohol to clean the area where the base of the skull joins the neck. The back of a caiman's skull has a bony protrusion to protect the space where the spinal cord connects to the brain. After palpating the tip of the protrusion, you carefully insert a needle between the hard skin scutes directly behind the point. The vein draining blood from the head dilates at the spot where it joins the neck and forms a saddle-shape sinus at the junction of each vertebra. You have to be careful not to go too deep and pierce the spinal cord. (Don't try this at home.)

After obtaining a blood sample, we untaped the animal and released it at the same spot it was caught. (We had to assume the caiman picked that spot for a reason.) The entire handling procedure took less than ten minutes. We paddled away in the boat, started the engine, and went looking for another. If caiman could tell stories, the ones at Lago Caiman would no doubt hear accounts of alien abductions.

In a good night we catch and examine ten or twelve. More commonly we get three or four in a few hours' work and head back to camp by midnight. I stay up for another hour or two, processing the blood samples. This involves microscopically evaluating the blood cells and using a centrifuge to separate the different blood fractions for freezing in liquid nitrogen. Solar-charged batteries supplied the electricity for the equipment. Rob, Lil, and

Zaire

John and me with radio-collared okapi

Okapi station
in Epulu

Aerial view of Garamba

Abdim's storks and buffalo herd

Biopsy-darting white rhino

Ear-tagged buffalo

Covering a darted rhino's eyes to calm him

Bolivia

Peccary herd at *salitral*

Mother and
"pecclet"

Wet and muddy: luckily she's sedated

Weighing a young caiman

Examining a bull forest elephant

Radio collar

Abandoned hardwood logs

At play high in the canopy

(Macaw) chick in a basket

Penguins, pelicans, and cormorants

Sea lion colony at Punta San Juan

Pulse oximeter (to measure blood oxygen) on seal's tongue

Bachelor number five back at work

Albino
penguin
chicks

Young orangutan at rehab center in Sarawak

Baby leopard cat with four broken legs caused by
malnutrition while being kept as a pet

Wild female orangutan in Sumatra

Slash-and-burn agriculture

Young rehabbed orangutan (Photo by H. Frazier)

Bornean bearded pig

Orphaned juvenille Asian elephant now cared for
by Sabah Wildlife Department

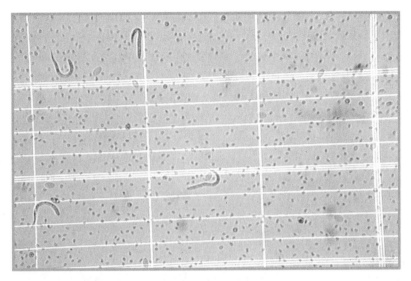

Microfilaria parasites in a caiman blood sample

some of the others always stay with me in the mud hut laboratory to help. By one or two in the morning we are all satisfied that we have accomplished something and head to our respective tents to get some sleep.

They're Back

We continued the nightly hunts for caiman as long as the moon allowed. Days were spent waiting at the peccary trap site. Seven days after their first appearance, the peccaries returned. By coincidence I was stationed in the hammock over the capture pen door that day. Once again, some of the herd went into the trap area and some of the others stayed outside beneath my perch. I dropped the door when it seemed that no more animals would wander in. The peccaries were stampeding around, clacking their tusks and snorting as usual, ready to shred any threat in their way. I was as excited and nervous as before, but this second time seemed a little more routine. I radioed the troops back at camp, jumped to the ground and chased off the peccaries in the immediate vicinity, plodded through the mud, and wired the trap door shut.

Within a few minutes Lil, Rob, and the team appeared. While I readied the equipment, they started to work their way around the huge pen, moving the peccaries down to the end where I could dart them. I had thirty darts prepared. But animals will be animals, and they always manage to prove you wrong. Or at least they don't read the directions. Only half of the captured group ran into the funnel-shaped corral at the end, allowing us to enclose them in a smaller area. These I darted as quickly as I could. The animals were excited, and I wanted to calm them down as soon as possible so they would not inadvertently hurt each other in the small pen.

Another ten peccaries were still running around in the huge

capture pen. Rob, Jose, and Yate had tired of trying to round them up from outside and had climbed over the fence. They were now confronting the peccaries directly and trying to herd them down to the darting area by yelling and thrashing the underbrush with sticks. The herd ran in our direction, then at the last minute turned and charged back past the three of them. I managed to dart another one each time they stampeded by. It was a little like shooting mechanical ducks at the county fair, except the staff was standing behind the ducks rather than safely in front.

Finally I filled my vest pocket with loaded darts and climbed inside the pen to track down the renegades. Wading through the mud and pushing through the thorny underbrush, the four of us in the pen called out sightings and directions of the constantly moving animals. The challenge was twofold: first, to approach them without getting attacked; and second, to dart only the peccaries that hadn't already been injected with the drug. I didn't want any of them to die from an overdose. I needed a clear view of both hind legs to check for either a dart or a spot of blood where a dart may have hit and fallen out.

While I was continuing to dart every animal, the rest of the team patrolled the large wooded corral in search of animals that had succumbed to the drug. Two people would then carry each eighty-to-hundred-pound sleeping peccary over to the small pen where the other anesthetized peccaries were being monitored. The team also had to maintain constant vigilance over the stream and flooded areas to ensure that no peccaries fell asleep in the water and drowned.

Within twenty minutes we had all of the animals darted. We lined them up side by side on the ground: fifteen peccaries sleeping in a long row, like soldiers bedded down in their barracks. We'd finally done it: the past three years of hard work had paid off. We

Lil and assistant weighing a peccary

were covered in mud and drenched in sweat. But it was not time to reflect on success or celebrate; for the time being, quick high-fives had to suffice. Fifteen animals under general anesthesia required our complete and immediate attention.

One of the Bolivian students attached a plastic ear tag to each animal. We were using the one-inch-long colored and numbered tags used by sheep farmers. The tags are inserted in the cartilage of the ear much like earrings. The plastic is safe and inert, reducing any chance of infection. The tags would allow us to keep track of the animals while we were examining them and also allow Lil to recognize individuals over the following years when she encountered them in the forest.

As soon as an animal was tagged, Yate and Jose slid it on a piece of burlap and hooked the corners of the material to a spring scale. The scale was then suspended on a six-foot-long pole and lifted by two people. Most of the animals were adults: the heaviest one, a pregnant female, was 105 pounds.

Two little ones, about four weeks old based on their size and red orange color, scampered around to escape being stepped on but quickly returned to stand next to their sleeping mother or one of their aunts or uncles. At five or six pounds they were small enough to handle without anesthesia. At first they squealed when I cupped my hand under their belly. But once I lifted one up and held it to my chest like a puppy, it would quiet down and just look around at the flurry of human activity with a slightly nervous but completely attentive expression. Baby peccaries are extremely cute, but their mud-drenched, short bristly hair and sharp little teeth prevent them from being cuddly.

I quickly went down the line and checked everyone's heart rate and respirations with a stethoscope. The peccaries', that is: I already knew the team members' heart rates were elevated. All the

Lil and me up to our ears in peccaries

animals were doing well under anesthesia, breathing clearly with regular and rhythmic heartbeats. I gave each animal a complete physical examination, checking mouth, nose, eyes, and ears and then progressing down the body to the stubby little tail. Using a digital thermometer, one of the students took their body temperatures rectally. Some were overheated from running around, so we cooled them off with buckets of water from the nearby stream.

Their long bristly hair does not cover their bodies densely, but it does provide a protective shield. When you lift it against the grain, you expose their tan skin. I had forgotten how soft to the touch they were, like a pudgy baby. A few had minor scratches and scrapes, but I didn't find any large scars or wounds. They were in good condition, no old fractures, no missing teeth or torn ears. As a vet, I always find it a joy to work on healthy animals.

On the center of their rumps they have a huge scent gland several inches wide that protrudes almost an inch. The gland secretes a thick, cream-colored, musk-scented exudate. When you squeeze the gland it responds like a huge pimple. The musky stench this gland produces is almost overwhelming. The oily exudate is rubbed off on the vegetation as the animals wander through the forest and probably marks their trails and territory. They also rub their faces on each other's glands, smearing the scented cream on themselves. The whole area now smelled strongly, but since we had the scent all over ourselves, we no longer noticed it.

Rob collected ticks from all the animals and stored them in alcohol for future identifications. The peccaries were moderately infested, most carrying ten to twenty ticks. This was normal and expected for any animal that lives in a forest and doesn't have hands, mouths, or beaks adept at picking off the bloodsuckers. If we later found signs of infectious diseases from the blood analysis, the ticks might be the cause, serving as a potential agent for spreading the diseases among the individuals in the group. Identifying the genus and species of the ticks and having specimens to test could be important in understanding the ecology or life cycles of the diseases.

After I examined each animal, I collected a blood sample from a vein on the inside of its thigh. One of the guys would lift a rear leg and give me access to the inner surface of the other leg. By sliding my hand in the groove between the muscle masses on the front and rear of the thigh, I could feel the blood pulsing through the femoral artery. Right in front of the artery runs the femoral vein. This was my target. You cannot see either the artery or the vein, but by understanding the anatomy and being able to palpate the artery as a landmark, you can carefully thread the syringe needle into the nearby vein. The blood samples would be processed later and then frozen for future laboratory analysis. For me, the samples were a precious derivative from our efforts. They were critical for understanding the health of the peccaries. Ironically, I would have to process and safely store these fragile and perishable samples in a remote and decidedly low-tech environment. Our camp couldn't be farther from the hospital and laboratory where this same study on humans would be conducted.

While I was examining and bleeding the animals, Lil was checking out their teeth. She could determine the age of the animal by evaluating the degree of tooth wear and the number of permanent versus baby or deciduous teeth present in the jaw. The older adults, who had all their permanent teeth, were lumped in age groups—four to eight, eight to fifteen, and over fifteen—based on how worn down their teeth were. This is an imperfect measure, however, because silicates in the soil can cause a degree of variance in tooth wear. These silicates are incorporated in the vegetation the animals eat and also are ingested when they eat dirt-covered fruits and roots. Thus the teeth of an herbivore that lives in an area with sandy soil will look older than those of a cousin that lives in an area with softer soil.

Next I examined all of the females with a handheld ultrasound device made for detecting pregnancy in domestic pigs. The Preg-Tone is a battery-operated unit about the size of a box of animal crackers with a three-foot-long cable with a small transducer head at the end. The transducer converts the electrical signal to low-frequency sound waves, which bounce off the body organs at different frequencies and intensities depending on the composition of the organ. If the Preg-Tone senses a fluid-filled space, like the amniotic sac in which a fetus floats, the unit produces a constant tone like a smoke detector alarm. The device is not as sophisticated or as fun to use as a real-time, two dimensional ultrasound machine that gives you a picture of the fetus. On the other hand, it weighs less than half a pound and clips easily on your belt. Five of the seven adult females we captured were pregnant, suggesting that reproductive performance was good. Lil's long-term studies could now track how many of these successfully gave birth and raised their young.

We were finished. All we had to do now was move them into the adjacent pen and wait for them to wake up from the anesthesia. Although they still had to be watched carefully to make sure they were breathing normally, it was finally time to relax. Everyone lit up cigarettes. Some of the guys put fresh wads, or "bolos," of coca leaves in their mouths. I had asked everyone to get rid of them when we caught the peccaries. My request had nothing to do with the effect of the mild stimulant. I simply was having a difficult time understanding what they were saying when they had a big wad of leaves stuffed in one cheek.

It was just getting dark as we finished. A couple of people would have to stay with the peccaries until they were all awake: sleeping, they were too susceptible to jaguar attack. We hoped that having several people standing around and talking would discourage a jaguar. We took turns hiking back to camp, washing up, and getting fresh water to drink. It had been a long, hot day.

Two hours later all of the peccaries were wide awake, alert, and coordinated on their feet. It was safe to let them wander off into the forest. They would bed down for the night and in the morning use their keen sense of smell to reunite with their herd mates.

Because of the large number of blood samples we had to process that night—the volume of the labwork we had to perform—we knew that the two twelve-volt truck batteries at camp would not offer sufficient power for our needs. This was a problem we had prepared for, and we had warned the staff at park head-quarters that we might show up one night to use their generator. So we loaded up the boat with the liquid nitrogen tank, micro-scope, centrifuge, crate of lab supplies, and extra clothing. Going with the flow of the river allowed us to make good time; by eleven we had arrived at the headquarters and set up our lab.

MR. WIZARD GOES TO THE AMAZON

At park headquarters we set up my lab in the screened dining area overlooking the river. I made thin blood smears on glass micro-scope slides and laid them out to dry before treating them with an al-cohol fixative that preserves the architectural structure of each blood cell. These slides would later be stained and used to evaluate red and white blood cells and to look for the presence of blood parasites.

Thin glass capillary tubes were filled with a few drops of blood and spun in the centrifuge. This forces the cell fraction of the blood to sep-arate from the serum or plasma fraction. After spinning, you can mea-sure what percentage of blood is made up of cells. This measurement, called the hematocrit, is a simple indicator of conditions such as ane-mia, dehydration, and shock.

A drop or two of the plasma portion from the capillary tube is put into another small device called a refractometer. The unit fits in your hand and has a glass plate at one end on which you put the plasma to be tested. After closing a little translucent flap, you point it toward a source of light such as the sun or a flashlight and look into the lens at the opposite end. It's reminiscent of looking through a kaleidoscope. The refractometer measures the bending of the light as it passes through a liquid. The degree of bending, or refraction, depends on the concentration of material dissolved in the solution (specific gravity). Using this basic principle of physics, the instrument focuses the bent beam of light on a little screen with a calibrated scale that indicates how much "stuff" is dissolved in the sample. With plasma, we are interested in knowing how much protein is present. Some of these proteins carry nutrients and wastes in the blood, and others are antibodies that fight off infections. All of these proteins serve an important role in maintaining the health of an animal (human or nonhuman).

Using another solution mixed with a carefully measured drop of blood (actually twenty microns, or less than half of an average drop), we can count the number of white blood cells. The solution is placed on a thick piece of glass that has been etched with microscopic lines to form a grid. A glass cover slip is laid on top of liquid and is supported on each side by two precisely formed glass ridges. This creates a chamber of exact thickness, and the gridlines provide exact length and width. Under a microscope you can count the number of white blood cells in a set area of the grid and then calculate the total number of cells in a milliliter, or "cc" of blood. White blood cells are essential in the functioning of the immune system, and the count provides an important index of overall health.

Finally, the remainder of the blood is centrifuged and the serum is separated from the cells and placed in high-density polyethylene

Dangling samples in panty hose into liquid nitrogen

screw-top storage tubes to be frozen in liquid nitrogen. At a later date the frozen samples will be distributed to different labs for a wide variety of tests, including nutrition, toxicology, genetics, and infectious diseases.

The samples from the fifteen peccaries took us only four hours to process. By three in the morning we were ready to bathe (cold-water showers were available) and go to bed. Park headquarters offered cots with mattresses. It was delightful to sleep in dry bedding above the ground for a night. The next morning we enjoyed another luxury, drinking coffee while sitting in real chairs. I never realized it while I was there, but in all the years we have been using the camp at Lago Caiman, no one has ever made a chair with a back on it or brought one in. We reloaded the boat and headed back to camp that same morning, excited about the prospect of catching more peccaries.

*After one more week of intensely hot days punc*tuated with downpours, another group of peccaries arrived. We captured fifteen, spent another night at park headquarters, and returned for five more days without making a third capture.

In total we had spent twenty-four days without a break. The team was tired, and it was time for me to move on to my next project. The experiment had worked. We had developed a technique to catch large numbers of peccaries that could be used by conservation researchers throughout South America. Later laboratory analysis of our samples provided the first information on wild peccaries' normal organ system values and disease exposure.

This baseline information enabled us to determine what is

normal. People take for granted their doctor's ability to interpret test results. This ability is based on thousands of samples obtained from one species, humans. For wildlife, we are challenged with gathering samples from thousands of species with whom we now precariously share the planet.

We found evidence of two viruses similar to those of domestic pigs that could affect reproductive success. We still must conduct long-term studies to determine the actual effects, but for now we at least know that these viruses exist in the wild. In roughly a third of the animals we found another agent that commonly causes still-births, abortions, and sometimes death in other mammals. This information is critical in developing models for population management strategies. Nobody can completely predict the future, but with good information we can prepare for various contingencies.

The capture of large groups of peccaries has also helped us develop an accurate understanding of the sex, age structure, and reproductive status of wild populations. Lil's studies will show how many adults and offspring survive, how different groups share the resources of the forest, and whether or not the individuals from different herds interact. Do they mix their gene pools, or do they remain separate?

It was a productive trip. Lots of peccaries, lots of caiman, and we'd enhanced conservation efforts in Bolivia. We were very proud of what we had accomplished together. Lil and Rob would stay on at Lago Caiman to continue their research with the help of Yate and Jose. I would miss my partners, my buddies. Sometimes I think this is the hardest part of my work. Once again it was time to make the long trip back to New York.

Crossing liana bridge

Part Four

Cameroon

The Race Against Entropy

*I celebrate Thanksgiving with friends
in the rain forest, share afofo with
some highly unusual drinking buddies,
and am almost killed by an elephant.*

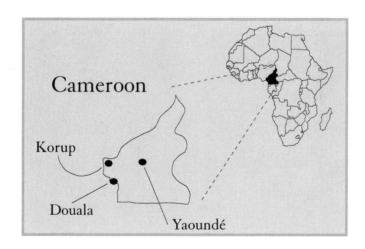

The Race Against Entropy

November of 1992 found me flying to Cameroon, deep in the heart of tropical Africa. Because the rain forests of western Cameroon were insulated from the ice ages, they are thought to be some of the oldest forests in the world, supporting a rich diversity of wildlife that has yet to be completely inventoried. Traveling with me was Fred Koontz, head of the Science Resource Center of the Bronx Zoo. A technology buff, Fred had helped to develop a plan to radio-track forest elephants in a new national park on the western edge of Cameroon. Our goal was to help in a multidiscipline approach to preserve the richness of the park.

My assignment was to attach radio collars to forest elephants so we could learn more about their ecology and behavior. Forest elephants are a different subspecies from their grassland cousins. They are a bit smaller and have thin, straight tusks rather than the thick, forward-curving tusks of savanna elephants. Unlike the huge, angular-shaped ears that help savanna elephants stay cool in the hot African sun, forest elephants have smaller and more rounded ears—like Mickey Mouse's.

The radio collars we planned to deploy would help us gather essential information on exactly how elephants used the forest. We knew elephants, like the peccaries of the Amazon, played a role in dispersing some plant and tree seeds and also in reducing the numbers of others. In addition, our study was important for public relations. Elephants are a flagship species; they (perhaps more than any other species) draw public attention to protecting the park. Our work would play a small yet significant part in developing and protecting the park.

Fred and I were heavily loaded with supplies to work with WCS's field biologist James "Buddy" Powell. The four radio collars (each seven feet long and made of rubberized five-inch-wide machine belting) alone weighed a hundred pounds. We packed tons of gear in six duffel bags, two suitcases, and four huge ice chests. Each 110-quart cooler was used as a shipping crate for the gear. Later we could use the coolers for dry storage at Buddy's field camp. In New York I had made a last minute stop at the little grocery store on City Island to buy a twenty-pound frozen turkey. I threw it in one of the coolers without telling Fred. Thanksgiving was six days away.

Our flight from New York to Brussels was first delayed, then canceled. We were shuffled over to a flight bound for London with the guarantee that we could get a flight to Paris and then to Cameroon. The Pan Am representative promised that our twelve pieces of baggage would be retagged and assured us we wouldn't be separated from our equipment and clothing. I was a little skeptical; Fred was moaning. Fred has perfected pessimism to a fine and humorous art form. In a tight situation you can always count on Fred to be muttering the worst-case scenario under his breath: "I'll be surprised if any of our things make it to Cameroon. I'll be surprised if *we* make it to Cameroon."

Fred had been to Cameroon a year earlier to help plan WCS's participation in the creation of a national park in the western part of the country, on the border with Nigeria. In addition to elephants, the area has a diverse and rare fauna. Drill baboons, a number of species of colobus and guenon monkeys, many types of rare forest antelopes, leopards and golden cats, eagles, hornbills, and an unknown number of yet unnamed reptiles and amphibians live there. The Korup National Park project was a joint effort of WCS, the World Wildlife Fund (WWF), and the Cameroonian National Parks Department. WWF planned to develop the southern part of the park for tourism, train the park guards for anti-poaching patrols, and develop a conservation education program for the local people. The U.S. Agency for International Development was providing several million dollars in support. WCS's role in the Cameroon project was to conduct biological inventories of the park to determine the abundance and diversity of plants and animals and to set up a long-term ecology research station in the more remote northern half of the park. All in all, this was a high-profile project in the region and among conservation agencies.

Buddy Powell was the leader of the project for WCS. The year before, he had finished a successful research and conservation project for WCS on the highly endangered West African manatee in the Ivory Coast. He had been looking for another conservation-related job in Central or West Africa and thought the Korup project would provide a healthy challenge. He would later learn that "challenge" was an understatement.

Buddy and I have a lot in common: we're about the same age, height, and build, and though Buddy was a bit leaner than me when I arrived, I usually drop five to ten pounds during the course of a project. Like me, Buddy had grown up in the Deep South and on the water. The first fifteen years of his career, Buddy worked with Florida manatees. During vet school I went to Gainesville to visit friends who were studying manatees. We ended up on Crystal River, in Buddy's houseboat. Fourteen years later I found myself on my way to Cameroon to work with him.

Eighteen hours after leaving New York, Fred and I arrived in Douala, the largest city in Cameroon. All of our baggage did not. The man responsible for lost luggage was more resentful than helpful. Later I would learn that anger was not uncommon. A brutal colonial history, as well as the precolonial slave trade, created a legitimate current of resentment. Moreover, our baggage may have contained more possessions than any single airport staff member would ever own. At any rate, the feelings emanating from the baggage manager made an immediate and lasting impression on me.

The missing pieces of baggage turned out to contain all of our clothing—not essential to the project, but helpful. I was lucky enough to have packed my bathroom gear in my carry-on as well as a surgical scrub shirt, but I wanted my hiking boots and work-clothes. One of the equipment bags that arrived with us contained the new zoo T-shirts that we had brought as gifts. At least Fred and I had a change of shirts, even if they did make us look like twins back from a class trip to the Bronx Zoo.

The next morning we went to the airline office to check on the bags. The clerk reported that our bags had been recovered in Paris and would arrive in Douala that afternoon. Time was tight, so we decided to drive to Yaoundé, the capital of Cameroon, meet with government officials, and return to collect our missing bags before leaving for the field in a couple of days.

Douala, Cameroon's main seaport, is not particularly clean, nor does it have that fresh smell of the open sea; but like most port cities, it is bustling with commercial activity. With its harbor full of cargo ships and its streets crowded with traffic and people, Douala retains the lively atmosphere of a buccaneer town. I felt at home and strangely comfortable there.

POSTCARD FROM CAMEROON

Cameroon is the most geographically diverse country in Central or West Africa, perhaps the entire continent. The three main regions are the rain forests to the south and east, the northern savanna, and the western hill region near the border with Nigeria—once the British Cameroons. French spoken in the eastern two-thirds of the country and English spoken in the west are the official languages.

Cameroon is approximately the size of Spain, though with only one-third the population—about 12 million people. More than 130 ethnic groups, each with its own language, make Cameroon one of the most culturally diverse countries on the continent.

Cameroon is able to feed its population without aid, and it's one of the richest sub-Saharan African countries. Its wealth comes principally from oil, though a thriving agriculture program feeds the economy as well as the people.

Until the middle of the nineteenth century, the slave trade was central to the economy and culture of southern Cameroon. This ended when the Germans established a colonial protectorate in 1884. The Germans were active colonialists, building a railway, wharves along the coastline, and schools. After World War I, the League of Nations awarded approximately 80 percent of the country to the French, two noncontiguous areas to the British, and a tiny area to the Germans (which they lost after World War II).

The 1950s witnessed Cameroon's long battle for independence. The Union Camerounaise Party from the north eventually dominated the political scene. In 1960 a full-scale rebellion was staged by the Bamieke and the Bassa tribal groups, southern Cameroonians and members of the opposition party. The French spent eight months quelling the uprising, during which thousands of Cameroonians were slaughtered. Finally, in 1973 East and West Cameroon voted to become a republic with one legislative body, and the struggle for unity and democracy within that governmental structure has been going on ever since.

Tribal life in Cameroon has not been destroyed by twentieth-century "progress." Many tribes remain isolated, intact, and highly hierarchical, with chiefs who are actually called sultans. (Arabic traders had touched the lives of Cameroonians long before the arrival of Europeans.) Tribal life remains traditional. Rituals are maintained, and native artwork, mainly wood carving, which varies from tribe to tribe, can be found almost everywhere. Wooden statues decorated with beads, cowrie shells, and bits of metal commonly depict the people and the animals of the region. A distinctly Cameroonian tradition is flamboyant elephant masks with round ears and elaborate glass beaded bodices stretching to the bearer's knees.

The logging industry in Cameroon has wreaked considerable havoc on the rain forest. The rate of destruction is approximately half that of Brazil—about 0.8 percent per year, far surpassing other countries in Central Africa. The French government recently relieved Cameroon of a large part of its foreign debt burden in exchange for exclusive logging rights for French-owned companies. We jokingly called this a "debt for nature swap," a term normally used when developing countries create protected areas in exchange for reduction of their foreign debt burden. The French deal with Cameroon reduces their debt burden in exchange for destroying their environment.

A Capital Offense

We took the project's Land Cruiser and drove inland from Douala on the coast, northeast to Yaoundé. Even though the road is in excellent condition, the hundred-mile trip takes three or four hours. Slow traffic, cattle, goats, chickens, and pedestrians along the highway slow the pace considerably. Yaoundé, located in the eastern two-thirds of the country, is predominantly francophone. It was chosen as the capital to establish a second economic center independent of the traditional commercial port of Douala. As a new center of government, it does not have the old flavor or beautiful but run-down architectural style of Douala. Basically it's a crowded, sprawling town.

Yaoundé has some of the worst traffic I've ever seen in a small city. Instead of buses, thousands of little yellow taxis are assigned circular routes through the town. They don't have signs depicting their route, so people have to stop them to find it out. When a cab stops, it blocks traffic, and since it carries only three or four passengers, the streets are choked with stopped cars talking to potential customers or picking up or dropping off fares. Luckily drivers do not blow their horns much. Mufflers, however, are not a high priority, so the traffic is loud and the air is thick with fumes. I'm convinced that Cameroon is the training ground for New York cabbies. A traffic circle can be a life-threatening experience; Buddy aptly calls them bangabouts rather than roundabouts.

The clogged traffic arteries delivered us to Yaoundé hot, sweaty, and dirty and too late to meet with officials at the Institute for Animal Research. The office closed for the day at two o'clock. Instead we went to the USAID office to meet with the American project officer. We reviewed with him our strategy for catching and radio-collaring the elephants. Buddy contacted camp with their short-wave radio and told the Cameroonian staff that we were trying to get permits and planned to drive to Korup within a day or two.

Buddy and his fiancée, Maureen, also from Florida, took us to a chicken house that night for dinner. Chicken houses take the place of restaurants in all the small towns or villages in Cameroon. Basically they're homes in which the main room has been converted into a communal dining area, providing a spartan but homey feeling. The families serve grilled chicken, fried plantains, and beer. The chicken house where we ate, however, had grown to become a more formal restaurant with a written menu. It included pangolin, a small anteater armored with scaly plates, and porcupine, both choice meats in Cameroon. Neither sounded particularly appetizing. Besides, wherever I work I try not to eat wildlife. Even if the animals are not endangered, they usually are overhunted and no game management strategy is used to control the harvest. Frequently, commercial hunting is illegal, and our buying the product would further encourage the trade. Professional concerns aside, the proprietors were welcoming and the atmosphere gave us a needed break from the day's tension.

We spent the night at a typical equatorial city hotel built in the seventies—modern but run-down and moldy. The next morning we were off at a frantic pace to complete our errands in Yaoundé, get back to Douala in time for a dinner meeting, and pick up our lost luggage. The first stop was the Institute for Animal Research to get our permits for radio collaring. Before they could issue the permits, however, we had to get a fiscal stamp from the Department of Treasury. A fiscal stamp? This was news.

We plowed our way through traffic back into the city center and found the Treasury Department for our stamps. A line hundreds of people long snaked outside and around the building, waiting to get fiscal stamps. Every official document, permit, or form requires a tax stamp, but none of the departments that issue the documents are allowed to sell the stamps. So everyone has to go to the Treasury Department to buy them. You'd be hard-pressed to design a less efficient system, though in this case I think the rationale is to reduce corruption. Seeing that it would take hours, Buddy walked directly inside and up to the front desk, where for a price of a dollar each they immediately sold him the necessary stamps. Buddy is a great problem solver.

We returned to the Institute for Animal Research. Twenty minutes after turning over the stamps, we received all the permits we needed. Driving back to town, however, we got stuck in the midday traffic. Even worse than the normal "stop and don't go" sludge that constitutes rush-hour traffic almost anywhere else on the globe, this was the two- to three-hour Cameroonian lunchtime; everyone seemed to be trying to go somewhere. Finally we reached the hotel, and after checking out and running a few more errands, we were ready to head back to Douala.

The drive was fairly uneventful except for an accident we witnessed. A bus had run over a pickup truck, which was now squeezed out from either side of the bus. The cab of the truck was crushed flat, and from where the driver's side door was supposed to be, a body hung onto the road. The passengers had climbed out and were milling around on the highway. It was a bizarre combination of gruesome death and casual routine. Buddy said that since foreign aid money had improved the road into a modern, wide, two-lane highway, accidents had become disastrous.

The next morning we returned to Sabena Airlines. Not only had they not received our luggage, they had no idea where it was. We decided to use the day to get supplies in Douala. If the luggage did not arrive the next day, we'd leave without it. We could buy some clothes locally, and besides, Fred and I were getting used to wearing our matching zoo T-shirts.

We bought a few tools at a hardware and marine supplier near the port. Telonics, the radio-collar manufacturer, had sent us the wrong-size wrench for the bolts used to fasten the collars. At $3,500 per collar, you'd think they could've given us the right wrench. But compared to the U.S. federal and state wildlife agencies that buy dozens to hundreds of units from them at premium prices, we were a small potatoes customer. As in the stories you hear about Defense Department contractors, there's no such thing as a free wrench.

Everything in Cameroon is two to three times the price it is in the United States. Supposedly the prices are driven up by European expatriates with huge foreign salaries. We had to pay over $200 for a socket wrench set. We had to have a wrench for our project, and we were willing to pay any price. We were much luckier than the vast majority of Cameroonians.

Miraculously, the next morning our bags arrived. Elated, we left Douala. We stopped for lunch at a technical training college near Buea, where our project is funding four students from the villages near Korup National Park. By providing young people living in and around the park with marketable skills, we may reduce their dependence on market hunting in the park and even provide incentives for families to move out of the park entirely. Next we stopped at another training school where Buddy and Maureen had also sent students. The Swiss-run school has a hugely successful twenty-year-old agricultural training program where students learn poultry, swine, and rabbit farming using locally available supplies and equipment. From Buea we drove another six hours to reach our next destination, the village of Nguti.

Buddy and Mo's house had a large living room/staging area, three bedrooms, a big office, and a kitchen. Simply built with cement blocks and a concrete floor, the house was located on a wooded hillside above the village of Nguti, with a very pleasant view of the town, far enough away to filter out the sounds of traffic and late night music blaring from chicken houses and outdoor bars. A small stream near the house provided cold running water, and solar-charged truck batteries provided electricity when the neighboring missionary medical clinic wasn't running their generator. This was to be our town house between trips to the forest over the next month.

Two Hired Guns

We spent the day following our arrival in Nguti, organizing equipment for the trip into the park. I did some cardboard box target practice with the new dart rifles I had ordered specifically for this project. Also, I had gotten some small radio transmitters that screwed into the tailpiece of the drug darts. I was hoping that they would help us track the darted elephant after it ran off in the jungle. Unfortunately the tailpiece transmitters were heavy. With a transmitter attached to a loaded drug dart, I could get an accurate shot from no more than thirty feet away. To hit an elephant I'd have to get too close for comfort. Without the transmitter attached I could shoot the drug dart sixty to ninety feet with a very high impact—enough to ensure that the needle would stick in the tough hide of an elephant and that the charge inside the dart would trigger the drug injection.

To both drug an elephant and keep track of it, we decided to use two dart rifles—one with the drug dart and one with a radio transmitter dart. I would handle the rifle with the drug-loaded projectile, while Philip, Buddy's best elephant tracker and forest guide, would be at my side and shoot the transmitter dart simultaneously.

Born and raised in next-door Nigeria, Philip had been working with Buddy since the Korup park project began. He was about five feet eight and well built, with a weathered face that made him look older than his forty-odd years. A reformed elephant poacher, he claimed to have killed more than 140 forest elephants before

Fred, Philip, Phillip, and Buddy at the end of the day

Buddy hired him to help study and protect them. He was excellent in the forest and boasted profusely of his knowledge and skills.

During our darting practice, Philip shared his view on elephant hunting. Philip had been a hired gun. When elephants were destroying a village's gardens of corn, bananas, and manioc, the community would arrange for a hunter to kill the elephants. This was dangerous work; over the years Philip had seen several of his assistants and colleagues trampled to death. As compensation for the risk, the typical arrangement allowed the hunter to keep the valuable ivory tusks. The villagers kept the meat. For centuries this was a normal routine, and no one called it poaching. Colonialization and Western culture changed the system. In recent years hunting elephants without a $500 license from the federal government has become illegal. As most local elephant hunters never have that much money, they work illegally—poaching.

Philip got comfortable with the feel of his dart rifle, and we practiced firing two darts simultaneously. Meanwhile Fred had shown Buddy a computer program that calculates the position of satellites we were going to use for the elephant tracking. The radio collars had to be programmed in synchrony with these satellites. By the end of the day we were finished practicing and organizing. We were ready for an adventure in the nearby jungle.

LIKE TWO SATELLITES PASSING IN THE NIGHT

The system we were using to track the elephants relied on two Argos oceanographic and meteorological satellites that are in low, circumpolar orbit. The Argos satellites are only six hundred miles high, and each makes a trip around the North and South Poles every six hours. The satellites' sensors can view an area a couple of thousand miles wide at a time, enabling the ground station to monitor a strip of the planet with each orbit. Like two painters stroking up and down on a spinning ball with a wide paintbrush, the two Argos satellites cover the entire surface of the earth three to four times daily.

From our perspective on the ground, the satellite rises on one horizon, transits the sky, and sets over the opposite horizon in a little over ten minutes. Near the equator, the overflight could be two thousand miles to the east or west, with the satellites too far away to "see" us. Our computer software, however, could calculate the exact date and time of each satellite pass over Cameroon. With this information we programmed the radio collars to turn on when the satellites were flying over and then turn off again to conserve the batteries when the satellites were out of range. We hoped to get three "fixes" a day. Our power consumption strategy would allow the transmitters in the collars to last up to ten months.

When activated, the collar sends a signal every minute. The signal identifies the individual collar (elephant) and relays information such as air temperature and activity level of the animal. The animal's movement is calculated by a computer chip and an electrical switch that uses a small drop of mercury to count how many times the collar has rocked side to side in a set period of time. If three or four signals make it through the forest canopy and don't get blocked by any nearby hills, the signals are relayed to computers on earth, where the data are interpreted and converted to longitude and latitude. Using a telephone modem, we can call from anywhere on the planet and download information from the system. Once we know each collared elephant's location, we can calculate its home range and thus determine how many elephants a given area can support—information critical for park planning and management.

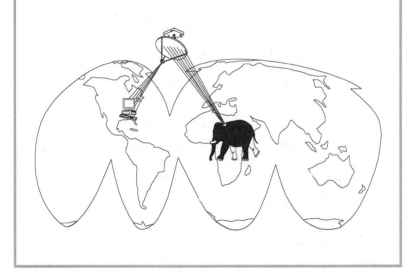

The next day was Thanksgiving, and we left for the field at about ten in the morning. From the house in Nguti it was an hour's drive to the trailhead near the village of Baro. There we spent a half hour negotiating with villagers for help carrying our equipment to the research camp deep in the forest. Theoreti-

Negotiating for lunch at Baro

cally these arrangements had been settled the day before by Buddy's Cameroonian project manager, but the locals had nothing to lose by reopening negotiations. Today they wanted a free lunch before starting work. As in any culture, price is determined by the level of need at the point of sale. Lunch was served.

With final agreements in place, we hiked the eight hilly miles through the jungle to camp with nine extra men helping with the equipment. We had to cross two hammock bridges spanning hundred- to two-hundred-foot-wide stretches of rivers too deep and fast flowing to wade across. The bridges were beautifully woven from sturdy rattan vines; remarkably, a three- to four-inch-thick bundle of vines can bear your weight. At shoulder height, two thin vines spanning the river are connected with a zigzag lashing to the vine bundle at the bottom to form a V-shaped bridge. The suspended macramé affair arches down gracefully from an elevated position on the cliffs along the river to within twenty feet of the rushing water and back up to the opposite bank.

As I crossed the bridge, an amazing optical illusion occurred. When I looked down at the thin vines, my brain tried to compensate for the apparent sideways movement by making it look as if the water were stationary—as ground would be—and that the bridge was rushing off to one side instead. I had to consciously force one foot in front of the other, squarely atop the vine, to keep from stepping off to one side. The bouncing of the stretched vines further complicated the crossing. By midspan a resonance pattern was established and the bridge was waving up and down. Walking with your weight even slightly off center makes the bridge swing side to side as it bounces up and down. For safety—since each person creates a different rhythm, and it's impossible to predict the state of decay of the rattan vines—only one person at a time crosses the bridge.

The people who live in this jungle casually cross these bridges while balancing heavy loads on their heads. Philip strolled across with a backpack and a cooler packed with equipment. I had a hard time with a fully loaded backpack, and Fred crossed without any load. I decided that kissing the earth on the other side would be a bit overdramatic, but only barely.

By midafternoon we arrived at the camp, which consisted of several buildings scattered in the thick forest, and began setting up for Thanksgiving dinner with the New York turkey that Mo had cooked in Nguti. Over the years I've come up with a few little tricks to help me cope with the constant travel. In addition to my favorite Starbucks Sumatran tiger coffee mug, I try to observe holidays from the States.

Mo heated up the bird in a domed-shaped clay oven she had built. In the embers of the open fire we roasted manioc or cassava tubers—one of the local starch mainstays—and cooked beans and rice. Mo had managed to obtain two cans of Ocean Spray cranberry sauce from the American embassy commissary. (All over the

Central African–style clay oven

world, American embassies maintain small stores that stock American brands such as Oreo cookies and Heinz ketchup for sale exclusively to embassy personnel.) Since the elephant collaring project was USAID funded, Buddy and Mo were allowed to purchase items. She had also made a pumpkin pie, which she had packed carefully in a cooler. At dinner, some of the Cameroonian field staff were amazed at the size of the "chicken" and how good the dark, rich meat tasted. I told them that all chickens in the United States were that big.

We had a magnificent dinner in the middle of the jungle—a wonderful way to celebrate the holiday. I talked about how Thanksgiving had begun as a feast to celebrate the way different cultures in North America had helped each other survive in a harsh environment (leaving out the part about how one culture then went on to systematically displace the other). Ironically, part of our effort to establish the national park was to eventually get the remaining residents to resettle outside its boundaries.

We finished up dinner and washed our plastic and enameled tin tableware in the nearby stream. The kitchen area was an open-air pavilion with a grass thatch roof and a packed-earth floor, but the rest of the research camp facilities were wood houses raised a few feet off the ground on wooden posts. Mo had designed and constructed the buildings. She had a surprisingly high energy level despite her calm appearance, and she had the ability to accomplish amazing tasks in the harshest of conditions. At Korup she brought a portable lumber mill saw into the jungle and cut up fallen trees around the camp area into planks for the buildings.

After dinner we discussed the procedure for darting the elephants. I laid out my basic needs. First I had to hit the animal with a tranquilizer dart, then find the darted animal again after it had run off into the forest. The radio dart would help with this. If the drug worked, and we were able to chase away the herd mates trying to protect the darted elephant, we could then attach one of the twenty-five-pound radio collars around its neck. First, of course, we had to find the elephants.

I asked Philip and the other guides what we should anticipate. They made it very clear that if we were fearful when we went after an elephant, we would be killed. Philip said that if an elephant charged, we should never, never run because the sound of our footsteps would alert it to our location and it would charge the area blindly. An elephant can crash through dense forest much faster than a human.

The guides agreed that the proper course of action when being charged by an elephant was to wait until it was almost upon us, then dodge to one side. This way, it would run by us and have to turn around. In that moment we might have time to prepare to repeat our "move" or find cover before the elephant charged again. I listened carefully. It certainly sounded simple. Simply ridiculous was more like it, but I understood the futility of running away and also the human need for faith (self-delusion) in a strategy to avoid being killed.

We awoke at dawn the next morning, dined on a hearty breakfast of Thanksgiving leftovers, and set out. Birds and insects were signaling another morning. A light rain had fallen at dawn, but now sunlight streaked through the canopy overhead, illuminating the steam rising from everything it touched. We walked through the jungle on narrow, leaf-littered footpaths used by local hunters. As usual, fallen tree limbs and branches, rapidly growing vines, and herbaceous plants impeded our progress. Often we had to stop and clear the trail with machetes. Between the rain-soaked foliage and sweat, it didn't take long to get wet. To stay a bit cooler, I chose to wear army fatigues or loose-fitting nylon biking pants with reinforced knees and seat and either a surgical scrub shirt or a mesh fishing vest. Others sacrificed keeping cool for the protection of long-sleeved cotton shirts.

According to plan, we were headed to a natural salt lick area the elephants frequented. Unlike the *salitrales* we used in Bolivia, these salt licks extended from small, natural springs scattered throughout the forest. The water that rises from deep in the earth is saturated with minerals, and this enriches not only the soil around the springs, but also the elephants that use it. The elephants excavate the fortified earth with their tusks and scoop up trunkfuls of the moist soil and muddy water to ingest.

We had made an early start to check on an area where one of the camp assistants had seen a group of three elephants two days earlier. Philip found this enormously disturbing. He didn't want anyone else suggesting which direction we should take to find an elephant. It took two hours to get to the site, then we followed ele-

Elephant salt lick

phant tracks over hills and through swamps for several more hours. It turned out that the disgruntled Philip was leading us in circles. At one point I spotted Fred's white T-shirt ahead of us in the forest. We had started stalking our own backup team. What a strategy. Philip was pleased: he had shown us the futility of listening to Sunday, one of the other Cameroonian field assistants, and would now take us to the place he thought we should have gone first.

When we finally arrived at the salt lick, we were excited to find lots of elephant dung and footprints. It was clear that a couple of days earlier elephants had been digging around this small, spring-fed pool with their tusks and trunks. Unfortunately we couldn't find any fresh trails to follow. The guides said the elephants had been warned of our coming. We called it a day.

Rather than taking the same trail home, we spent the next four hours hiking back to camp, following Philip's elaborate "shortcut" that involved an hour of bushwhacking through the jungle without a trail and crossing a major river through rushing rapids. I finally began to understand how the guides operated. They derived great pride from leading us through the forest, while suggestions on which way to go (even the mention of a compass) were considered insulting. The others would question the head guide as a challenge and to prove to Buddy and me that they knew more than the leader. Finally, they would never, ever admit to being wrong; they would use any excuse, however irrational or ridiculous. Reluctant to expose his secret survival strategies to the rest of the group, Philip later told me in private that he never returned home the same way he left. That way, he explained, "you can never be ambushed by your enemies."

Twenty days later we were still hiking and hacking our way through the forest, wading across rivers and streams, and listening to the Cameroonians argue with each other. While this was frustrating, I eventually grew comfortable with the confusion and disharmony. Days passed, and we never saw or heard an elephant. On some days we broke up into teams and searched different areas. Almost every day some of the guides would break from our plans, and in the evening a big argument would ensue about whose fault the misunderstandings were. All this appeared to be normal social interaction. Buddy wrote instructions for each team member every night: it didn't help, but it gave Buddy something to do.

One day we found fresh elephant footprints and feces. Philip picked up a big wet ball of dung, smashed it under both of his armpits, then turned and did the same to me. The hunt was on. Even with our natural odors well masked, we pushed our way through the thick forest another full day without seeing an elephant. I asked Philip not to do it again.

The simple truth is that forest elephants can be very hard to find. Where there is poaching, the elephants will frequent an area for a while and then move on. When people encounter elephants accidentally, they seem to think finding them is easy, but spotting elephants half a dozen times in the course of a year does not really provide the predictive capabilities I needed to find them. Had forest elephants been easy to locate, biologists would have studied them decades ago, as they did the elephants of the African savannas. Nor would we have to smear ourselves in elephant dung and wander endlessly through the jungle to find them.

The time I had available for this project was running out, and we still hadn't located any elephants. We altered our hunting strategy by camping out in the jungle three or four nights in a row. We covered more territory this way but also had to carry more gear and food. At the end of the day we cleared a small area, set up some tents and a tarpaulin, and made a few stick benches from saplings.

A new camp attracted a tremendous number of insects. Within half an hour the site swarmed with bees, tiny blackflies, deer flies, and tsetse flies drawn by the disturbance of the understory and the smell of animals (us). The tsetses carried African sleeping sickness. The blackflies transmit the parasite that causes river blindness. The larvae of this parasite normally encyst under the skin, but when they deposit themselves in the back of the eye, they cause blindness. The tiny, biting blackflies are common along rivers and streams, and almost everyone is infected. Getting bitten is unavoidable if you spend time near flowing streams. Luckily a modern horse deworming medication provides an effective cure.

Least dangerous were the African honey bees. Because we were salty with sweat, the bees went into a feeding frenzy. They did not sting me intentionally, but inevitably a few would crawl in-

Stick benches at camp

side my shirt and sting when they felt trapped. Try as I have for years now, I've never got completely used to this annoying occurrence.

Bathing in the streams and rivers provided a refreshing break from the heat and the insects. However, these streams contain schistosomes, the larvae of a parasitic fluke that looks like a flat leech. The larvae in the water burrow through human skin and migrate to the liver and abdominal cavity, where they spend the rest of their lives (years). They are different from the avian schistosome larvae I swim with in Zaire and Bolivia, which just burrow under your skin and die. Fortunately this schistosomiasis is eventually curable with modern medicine (a common dog deworming treatment), so bathing was definitely worth the risk.

Within a week of my being in the forest, my arms and lower legs were covered with insect bites and my feet had a red burning rash from being continually wet and hot. The skin on my feet was waterlogged and peeling, and as it dried at night, it cracked and bled and itched incessantly.

If it wasn't raining, we spent the evenings around the campfire. Korup is one of the wettest rain forests in the world, receiving over six hundred inches of precipitation a year. To pass the time, we told stories. Philip talked about growing up in Nigeria, serving in the army during the civil war, moving to Nguti in 1980, and working as an elephant hunter. He said it was all legal; he had bought the proper hunting and gun permits from the government. Because the international ban on selling elephant ivory applies only to trade between countries, not internal trade in any one country, he would sell the tusks for about $50 per pound. According to my calculations, Philip should have become a relatively rich man, but I knew he had family in Nigeria; maybe he had sent much of the money back to them. Philip and I talked a lot, possibly because we were partners in the riskiest part of the effort, or maybe he was more comfortable speaking with outsiders thanks to his other experiences in life. Also, his English was very good.

Because the rest of the team spoke only pidgin English, simply understanding them when we were working in the forest was difficult. I tried to learn the basic grammar and verb conjugations during the evenings at camp so I could communicate with them and with U.S. Peace Corps volunteers, who speak strangely to impress me with the fact that they have worked in Africa. This is a basic example, or at least the way it was explained to me:

Pidgin	American English
I di go	I go
I don go	I'm going
I bi go	I went
I no bi go	I did not go

I no go go	I will never go
de or da	the
boss	cross or across
small small	very small or slowly

Then I practiced a sentence. "I no go go small small boss da bridge."

Beam Him Up, Scotty

Fred needed to get back to his regular job at the zoo in New York. A technology buff, he had lobbied heavily to try the satellite tracking on forest elephants at Korup. At the time, it certainly seemed a worthwhile endeavor. After scores of scientists produced decades of research and popular books on every conceivable behavior of savanna elephants, little was known about forest elephants and nothing about their ranging patterns and habitat needs. But Fred's proposal called only for a couple of weeks in the forest and, afterward, data collection via the computer in an air-conditioned office at the zoo. Our frustrating inability to find elephants didn't fit Fred's computer model.

Fred's father, Charles, a retired engineer with an understanding of computers and a keen interest in conservation, had volunteered to do the computer tracking. He was going to download the data every day and convert it to something comprehensible by generating color maps with the elephants' movements superimposed on the park's streams, trails, topography, and vegetation, which he had spent weeks hand-digitizing into his computer. Fred would then present the results at meetings.

I had to stay behind to try to get the collars on the elephants—the low-tech part of the operation, without which all the high-tech plotting and planning would be for naught. Buddy and Mo would stay for a few more years to figure out why the elephants were going to the places the satellite said they were, and also to manage the other parts of the park project, such as conducting inventories of the plants and animals, setting up other research projects, and training Cameroonians to take up these tasks. We packed Fred off to Douala to catch his flight back to New York. Then the rest of us hiked out of the forest to take a break for a night or two. Three full weeks had passed.

We stopped in the small village of Baro, where the trail from camp meets the new dirt road across the river. Before the logging road was cut, Baro had been eight miles from the nearest road. In Baro we radioed to Buddy and Mo's base in Nguti and asked them to send a vehicle to come pick us up. With an hour or two to wait, we decided to spend some time in town to investigate what the new road and the park development project had brought to Baro.

Many different approaches to conservation are tried around the world. WWF, for instance, is excellent at marketing, generating awareness, and creating the sometimes necessary office bureaucracies. However, only a small percentage of the money they raise goes into field projects. WCS's strength, on the other hand, is in the wilderness, which is why we collaborate on projects with WWF and other city-based conservation organizations.

A group of Exxon executives and engineers, acting independently, wanted to contribute to Korup and felt their expertise could add substantially to the project. They contacted the WWF office in England and subsequently built offices for WWF outside the southern section of the park. Pleased with their contribution, the two groups decided to take on a second project. Through Exxon's international network, the volunteers put together a multidisciplinary project team and spent two years planning a steel suspension bridge at Baro to make the northern section of the park more accessible. They raised roughly $350,000 in cash and equipment to make it a reality.

Sadly, as a conservation project the plan did not make much

sense. The northern part of the park was designated a core protected area, to be used for long-term research and not for tourism or harvesting forest products and wildlife. No one told them of the misdirection before they arrived in the middle of the jungle with three shipping container loads of equipment, supplies, and machinery.

The team and the WWF people thought that a bridge would make living inside the park easier for the Cameroonian villagers. They could bring their forest products out to the new road for sale. It was a nice idea, except that people were not supposed to be living in the park; they were supposed to move out to buffer areas on the new road. Not only were these same villagers heard hunting every day in the protected area, but they cut down the trees to grow crops. The bridge would only make the remaining protected area easier to exploit.

Furthermore, a bridge and the new road to Baro would support the bushmeat (wild animals killed for food) trade. For centuries meat has been smoked over campfires and used to feed a family for days. In modern times, however, roads and access have made it easy to send this bushmeat to urban areas. Growing urban populations with cash incomes, no place to hunt, and traditional tastes have created a steady demand for bushmeat. The demand can be supplied only by exploiting the forests beyond their capacity for sustainability.

When we hiked out of the jungle, the Exxon team already had been hard at work for three weeks and had accomplished a major portion of their task. They were also building a water supply system and wiring the village of Baro for electricity—with a single power line and light bulb for every hut. They even had erected electric street lamps throughout the village.

Amazing changes were taking place in Baro. The Exxon volunteers brought a diesel generator the size of a tractor, a ditch dig-

Roadside sale of bushmeat

ger for laying underground pipes and electric lines, a fully fabricated steel-and-aluminum bridge to span the hundred-foot-wide river, and all the hardware you could buy at Sears. They had brought computers, radios, refrigerators, an ice machine, a microwave oven, video equipment and a high-resolution monitor, and kitchen and bedroom supplies to outfit a complete household of twelve (themselves) for a month. They enjoyed being able to entertain us. When we wandered out of the forest, we were spoiled with ice-cold Coca-Cola. Many of the villagers had never seen a white person or ice in their lives, much less a TV, movie, or videocamera. The modern world had arrived in Baro. How long it would stay remained to be seen.

The villagers' lack of technological savvy did not handicap them in dealing with their foreign visitors. They assessed the situation and within a week were demanding higher wages to build the bridge and insisting on being paid to help fix up their own village and set up the donated pumping station. The villagers knew that the Exxon team had a deadline and, to be successful, needed to get all the work finished before they left. The Exxon volunteers were under a lot of pressure—and the extortion worked. The villagers got running water, a huge diesel generator, electricity in all the homes, and a new bridge. They also got paid.

A week after the team left, the generator broke. No matter. The villagers would have run out of fuel in another week or so and would not have spent their own money to buy fuel or have it trucked in. The street lamps could be used for drying the laundry, which was still washed in the river, as it had been for centuries. The water pump would not work without power, so there was no more running water. Within another month the rains had softened the banks of the river, and the new steel bridge listed. No one dared use it, so the villagers rebuilt their rattan vine hammock bridge.

Maureen had often observed this constant struggle between high-tech foreign development projects and the natural human drives of self-interest, habit, ritual, and even self-destruction. Saddened and sometimes bemused by this collision of cultures, Mo jokingly called working in Cameroon "the race against entropy." The Exxon team had lost this leg.

Dances with Elephants

When Buddy, Mo, Philip, and I returned to the park, we met with more of our team in Baro before hiking in to the research station. They informed us that the major obstacle in our search was that villagers were transforming themselves into elephants and warning away the wild elephants. The villagers were concerned that we might drug one of them while they were in their elephant state and they would die. Okay: some villagers turned into elephants. I've heard stranger things.

Acting as if this made perfect sense, we replied that we would be patient. Perhaps over time the villagers would forget why we were there and stop warning the elephants. We shared this new information with the Exxon team, still hard at work in Baro. They thought we were crazy. I thought the pot was calling the kettle black.

The Baro elders told us we should have come to them in the beginning—they could have arranged the elephant search properly. Then they explained the elephant transformation story. In each village the older, wiser men learn how to transform themselves into animals. Usually at night after drinking alcohol, they leave their human bodies and enter those of certain animals. Some become leopards, some pythons, and some elephants. Not coincidentally, they transformed only into animals that frightened the locals. The ability won them the respect—and fear—of their neighbors.

As leopards or pythons, the transformed wise men might attack and kill enemies' goats or chickens or the enemies themselves. As elephants they would sometimes kill people and sometimes get killed themselves. The older brother of our guide Sunday reportedly had been shot while in his elephant state and died a few days later. No one doubted the plausibility of this story.

Often, when a village's crops are destroyed by elephants, blame falls on transformed men from another village. This belief is deeply rooted in hundreds of years of tribal cultures and contributes to the strong antagonism and distrust among the different villages. That these tribes captured and sold each other into slavery for hundreds of years does not help community relations, either.

LAYING BLAME

The belief that people can cause bad things to happen (whether it is an elephant raid, a tree falling on your hut, or an illness in the family) seems to be prevalent among the people I've worked with in the Central African forests. Events don't occur naturally or by accident; a person must be blamed. As in many religions, this is another way to make sense of random tragedy.

When Terry Hart first started working with the Pygmies in Congo-Zaire, she received a small grant from a pharmaceutical company to find medicinal plants. Unlike the healing forest products used by South American Indians, most of the plants the Africans showed her caused either vomiting or diarrhea. The traditional Central African approach to curing disease is to purge the bad spirits or the curse from the body. After this unpleasant but dramatic treatment, the healer tries to find the villain who cast the spell (or paid for a witch doctor) and punish him or her with a counterspell or public flogging. When something bad happens in the jungles of Africa, someone has to be at fault.

The Baro village elders would have liked to negotiate with us for further spiritual assistance. However, we knew that the research camp and the area in which we were most interested in radio-collaring elephants was around Ikenge, a village in the center of the park. Eventually Ikenge was slated to be moved outside the park; this may sound alarming, but all the villages moved every few decades after farming and hunting depleted the soil and wildlife. Their mobility was their means of maintaining sustainability. Development, logging, and population growth, not the creation of the park, has changed their customs irreversibly.

Over the years the villagers had cleared a tremendous amount of forest for their crops of bananas, cocoa, and cassava, as well as for small amounts of vegetables. As in much of sub-Saharan Africa, the women do all the easy work—farming, washing, hauling water from the nearest stream, carrying firewood, and raising the children. The men do the hard work: they sit around making important decisions, hunt or fish occasionally, and, on really productive evenings, get drunk and transform themselves into threatening animals.

Ikenge consists of a strip of mud huts lining a dirt road about seventy-five yards long. As in Baro, it's strange to see a stretch of what looks like a road in the middle of the forest. Baro's main street was suddenly connected to the outside world, but Ikenge's main street just ends in a footpath. If you take the shortcut, it's a four-hour walk to Baro. The 150 people who live there could count on one hand the number of white people who have ever visited their village.

Buddy sent a note to the village elders requesting a meeting, and the next morning we hiked to Ikenge. First we met with the traditional chief, who is the ultimate authority for the village. The power is passed along father to son. The chief listened to us and then to our interpreter, Elias, who was born and raised in Ikenge and worked for the WCS project under Buddy. Elias was also the elected chief of the village. The elected chief takes care of daily affairs such as dealing with the government, running the school, and collecting taxes for village projects. After someone ran and borrowed three chairs for us, we sat down and explained to the traditional chief what we were trying to do with the elephant collars and asked for permission to "hunt" in the Ikenge area. Elias translated into pidgin, though I think the old chief could understand most of what we were saying.

The chief yelled at us. The intensity and speed of his diatribe in pidgin made it impossible for me to understand him. But whatever he was saying, it didn't sound like a gracious welcome. Elias assured us that the chief was, indeed, very happy that we had come to ask for his advice and support. However, he said we should have come in person the day before, instead of sending a note.

Buddy explained that the note was a courtesy to inform them that we were coming today and to request a meeting. The chief countered that while it was nice to send a note saying we wanted to hunt elephants, we should have come ourselves. We gave up trying to explain and said thank you.

The chief informed us that he would have to call together the village elders. Before a final decision could be made, we would have to meet with the elders and discuss the whole operation and the reasons behind it. A young man left the hut, and then we heard a drum beating outside, calling the elders to the meeting hut right away. After thanking the traditional chief repeatedly, we walked to the meeting place. Three young village boys wearing only tattered short pants ran behind us, laughing and carrying our rattan chairs.

Buddy and I sat outside the hut and waited half an hour for the elders to gather. The hut was made of ocher-colored mud clay

Ceremonial hut in Ikenge

My drinking buddies inside the hut

and had a dirt floor. The roof of corrugated tin, coincidentally acquired when Mo was building the research camp huts, illustrated its importance in the community. There were two doors at the front of the hut. The elders entered the door on the right in a short procession and sat in a line on a clay ledge along the right side of the room. The younger men of the village came through the left-hand door and sat on a ledge along the left. Buddy and I were ushered through the left door, and our chairs were placed against the wall in the center of the room between the two front doors.

Buddy and I sat in the dark room facing a simple wall shrine that consisted of a sooty collage of woven sticks; a collection of feathers from what looked like hornbills, eagles, and pheasants; a skull with horns from a sitatunga antelope; a forest hog skull with large curved tusks; and a miniature bow and arrow. Below was a tiny, very crudely carved human-faced mask, about three inches in diameter. Ten hornbill feathers were stuck in it, forming a miniature headdress. Two sticks with double-curved crooks at the top leaned against the wall, and a four-foot-long log drum lay on the floor.

When the eight village elders were finally settled in position, a younger man came in with two large bottles of beer and pinkish purple cola nuts, a potent source of caffeine. Buddy leaned over and quietly reminded me to use only my right hand, a custom probably brought to Cameroon by Arabic traders centuries ago. The beers were given to us and the cola nuts peeled, cut up, and passed to everyone in the hut. I was happy to see the cola nuts; I hadn't gotten enough coffee that morning. I was not as happy about the beer; I knew it would be rude to refuse, and since it was only midday, I also knew the combination of beer, heat, and dehydration would give me a pounding headache.

After taking the cola nut and drinking some beer, we again had Elias explain that we planned only to examine the elephants and did not want to kill any. Because we would not have any meat to share after the hunt, we offered a goat in symbolic deference to their authority over the territory. One old man, the blind village herbalist, harangued us for several minutes. Elias reported that the old man was pleased we had come to ask their permission. He also said we should have come a long time ago because it would be hopeless to hunt an elephant without their help. After having endured three weeks of fruitless searching, I had to agree. Then another of the elders said we should have come to visit ourselves rather than write a letter. I started thinking we were in the Twilight Zone.

We agreed to their request to provide *afofo* for the village. *Afofo* is a fermented brew made from the juice of the palm tree. The palm is tapped near the top, which kills the tree, and gallons of juice are collected and fermented at the hot, ambient temperature. In just a few days it's quite potent. The *afofo* the Ikenge villagers liked was made in Nigeria and carried across the unmarked border through the jungle on traders' heads in 15-gallon plastic jugs weighing 130 pounds. I'm not sure why they preferred the imported mix to their local brew, but I assume it's similar to the reason Americans prefer imported beer or bottled water shipped in huge oil-guzzling ships across the ocean. With everything settled, we were told to go wait in the village while the elders decided what to do.

An hour later someone came for us and asked us to bring along the dart guns. Back in the meeting hut, we handed over our guns to two elders, who leaned them up on each end of the drum log. They had agreed to help us, but the traditional chief said we had to offer them a pig instead of a goat. A pig? A goat? This was as complicated as a UN peace treaty. Buddy agreed to a pig, and the deal was finally struck, again.

Now the elders would have a ceremony to bless us and our guns for a successful hunt. A pedestal adorned with about a hundred or so hornbill feathers had been placed at the front altar, behind the drum log, and some fresh herbs had been placed on either end of the log. The traditional chief knelt before the log and started chanting. A young man entered with three old bottles filled with water. I knew it had been neither boiled nor filtered, and I had a funny feeling that I might have to drink it. Then again, it had been a long hot day, and I was parched.

Someone handed the chief a glass of water. Chanting, he threw the water on the drum, the pedestal, and the mud wall. Then the old chief flailed the herbs on the drum and our gun stocks. After this he ground a chalky stone called *fembe* over the guns, dusting them with a white powder. He went back to his place on the ledge and told a young man to pour some more water in the glass. The chief drank it straight down and asked for a little more, which he also threw back in a single gulp.

The young man poured out the last few drops in the glass on the dirt floor and refilled the glass before giving it to the next elder, who likewise drank it straight down. This continued along the line, with several of the old men coughing deeply and spitting big wads of phlegm on the floor before drinking. I realized that Buddy and I would probably have to drink out of this glass and contemplated all the contagious diseases we could be exposed to. Water quality and my thirst were no longer my biggest concern.

I kept smiling and looking relaxed as I checked out the elders. All were thin, though some had potbellies; none was taller than five feet eight; and all were dressed in old, tattered shirts and pants cut off at the knee or above. None of these men looked healthy. Their legs and feet were swollen from years of filarial parasite infections clogging up their lymphatic system. This parasite is related to the organism that causes elephantiasis in Asia and a close kin to the Central African one that causes river blindness. Most of the men had lost the dark skin pigmentation on their lower legs from the lymph node blockage and chronic swelling, along with other miscellaneous wounds and subsequent infections over their lives. None of them could walk very well, and most of them were coughing intermittently as if they had tuberculosis.

I was excited at the opportunity to participate in the ritual—a ritual that might not exist much longer in this world. I'd never had my dart guns blessed before, and I thought that it would be a special event. But as the dirty old glass got closer and closer to me, I started wondering if the experience was really worth it.

I whispered to Buddy, "I guess we are going to have to drink from that glass."

He nodded.

"Is that water?" I whispered.

"I don't think so," he whispered back, smiling as he was handed the glass.

He gulped it all down and gave a small gasp as he exhaled. I realized suddenly that this was *afofo*. It was now my turn, and as I brought the glass to my lips, I was relieved to catch a whiff of what smelled like pure grain alcohol. This stuff would sterilize just about anything it touched. Actually the *afofo* was good, with a thick texture and the smooth taste of well-aged tequila served at ninety degrees. The hardest part was drinking the whole six-ounce tumblerful without stopping. The glass made the rounds until all three bottles were finished and we were all a little drunk. At least I was.

The blind herbalist chanted loudly, leading the old men sitting along the wall on the right. The young men on our left joined in occasionally with a duet of humphlike calls. One of the elders who was a bit more crippled than the others got up and took one of the crooklike staffs from the front wall. He started singing and dancing around the room—obviously he was doing an elephant dance. The double-curved staff mimicked an elephant's trunk. Gesticulating with his arms and the staff, he indicated that we would be led to the elephants. When his dance finished, the ceremony was over. Afterward the elders added a caveat to their promise to bring the elephants to us: Since it was already the start of the dry season, they explained, the elephants had gone very far and might be difficult to bring all the way back to us. I had been wondering when the excuses would begin.

The old man who had done the elephant dance came and chatted with us for a while. He seemed like an unusually nice, pleasant man. We found out he was the leader of the transformed elephants, which was why he did the dance. That night he and the other elders would transform themselves into elephants and bring the herds back to us. I asked how we would know which elephants to dart. The old man laughed and assured us that they would be aware of us and would stand behind the empty (real) elephants.

It was now late afternoon. I was still drunk and getting a headache. All in all, it was not a good time to go elephant hunting, so we hiked back to camp. When we got to the hammock bridge between Ikenge and the research camp, I remembered Fred telling me that the bridges were easier to cross when you were drunk. This bridge was the worst I had encountered: we were crossing at the end of the rainy season, and no one had repaired it for months.

The bridges are rebuilt at the beginning of the rains, when the rivers start to rise. Over the rainy season they slowly break down or decompose. Once the rains stop and the rivers can be crossed on foot, no one bothers to repair the bridges. This particular bridge was very flimsy, with only a few strips of rattan to walk on and very few side supports. But Fred was right: crossing was much easier under the influence of alcohol. The rushing of the river below was much less noticeable, and I could get into the rhythm of the swinging and bouncing of the bridge under my feet. It wasn't as good as dancing, but this time around it was almost fun.

Success at Last

The next morning, while hurrying to get ready before dawn, I managed to pull a muscle in my lower back. At first it felt as if a hot dagger were cutting me in half, but later it hurt only when I moved or took a breath. Nonetheless, it was time to set off. Within two hours we heard the characteristic tree rustling of elephants feeding. They were tearing small branches off the trees and munching on them. Philip and I went ahead while the backup team waited for our signal to advance. My heart was racing.

Through the dense undergrowth we didn't see the group of three elephants until we were twenty yards from them. Elephants have poor eyesight, but the thick underbrush put us at a disadvantage, too. In this environment their acute sense of hearing and smell gave them the edge. To make matters worse, at this distance the dense bushes and vines would prevent me from darting the elephants. I needed to get ridiculously close. Forest elephants are particularly dangerous—they kill people. When elephants detect humans close by but don't feel threatened, they will leave, thus eliminating the threat without conflict. But if you're five or ten yards away, an elephant's best defense is a good offense. Elephants have been known to stomp people and head-crush them—using their heads to crush the bodies of trespassers. Sometimes after they knock you down, they gore you with their tusks before they crush you. Sometimes they just crush you. It's actually more simple than it sounds and takes place within a few seconds. Their defense strategy is excellent. The only problem was that my work put me on the visiting team in these particular elephants' survival game.

Philip and I slowly and silently advanced to within ten yards (about three seconds' reach) of one of the three elephants. She was at least nine feet tall and must have weighed over five thousand pounds. But she was facing us directly—the wrong direction to get a shot. I needed to dart her in a large muscle mass like a front or rear leg. By now the pounding of my heart was almost deafening to me. As we snuck around the animals, desperate not to be seen, heard, or smelled, I was thinking how completely insane this was. After three grueling weeks in the jungle, we had finally found elephants and now could not get a shot.

We crept silently back around the group, this time ending up in a spot about ten yards behind a medium-size female elephant who was calmly munching on leafy branches she was tearing from a small tree. I guessed she weighed between five and six thousand pounds and was close enough to kill at least one of us. We both raised our guns slowly, but before I even had the chance to look down the barrel of my rifle, Philip fired his radio transmitter dart. I had no choice but to fire my drug dart immediately.

Suddenly there was a tremendous thundering to my right, and out of the corner of my eye I could see Philip running away. The other two elephants trumpeted and stampeded through the thick bush. Even as my body tried to turn and flee, my mind kept repeating, "Don't run, don't run," and forced my feet to stay planted. A second later I could tell that the stampeding elephants were heading away. I caught a glimpse of one of them disappearing back into the forest.

I ran over to the place where the elephant had been standing and radioed Buddy to advance with the backup team. My drug dart had pierced straight through a one-inch-diameter liana exactly at elephant rump height. I don't think I could have hit such a small target if I tried. Philip ran up, and I showed him the dart. He insisted that his dart (the radio transmitter) had hit the elephant. "You missed, I no did," he said. I was pretty embarrassed.

I quickly began making up a new drug dart so we could track the animal carrying Philip's radio tag and dart it with the drug. Moments later Buddy arrived with the radio-tracking receiver and declared that if the radio dart was in the elephant, we must be standing on top of her. We looked around, and sure enough, Philip's dart was stuck in the ground. We spent the next seven hours hiking in search of the elephants, to no avail.

The village elders had done their part, but it was becoming increasingly obvious that finding the elephants was only the first stage of an increasingly difficult task. Despite our failure, I returned to camp that night almost euphoric from the adrenaline high. Sneaking up so close to such a massive, uncontrolled beast had pushed me to my psychological limits, and I felt exhilarated. I was hooked, ready to do it again and again for the rest of my life.

TERMITES

Biomass is the total weight of all the individuals of one species in a given place. While it seems as though elephants or hippos should have the highest biomass, more frequently the title is won by termites. By converting woody plant material into usable organic matter in the soil, termites play one of the most important roles in many ecosystems. In grasslands and rain forests they build castlelike nests, sometimes ten feet high, which protect them from the elements. Aboveground a termite mound is structured to create air currents that precisely control the temperature and humidity of the underground nest tunnels. To make their termiteriums weather resistant, termites carefully select only certain minerals from the soil. Years later these mineral-rich mounds may be taken over by mongooses to use as a home or will be broken down by elephants or other mammals searching for nutrients. Even after the huge mound finally collapses into the underlying tunnels, the termites have still contributed to their environment. A salt-rich mud wallow remains to be used by rhinos, peccaries, and dozens of other species.

Giant termiteria (Marianne Howard/IMAGEQUEST©)

Despite the serious work that lay ahead, finding the elephants at long last was cause for celebration. I was happy to give credit to the Ikenge village elders and their elephant dance, but Philip insisted that our success was due only to the fact that we had left early without telling the other guides where we were going, thus protecting our secret. At that point, the real reason was not important to me: my back was still killing me. Luckily Maureen had studied more than carpentry when she'd lived in Florida: she was also a trained, licensed massage therapist. I stretched out on the wood-planked porch of the main house, and she worked wonders on my lumbar muscles.

The next day we hiked twelve miles north of the research camp and found a good site to camp for the night. Our destination was a salt lick area another couple of hours north. I'm not sure why we had chosen another site—I'd stopped trying to figure those things out. We woke early again the next day, had our usual hearty breakfast of cold rice and beans left over from dinner, and started on our merry way. After a brisk two-hour walk through the forest, we reached the Miri River. The Miri is beautiful, wide, and crystal clear. It's also fast flowing, with long sets of rapids. Nevertheless, crossing the river is possible. By snaking through the rapids, we could stay in water that reached only to our thighs. The salt lick area was fairly extensive, consisting of two main springs where water seepage and elephants had created mud wallows that drained into small streams flowing into the Miri. Fresh feces and footprints in and around the muddy pools of the salt lick showed us that elephants had been there recently. You could smell them.

Then Philip signaled me silently—we were close. Years of experience with forest elephants had honed his senses. His body betrayed his attempt to appear calm. I signaled the rest of the backup team to wait five minutes before following us. I didn't want to risk alerting the elephants to our presence. Philip and I had walked only a short way when I saw an elephant browsing on the tender leaves of a sapling. I tapped Philip's gun stock and pointed to the animal. Philip quickly and quietly led me through the dense undergrowth in a semicircle around the elephant until we came to a spot near a large tree, about eight yards from the rear end of the elephant. He was a big bull, and so far he was unaware of our presence.

In my peripheral vision, I caught sight of Philip lifting his rifle. As I heard Philip's shot, I raised my gun and, without taking aim, fired my dart through a small gap in the undergrowth. Once again Philip had lost his composure and shot out of instinct. The elephant trumpeted and turned but did not run away. He stood with his flank toward us for a few minutes, trumpeted again loudly, then turned and charged.

Philip and I jumped to get behind the nearest large tree. My heart was pounding so loudly that I couldn't hear the animal's trumpeting, though I felt the ground tremble from his charge. He stopped on the opposite side of our tree. We froze: first an elephant ear appeared on one side of the tree and then another ear and shoulder on the other side. When he leaned around the tree on one side, we leaned to the other. When he leaned back to the other side, we leaned the opposite way, trying to stay on the dark side of the moon, so to speak. If it hadn't been so dangerous, it would have been like a scene from a Keystone Kops comedy. However, I wasn't thinking about any of that at the moment. The standoff dragged on forever.

I covered the speaker of my walkie-talkie with one hand so the elephant wouldn't hear the click as I turned it on. Situations such as this one were the reason I kept my radio turned off. If someone called me, I would have been immediately exposed. I pushed the transmit button four times to signal the backup team to stay away for their safety. If they approached now, they could be killed. Their arrival might provide a brief distraction, but I didn't want to put more people at risk. Philip and I needed to cope with this ourselves.

Suddenly Philip ran to another tree thirty feet away. (Ironically, the night before, Philip had reminded me, "Whatever you do, don't run.") The elephant heard Philip's feet breaking the brush, trumpeted, and ran after him, but Philip got behind the tree. The elephant wheeled around and ran back toward me.

Once again I could see a part of the elephant on either side of the three-foot-wide tree trunk. Buttress roots, each a few feet high, radiated out in all directions to support the massive tree. For me, they were hurdles I would have to jump if I needed to get around the tree. I crouched between two of the buttresses, realizing that trying to avoid the elephant by quickly circling the tree was impractical. I couldn't move faster than an enraged elephant, and eventually I'd stumble over a buttress. I finally accepted that all I could do was sit tight. The elephant was in complete control of the situation. I can't say this was a moment of complete liberation, but, paradoxically, I did feel calmer.

The adrenaline surging through my body made the time pass extremely slowly. As the elephant and I continued our awkward dance—first leaning to one side and then to the other—I had what seemed like a billion seconds to contemplate life. I thought about fear. I had always tried to be above fear, to push it away. I told myself I couldn't afford fear's distractions. But finally, crouched on the opposite side of a tree from an angry elephant, I came to accept fear as a source of energy, as a means to sharply focus concentration, and as a very healthy and natural response to life-threatening situations.

The thrill of the hunt had long since gone; it had vanished when I lost my participation in determining the outcome. I was in the unenviable position of being the hunted. Am I really getting paid enough to do this? I asked myself. I had accepted the obvious risks of traveling and working in the bush, as well as the challenges of remaining healthy and avoiding accidents. But placing my body an arm's length away from a pissed-off elephant seemed way beyond the call of duty. The elephant continued to bash the tree with his head. It amused me that I used to believe that working with zoo elephants was dangerous. Everything is relative.

Finally, either bored or frustrated, the elephant trumpeted loudly and thundered back into the forest. I jumped over the buttresses to the spot where the elephant was first darted. The drug dart had ejected its contents. Although the needle was bent, it showed no signs of blood or tissue, and the barb, two-thirds of the way back on the needle, had definitely not pierced the elephant's thick hide. The hub of the needle was stained green, as if it had hit a branch and ejected the drug. But despite evidence to the contrary, I had to assume he had gotten the drug dose. That meant I needed to find the elephant for his own safety.

Only Buddy and Mo were helpful. Everyone else in the group knew someone who had been killed by elephants in this forest. Buddy, Maureen, and I led the way, and the team followed slowly, suddenly unable to find the elephant's tracks. We scoured the area, following every set of elephant footprints we could find. There was no signal from the radio transmitter dart; either it had broken or the elephant was so far away that it was out of receiver range. After two hours we called off the search. Had the elephant gotten the drugs, he would have fallen somewhere nearby.

The long hike back to camp gave us time to reflect on the day's events. In the army they would have called our discussion a debriefing. We all told our versions of the story. Needless to say, Philip's story was very different from mine. Buddy and Mo had seen nothing, since they were fifty yards away in the forest, but they had heard the elephant trumpeting. Ironically, they had been privy to the experience I had missed. Either the pounding of my heart or my own concentration had kept me from hearing the elephant's roar. Maureen played back a cassette tape she had made

The house that Maureen built

during the incident. The sound was a bugle call, bringing me back to the reality that we were still carrying the radio collars.

I told Buddy we had to change our approach before I would continue our mission. Since the guides would not track an elephant after it was darted, we would have to rely on the radio dart as our primary means of finding the animal. Thus the dart needed a much longer transmission range than three hundred yards or so. Also, I had to be in control of the darting, which meant we had to have a gun strong enough to combine the drug dart and the radio dart into one unit. I was tired of shooting before I had time to take aim. I was also too tired to discuss it much more that day.

About halfway back to our temporary camp, a runner met us with a radio message from Fred, who was back in New York. The day before, his dad had realized that the radio collars were no longer transmitting. So Fred had sent a fax to the USAID office in

Douala that was radioed to the house in Nguti and then to the research camp and hand-delivered to us. It read, "Do *not* use the radio collars, they are *not* working." Great. It was time to head home. Despondent, we walked back to our tents. The next day we hiked the eight or ten miles to the research camp.

A few days later I was flying back to New York with the malfunctioning radio collars. Fred's father got a satellite fix on me at the Frankfurt airport and alerted everyone at the zoo that I was on my way home. I didn't find it particularly amusing.

The successful completion of this project took more than three years, which is not unusual in this line of work. The first year, the collars didn't work. The second year, I returned, but without the help of the elders we were as unlucky as before. The third year, Buddy arranged for a French vet working in Cameroon to assist on the project. Eventually we were able to get radio collars on three forest elephants.

The tracking data provided the first information ever available on the home range patterns of forest elephants. We found out that each elephant used about two hundred square kilometers of forest (about twice the size of Manhattan), and they avoided areas of the forest close to small villages. This means that despite how many acres we protect, villages in or near reserves limit the amount of land usable by the elephants. The home range measurements showed that forest elephants thrive in much smaller areas than their grassland cousins, apparently owing to the lush vegetation of the rain forest. Savanna elephants, we had learned in earlier studies, need ten times as much land—two thousand square kilometers of grassland and dry forest patches—to find enough food for survival.

It took three years to get the needed information about the land use patterns of forest elephants. The Korup project was fraught with problems throughout this time. Villagers living within the national park never moved out and continued to farm and hunt. While we gathered a tremendous amount of information about elephants and other wildlife that could be used throughout the forests of Central Africa, our project partners were able to protect the forests of Korup only on paper. Early on, Buddy began working in Banyang-Mbo, another forest reserve near Nguti, while he was finishing the Korup project. In fact, Banyang-Mbo was where the elephants were finally radio-collared, though they cross into the park whenever they wish.

Buddy and Maureen married, finished up four years of work in Cameroon, and moved to the Caribbean. They developed and managed WCS's research station on the barrier reef twenty miles off the coast of Belize, raised their first child, and smiled a lot more. Buddy is back to studying manatees and spending his days in small boats on coastal lagoons and the open ocean. Buddy and Mo have gone home to roost for a while, more evidence to support my theory of early childhood environmental imprinting.

Guanay cormorants

Part Five

Peru

Two Sides of the Andes

I make pediatric house calls to rare
baby macaws a hundred feet up in
the forest canopy and to boisterous
seal pups on the arid, windswept coast.

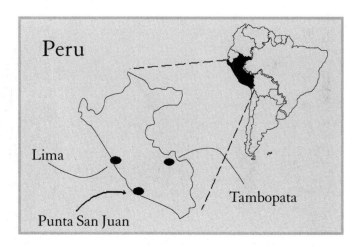

Two Sides of the Andes

I arrived at dawn in Lima, the capital of Peru. I've made the flight so many times, I've lost count of the number. I spend almost every November on the stark desert coast of Peru, working with fur seals and penguins. On this trip, however, my first stop was the jungles of southeast Peru to evaluate a novel bird conservation project involving macaws, the brilliantly colored Latin American cousins of parrots and cockatoos.

At the airport I was expecting to find Eduardo Nycander, the architect turned biologist and ecotourism entrepreneur who had asked me to come work on his macaw research project. He decided at the last minute to go to the United States for a pet parrot breeders convention and hadn't bothered to let me know. Instead a young Peruvian biologist named Augustus Malanovich met me at the airport. Clearly not of indigenous descent, Augustus was big, blond, and blue-eyed. His paternal grandfather had immigrated to Peru from Russia, and his mother's family arrived with the first Spanish colonists. We had never met before, but he was holding a paper sign with my name on it. His English was as bad as my Spanish, so this promised to be an interesting trip.

Macaws are much larger than their parrot cousins and much sought after for their beauty. Because huge populations of these distinctive, brilliantly colored birds have been plundered throughout the continent for the pet trade, they are now designated an endangered species. The sad reality of the bird trade is that ten birds die for every one that survives the trip from the wild to its destination in captivity.

The macaw conservation and research project had various components. The biologists were experimenting with increasing macaw reproduction by building artificial nest boxes for wild macaws and also hand-rearing chicks and releasing them in the area. Eduardo, my missing collaborator, had asked me to evaluate the health of the wild and hand-reared birds at their study site and to suggest improvements for their research and tourism programs. Eduardo and his Peruvian partners had built a lodge for tourists to explore the forest and observe "scientific research," with a guaranteed abundance of macaw viewing. Employing local Indians to run the lodge and give tours encouraged nonconsumptive uses of the forest among the indigenous people, and inviting Peruvian biology students to work at the research site helped develop in-country biological expertise. This approach is called an integrated conservation and development project (ICDP).

Lima has only a few high-rise buildings, but the city spreads out for miles along the coast. Warm and dusty from the desert sands, it's a city of sepia tones. Most Peruvians seem like gentle people who tend not to rush around. The atmosphere on this trip, in 1994, was much more relaxed since the capture and imprisonment of the Shining Path's leader the previous year. Though many of the guerrillas were still at large in the countryside, the bombings in Lima had subsided. The concrete street barricades used to slow traffic for inspection and reduce the risk of fast, drive-by shootings and bombings had been removed, the nightly curfew had been lifted, and police wearing helmets and bulletproof vests were no longer standing on every corner. People on the streets smiled more and seemed happy. Lima was a city transformed.

INTEGRATED CONSERVATION AND DEVELOPMENT PROJECTS

ICDPs are all the rage among the big international development funding agencies such as the World Bank and the United Nations. Millions of dollars are being funneled into foreign aid projects claiming to use this approach to development. In theory, and sometimes even in practice, economic development of an area or group of people is piggybacked onto some type of conservation project. A good example of this is ecotourism, especially if local people rather than a wealthy tour operator get a large share of the economic benefit. Ultimately success must be measured on more than financial benefits, making the evaluation more complicated. Because many aspects of the basic biology and health of the local plants and animals are so poorly understood, we need to establish benchmarks against which conservation progress can be measured. Time and money are required to establish this knowledge base, but often project funding agencies do not want to support ecological studies because they are interpreted as "research." Instead development agencies are more comfortable with the traditional approaches to foreign aid, which focus funds on management consultants, equipment, construction, and training. As a result, unfortunately, only a small percentage of the money in many integrated conservation and development projects is directed toward the wildlife and habitat studies needed to evaluate the success of this new approach to conservation.

We spent the morning shopping for food and a few medical supplies for the fieldwork, including formalin, alcohol, and liquid nitrogen. Augustus then dropped me off at my hotel. I'd been traveling since the day before and needed a shower and fresh clothes. The Hotel Señorial is a beautiful old Spanish colonial house complete with a central courtyard. Although it's a bit musty and doesn't have telephones in the rooms, the place is immaculate, inexpensive, and homey. A beautiful young woman with a cascade of jet black ringlets greeted me at the front desk. Her parents, the owners and managers of the hotel, had sent her to the United States for a college degree in hotel and restaurant management. She charmed me immediately, and I've never stayed at another hotel in Lima since.

Down the street from the hotel is my favorite park in Lima, El Parque de Amor. Set on cliffs overlooking the Pacific, it's both beautiful and appropriately named. Couples of all ages sit on the grass and along the stone wall, holding hands and kissing. Dominating the park is a thirty-foot-tall stone sculpture of a reclining man and woman embraced in a kiss. After getting settled at the hotel, I walked to the park to watch the sun set over the ocean.

The ocean was extremely calm, with gentle waves breaking on the wide sandy beach five hundred feet below the cliffs. You can see up and down the coast for miles and miles. I watched the small fishing boats out in the water until the giant orange ball of the sun sank into the clouds on the horizon. Once again, being alone in such a romantic setting reminded me of the two-sided coin that is my job. My work enables me to have awe-inspiring experiences in some of the most beautiful places in the world, yet I'm unable to share such romantic experiences with someone dear to me. Although over the years I've become involved with women in the countries in which I've worked, I'm acutely aware of how lonely the work can be. I now find myself avoiding opportunities to visit yet another beautiful vista and realize that often I'm happier skipping the sites and interesting museums, finishing my work, and getting back to friends in New York.

POSTCARD FROM PERU

Peru, the third largest country in South America, is often referred to as "the Land of the Incas." The Incas built the largest empire on the South American continent. Their legacy includes the magnificent ruins of the world-famous Machu Picchu. Less well-known is the fact that the Incas were only the last in a long line of highly developed Peruvian civilizations, the ruins of which may also be seen today.

Famous for its geographical diversity, Peru is divided into three distinct and dramatic geographical regions—the narrow desert coastal strip, the Andean mountain range, and the Amazon rain forest. While Peru is famous for the magnificent Andean mountains, fully half of the country lies in the rich Amazon basin, and the tropical rain forest that borders the Andes is home to the greatest variety of birds on earth. Although half the size of Texas, Peru contains more than twice the number of bird species that exists in all of North America. Peru has close to 120 species of hummingbirds alone. The forests of Peru are also home to a few indigenous lowland Indian groups that survived Spanish colonization.

The capital city, Lima, is located in the center of the thin band of desert that runs the length of the thousand-mile coastline of Peru. Like steps on a ladder, small rivers flowing from the Andes to the Pacific create oases in the desert that supported many civilizations. One of the world's most interesting ruins lies in the north of this desert area— Chan Chan was the greatest adobe city in the world and the capital of the Chimu empire, one of the oldest in Peru. In other areas such as Nazca, pre-Incan cultures built stone-lined aqueducts twenty feet underground to conserve irrigation and drinking water. These pipelines from the mountains to the desert have survived centuries of earthquakes and still function today.

Since Spanish colonial times, Lima has grown to be the population center for the country; at least one-third of Peru's twenty-four million citizens live there. Lima offers fine museums, historic neighborhoods with beautiful architecture, colorful local markets, and some of the friendliest people in the world. It is the seat of the national government, now a capitalist democracy. Peru spent decades under the Communist sphere of influence, which provides the Maoist and Marxist underpinnings for the opposition parties and the guerrilla movements today.

The heritage of the Andean or highland Indians is represented in music and dance as well as in colorful tapestries, handwoven garments of wool and alpaca, and beautiful silver and semiprecious-stone work.

Early that next morning I went to the wildlife department headquarters to meet its new director and obtain research permits. According to rumor, the new man, a veterinarian by profession, had treated the pet snake belonging to President Fujimori's son, and this connection had eventually led to his current appointment. I didn't know if it was true, but it made for a great story.

Our common veterinary backgrounds helped break the ice when we met. He understood the need for more wildlife health studies, and he wanted to help facilitate our work. He also told me of his personal interest in wildlife preservation; to prove it, he reached behind his chair and produced a stuffed and shellacked baby caiman. At first I was speechless, but I managed to regain my composure and explain how our approach to wildlife conservation was a little different. I think Spanish to English wordplay—preservation and conservation—contributed a bit to the confusion, but misunderstandings aside, he was illustrating what he thought to be a good example of economic utilization of wildlife: integrating conservation and development.

In any case, the permit to work on the macaws was issued. Despite the scope of the macaw research project and the number of foreign scientists conducting research in Peru, I had just become the only person in Peru with a valid permit to study macaws. Jurisdiction over wildlife studies was just being clarified in Peru, and the new administration in the wildlife department had only recently declared its authority over all protected areas. The group with which I would collaborate had yet to recognize the wildlife department's newfound authority over "forest reserves."

PERMITS, PERMITS, PERMITS

Many developing countries are grappling with establishing more protective wildlife regulations, and sometimes this inadvertently slows conservation projects. Even in the United States, five to six months are required just to obtain a permit from the Fish and Wildlife Service to import blood samples from endangered species for health evaluations. The regulations were developed to control the illegal trade in endangered animals and their body parts such as skins and ivory. Since even a small blood sample is considered an animal product, the exact same process applies. Museums can kill thousands of animals and ship the specimens around the world, exempt from international permit regulations as long as the transaction is called an interinstitutional loan; I, on the other hand, may wait up to a year to get a permit to import blood samples to determine if an endangered population is healthy.

With our errands in Lima accomplished, Augustus picked me up at the hotel before dawn the next morning for what should have been an uncomplicated journey. We were going to fly from bone-dry Lima to the wet lowland forests on the other side of the Andes. With the exception of being stopped and interrogated by a military policeman holding a Kalishnikov to my stomach, the drive to the airport was uneventful. It was still dark when we arrived, and a small group was waiting to accompany us. Two Peruvian architects, a husband-and-wife team, were coming to help Augustus design a butterfly facility at the site. Raising butterflies for export to collectors in Europe and North America has become a lucrative business in a few tropical countries. Some chrysalises are worth thousands of dollars each. Augustus was trying to set up an operation that could be owned and managed by some of the indigenous Indians in the area to provide a source of income as an alternative to poaching animals for the meat and skin trade or capturing them for the pet trade.

Two Dutch women who had been traveling the west coast for a couple of months were also waiting at the airport to join our group. Both were bird-watchers, one an artist who wanted to collect leaves and plant fibers to use in her collage paintings. A Peruvian college student volunteering for the macaw project and a graduate student from the University of California rounded out our group.

As we stepped off the plane in Puerto Maldonado, the thick heat and humidity of the tropical jungle hit us. Without the dense cover of the forest, the airstrip had already heated up to close to a hundred degrees. Within a few minutes my shirt and pants were wet with sweat. The air was heavy with the sweet, wet peat odor of decomposing organic matter. The smell of the rain forest gives me the warm sensation of being someplace I belong.

Puerto Maldonado is located at the confluence of the Tambopata and Madre de Dios Rivers, which then flows to the Amazon. With a population of a few thousand people, it's the capital of the state of Madre de Dios. The town is characterized by muddy

Puerto Maldonado

dirt roads and, along the river, mudbank ports rather than docks and creaky wooden buildings on stilts. The local Indians arrive in small wooden or aluminum boats to trade fish, meat, and vegetables for supplies or cash. Like any poor river town in the world, Puerto Maldonado is a small, dirty trading center that represents the outside world to the people living in the vast stretches of the surrounding jungle.

Some of the project staff had met us in town, so now our group had swollen to twelve. By ten-thirty that morning we had loaded up a long skinny riverboat with our gear and taken off up the Tambopata River. Around Puerto Maldonado, the river is fast flowing and about 100 to 150 meters wide. The river was running pretty high from the fall rains, and the water was muddy from topsoil washed off the land cleared by logging and agriculture. Even though we were on a tributary thousands of miles from the mouth of the Amazon River, I was immediately impressed by the enormous volume of water that flows from the rain forest across the continent and to the sea. One-fifth of all the fresh water on our planet makes the trip down the Amazon.

Our boat driver skillfully avoided the occasional turbulent sections, where gravel bars were close to the surface or fallen trees were submerged. Over the first six hours of the trip we passed by the raised, wood-planked, palm-thatched homes of Esheaja Indians (pronounced Esh-why-a) living along the river. We could see the surrounding areas they had cleared to grow corn, potatoes, and other fruits and vegetables. Thick rainclouds provided intermittent relief from the sun, and a plastic tarp the length of the boat was stretched overhead for shade.

In the afternoon we stopped for a short break at one of the original ecotourism lodges on the river, the Explorer's Inn. Its houses with their stilts and palm thatch roofs were just like those of the local Indians. The grounds were thick with tropical fruit trees, dense vines, and vegetation; and semitame colorful parrots, macaws, and small songbirds fluttered among the buildings and boardwalks. The lodge was established in the early 1970s when the area was still remote jungle and interest in the "Amazon adventure" was just beginning. As trade and the economy developed, helped in part by tourism, people migrated to the area, settled the surrounding land, and cleared it for crops. Although tourists can stroll around the lodge to see patches of forest, boat trips are now scheduled to take them to more remote areas such as the Tambopata Reserve, where we were headed, to visit unspoiled areas. In this case, forest protection had not been integrated in the plans for the privately owned tourist lodge, so economic development eventually displaced their conservation effort.

WHAT'S ECOTOURISM?

Ecotourism is one of the newer approaches or tools of conservation. The theory is to establish an economic value for protecting natural habitats. East Africa has done a remarkable job in this regard. Wildlife viewing is a major source of revenue for Kenya and Tanzania. While I fully support the concept of wildlife generating revenue for a country, I am nervous about basing conservation on commercial ventures. Even before the infamous embassy bombing in Kenya, political turmoil caused a drastic decline in tourism and, hence, income. In response, the government cut the wildlife department's budget by $3.5 million, resulting in staff reductions of over five hundred people. Wildlife and parks require constant care and can't be opened and closed like a wing of an art gallery. Long-term financial commitment must be ensured, independent of fluctuations in revenue.

Ecotourism sounds so good that it has spread around the world. On the African savannas, tourists loaded into minivans can see hundreds of thousands of wildebeest and zebra, prides of lions, elephant herds, and giraffe and then drive back to a comfortable lodge for cocktails by the swimming pool or simpler accommodations if they wish. Profits come from either small numbers of people paying a great deal of money or the capability to handle huge numbers of people at lower costs. It takes a special tourist, however, to appreciate a rain forest. Animals are difficult to see, basic luxuries are few and far between, and transportation is rarely sophisticated. The intrepid bird-watcher will make the effort and pay well for the opportunity, but tourists will never come in the millions as they do to the plains of Africa. This is probably appropriate given the negative impact that large numbers of visitors can have. But the promise of fortunes could be misleading, and when reality sets in a decade from now, the concept of protecting the environment based only on tourism profits may backfire. As with any commercial venture, promoters' hype can foster an expectation of spectacular success; thus, any modest

achievement (which would otherwise merit a healthy degree of appreci-
ation) is sure to disappoint. Nonetheless, entrepreneurial spirit as well as
hope prevails in South America, and tourist lodges are popping up all
over its rain forests.

We were still traveling upriver by boat and had finally gotten
past human settlements. Sunset was prolonged by the stormclouds
off in the distance, giving us a purple-and-orange-streaked dusk
that lasted almost two hours. Because it had not rained for a day or
two, the river narrowed and the sand and gravel bars became more
exposed as we headed toward the river's source. Nevertheless we
were clipping along at a fast pace up the river, hoping the ten-year-
old Indian boy driving our boat would continue to avoid the submerged tree limbs and floating logs.

The last time I had taken a riverboat trip at night through the
jungle was a couple of years before, during a memorable thunder-
and-lightning storm in Borneo. Branches and entire trees were
crashing down around us, and the tiny river had flooded its banks.
We couldn't tell where the river went through the forest.

In contrast, this night's ride was beautiful and calm. We
skimmed up the wide river, peacefully enjoying the evening. As
long as we didn't hit an overturned log, the trip would be a pure
delight. With no moon it soon grew very dark; only the light of my
laptop computer brightened the area around me while I did some
writing. A few small flying insects not blown away by our speed
were hanging out on the backlit screen.

By seven in the evening we had gone about as far east as you
can go in Peru without crossing into Bolivia and reached the research station in the Tambopata Reserve. The extreme remoteness
protects over 100 species of mammals, including jaguars, ocelots,

The main house

tapirs, and peccaries; more than 900 species of birds; an estimated 1,200 species of butterflies; and more than 20,000 types of plants. Numbers like that make people interested in biodiversity salivate.

The main house, like all the buildings, was a hundred-foot-long platform raised on posts about four feet above the ground, with no walls and a high thatched roof. Two rows of cot mattresses ran the length of the platform floor. Above each mattress hung a mosquito net on a rectangular wood frame. A ten-by-ten-foot entry area at the center of the building had a slatted wood floor where you could leave your muddy boots and wet raingear. Shoes were not allowed in the "bedroom."

Raised boardwalks with thatched roofs connected the outbuildings. One was a large cooking area. Another mosquito net–enclosed room was a laboratory, used for incubating and raising baby macaws. A third building, attached to the back of the kitchen, was used as staff sleeping quarters. Thirty feet away, the thick, wet jungle surrounded the entire complex, and the chorus of night sounds was in full force. Everything you touched felt damp. Even though the night had begun to cool off, the humidity made it feel warm. The smell of mildew and fungus permeated the place.

Eduardo and his partner, Kurt, who lived in Lima, had assembled a big team. To keep the operation running, Fernando, his three sons, some other men and women from the nearby Esheaja Indian communities, and several college students from Lima worked at the station and helped with the research on the macaws. One Peruvian student was studying hummingbirds. An Argentinean student attending college in Lima was collecting plant specimens for research on their chemical compounds. Three Peruvian botany students were collecting specimens for a biological inventory project. And Augustus, with the help of the two architects who had traveled with us from Lima, was preparing to design and build a prototype butterfly-breeding facility.

The lodge operation required a lot of hard work, and the living conditions, while comfortable, were certainly not luxurious, so the enthusiasm and dedication of the students were encouraging to see. Sometimes I'm disheartened by the lack of environmental awareness and interest in conservation I so often encounter overseas as well as in the States. At Tambopata I knew immediately I had found another group of dedicated people hoping to make a difference and doing their part to secure a future for the natural world.

HUMMINGBIRDS

Peru hosts about 120 different species of hummingbird. The names of certain species are almost as beautiful as the birds themselves—the green-tailed golden throat, the amethyst-throated sunangel, and the spangled coquette, for example. The heart rate of hummingbirds is almost four hundred beats per minute—close to the physical maximum of how fast a muscle can contract and relax.

The Real Macaws

The site for the Tambopata Project was chosen because of its proximity to a clay embankment along the river. Ornithologists have observed that hundreds of macaws and parrots frequent these clay banks throughout the Amazonian basin. From the river dozens to hundreds of birds could be observed flying in and eating the clay. As an added benefit, having the station close by deterred poachers from catching birds for the pet trade.

Why these birds feast on clay is not yet completely understood. Mineral compounds in the clay are thought to neutralize some of the toxic secondary plant chemicals found in the wild foods the macaws and parrots eat. This may also be the reason peccaries, tapirs, and elephants eat the muddy soil at "salt licks" in the jungles elsewhere. Regardless of the reason, the large congregation of forest birds out in the open creates a windfall opportunity for ornithologists and recreational bird-watchers alike.

The center's primary research focus was on the habitat use and reproduction of wild macaws. Three large macaw species live and nest in the area. The blue and gold macaw has a brilliant yellow neck and breast, with turquoise feathers covering the rest of its body, trailing off to foot-long tail feathers. These stately birds build nest cavities only inside the top of dead palmetto trees. The other two species, scarlet macaws and green-winged macaws, nest in hollows of tropical hardwood trees. Roughly three feet long from beak to tail tip, both scarlet and green-winged macaws are similar in size and appearance and are slightly larger than the blue and golds. Their bodies have bright, rich red feathers with patches of brilliant blue and gold feathers on each wing. The green-wings are the larger of the two species and have an added patch of green feathers on each wing next to their blue-and-gold shields.

The macaws use their powerful beaks to crack nuts, rip open fruit, and carve out their nests. They excavate a four- to five-inch entry hole into a hollowed-out chamber fifty to a hundred feet above the ground in their preferred tree type. The only predators that can easily reach the nests are snakes and, less easily, humans.

During the initial research on the birds at Tambopata, the students used rock-climbing gear to ascend to the nests, count eggs, and measure the hatched chicks to determine growth rates. They found that in this area, only one chick per nest survived to fledging—the stage at which they have grown flight feathers and can leave the nest. For macaws, this occurs at about two months of age.

The student researchers experimented with two methods to increase macaw reproduction. The first was to create artificial nesting opportunities by splitting and carving out six-foot sections of fallen trees, then banding them together and raising the "nests" back up into the canopy with ropes. Scarlet macaws and green-winged macaws, who nest in the hollows of hardwood trees, readily used the fake nests. Blue and gold macaws nest only in dead palmetto trees, which were scarce in the area. To increase the number of nest sites for the blue and gold macaws, the students found very old or dying palmetto trees and cut off their tops to make them look dead. Both approaches worked, and soon more macaws began to nest. The lack of good nesting sites was a limiting factor for reproduction; providing the nest boxes allowed more wild macaws to raise their young.

Macaws normally lay only two eggs each breeding season. Finding that almost without fail only one chick in each wild nest survived prompted the researchers to conduct a second experiment: they removed one chick from each nest and hand-reared them at the lodge and let the adult pair of macaws raise the remaining chick in the nests. The experiment worked very well—effectively doubling chick survivorship. The young hand-reared macaws were free to fly off to the forest as soon as they were able. However, these birds remained tame after release and frequently came back looking for food or to spend time with their human flock mates.

The students took shifts feeding the young chicks every two hours. When I arrived some chicks were already two months old, and all of the students were showing signs of long-term sleep deprivation. Everyone was disturbed throughout the night by the changing of the guard. That half of the people sleeping on the raised wooden platform pavilion sawed logs snoring did not help the situation—I'm sure I contributed to the nighttime logging activities.

In previous years the students left both eggs in the parents' nest and collected one chick after the two eggs hatched. They took the smaller of the two chicks—the one less likely to survive competing for the food the adults brought back for them. Then they noticed that eggs were disappearing from the wild nests, possibly eaten by snakes. Consequently they decided to collect one or both of the eggs and artificially incubate them—replacing the real eggs with dummy eggs to appease the adult birds. The adults never knew the difference; they stayed in the nests, waiting for the dummies to hatch. When the real eggs hatched, one chick was returned to the nest and exchanged for the dummies. Since egg and chick loss is so common, the parents accepted the exchange and dutifully raised their one remaining chick. The second artificially incubated chick from each "clutch," or for macaws a pair, of eggs was kept at the lodge to be hand-reared as in previous years.

Eleven chicks were in the brooder room when I arrived, rang-

Tourists, students, and macaws entertain each other

ing in age from one day to two months. They all looked great, but the surrogate parenting job had taken a hell of a lot of work. The student researchers' efforts had significantly increased the production of young macaws. Years of illegal poaching of chicks from the nests near the settled areas downriver would create a lot of vacant trees for these young birds to find homes when they grew up. Since macaws can live to forty and produce offspring every year, the released birds could significantly contribute to restoring the wild population. So far, this novel approach appears to be successful. It is certainly safer and much more cost-effective than raising birds in zoos or private collections in the United States and shipping them to completely foreign environments to be released.

The juvenile macaws raised and released the previous year still fly in to visit the lodge. For days or weeks at a time they might not show up, then one day they appear, begging for food, which is given to them in generous amounts. They explore the place with a peculiarly intense curiosity. Their visits are a wonderful experience for the tourists. When it is raining, the macaws swoop in under the eaves of the pavilion and spend much of the day flying or walking around the lodge.

For the first hour or so they're very entertaining. After that they become a real nuisance, chewing on everything you leave out, easily destroying any item with their strong beaks. They make extremely bad houseguests—like a miniature urban street gang dropping in for a visit and then taking over the place. Shoelaces get snipped off almost immediately, pens and pencils snapped in half, canisters of film pried open, books and magazines ripped into strips, and field data notebooks shredded. If you try to push them away with your hand, they bite you. They also hang around the dining area and the kitchen, looking for interesting things to taste. Bananas, mangos, and oranges are all fair game, but rather than eating only one, they take a little bite from a dozen, effectively ruining the snacks or meals for the ecotourists. Plastic containers are no challenge, and tins of food are simply pushed off the shelves. When the rain stops and they get bored, the gang suddenly flies off into the forest again, squawking loudly as they go.

One other native bird, a white-winged trumpeter chick, was running around the lodge while I was there. Trumpeters have long necks, long delicate legs, rounded bodies with broad, short wings, and dark, iridescent bluish black feathers. Like pheasants, trumpeters won't fly unless they're spooked or want to perch on a branch. But they can run very fast along the forest floor.

Adult trumpeters are just over a foot tall, and this chick was already standing at about ten inches. He towered over me when I was in bed. Raised by humans, he had imprinted on people and followed us around as if we were his parents. He was also fond of standing close to us when we were sitting or lying down. Like most small birds, he defecated every ten to fifteen minutes. The big challenge, of course, was to keep him from standing on my pile of clothes, my mattress, or my pillow—his favorite perch.

My first morning at camp I was awakened before sunrise by the calls of red howler monkeys in the forest. Their deep-throated howls and whoops blended together to form an eerie roar, as if an interstate highway were nearby. It's a haunting sound, particularly in the dark. By five-thirty the new students and tourists were up and around, getting ready to hike over the clay licks to watch the macaws fly in just after sunrise. I walked down to the gravel bar near the lodge to bathe in the river. The oranges and purples of sunrise still colored the clouds on the horizon.

Despite recommendations to the contrary, I decided to take my first bath at Tambopata in the buff. Everyone talks about the skinny Amazonian catfish with modified spinelike whiskers that can swim up your urethra, vagina, or anus and lodge there. Supposedly that's why everyone wears a swimsuit while bathing, though I think it may have more to do with the influence of missionaries. To reduce the risk of such an intimate invasion, I tried to deny them access by not urinating while swimming. Even more important, I tried not to think about it.

While I bathed, several of the juvenile green-winged macaws and a few scarlet macaws flew down to the river's edge. One tried to destroy my tennis shoes while the others worked on tearing open my shampoo bottle and soapbox. Intermittently they climbed onto my towel and tracked mud all over it. I finally had to carry my things out into the river with me and balance them on a small rock poking above the water's surface. After I splashed one that tried to land on my pile, the macaws waited patiently on shore until I had finished bathing, dried off, and got dressed. Once the entertainment was over, they flew screaming into the trees on the opposite bank and I returned to the lodge to prepare for work.

At the site, my companions, Alvarro and Krista, set up the climbing gear. Alvarro del Campo is a Peruvian from Lima. Normally in charge of the macaw project, he was now also responsible for managing the lodge, since Eduardo and his partner, Kurt, were busy in Lima developing the tourism business.

Alvarro has short black hair and usually a day-old shadow of a beard. Krista Lee is a fair-skinned, redheaded American graduate student from Louisiana with a southern accent to match. Her project concerned the taxonomy, or scientific categorizing, of macaws based on genetic samples she was going to collect. She had come to Tambopata and fallen in love with raising baby macaws and, possibly, with Alvarro. They seemed extremely in tune with each other as we got ready to ascend into the canopy.

Romance in the jungle (or the grasslands or mountains, for that matter) can be intensely passionate, although for me it's never been very long lived. The intimacy that develops from working and living together in such remote places and harsh conditions is almost impossible to maintain later over vast distances. E-mail is not a satisfactory substitute. Also, one of the nicest parts of a relationship is being there for the other person. With my schedule, that's often a problem. More than once I've been told . . . well, I've tried to forget the details, but it almost always includes a part about a man who actually lives nearby.

The sultry atmosphere at Tambopata was certainly conducive to passion. The forest was dense, wet, and hot. It had been months since I'd been in the thick organic broth of a steamy jungle, and I had almost forgotten how much I liked the smells, weight, and feel of wet air against my skin. The environment enveloped me in an intimate embrace.

Alvarro knew the area as if it were his own backyard and

Tree climbing

quickly led us through the jungle to the first nest. Every macaw nest in the area was identified by a number. Each had a thin nylon cord running from the ground to a limb above the nest and back down again. The thin lines were used to hoist our heavier rock-climbing ropes up and over the limb. We stored the climbing ropes at the lodge each day because they were expensive and, more important, our lives depended on them. They could not be left exposed to the elements and animals. Once the heavy rope was slid over a limb high in the canopy and the ends were secured to a nearby tree trunk, one person would make the hundred-foot climb to a nest.

The approach is not unlike rock climbing, though your hands and feet never contact the tree as you ascend. The equipment is exactly the same, a slinglike harness that you step through and then sit in—supported by a strap under each cheek of your butt and a strap around your waist. To climb, you use two ascenders, hand-size oblong aluminum grips, which clip on the rope. One ascender has a line connected to your harness. The other ascender has a loop of nylon webbing through which you slip a foot.

Now all you have to do is climb 80 to 120 feet up into the air by shifting your weight and advancing the two ascenders up the rope. It sounds simple, but you can't really outsmart the simple law of physics. You are truly lifting your body weight to whatever height you can achieve.

The two hundred feet of climbing rope stretches a great deal under your weight. If you are skilled like Alvarro, you can use this elasticity to help propel yourself elegantly up the line, quickly shifting the ascenders in rhythm with the stretching and contracting of the rope. If, like me, you are not very savvy with the free ascending, you waste a tremendous amount of energy bouncing up and down.

This Pediatric Team
Makes Nest Calls

Suspended a hundred feet up, Alvarro pulled himself over to the tree trunk and hooked a leg around it to hold himself steady. After reaching deep into the macaw nesting cavity, he fished out a chick and placed it in a blue plastic bucket and attached to the side of his climbing harness. He put a lid on the pail so the chick wouldn't fall out accidentally, then lowered the bird down to us on a long, thin cord. While we worked on the bird, Alvarro hung in the canopy, carefully scrutinized from a nearby tree by the vigilant parents.

The first chick I examined was a two-month-old scarlet macaw. It was fully feathered and weighed about two pounds. Most birds weigh a little more than their parents before they are old enough to fly, or fledge, from the nest. Many species, even some large ones such as eagles, reach full size and skeletal growth at six weeks. When their flight feathers finish growing out, they drop a bit of their baby weight and are ready to fly. In order to catch them, we had to schedule the work before they left the nest.

Krista held the baby bird still for me while I gave it a perinatal examination. The chick's big, curved beak was softer than an adult's and easy to open to check its mouth and throat. Its bright red feathers and striking yellow wing patches had already grown in, even though the long flight feathers had not fully emerged and unfurled from the quill-like sheaths in which they grow. We took

Blue and gold macaw chick

great care not to damage these exposed quills because they have a rich blood supply and any trauma can result in extensive bleeding and a deformed feather. This bird was in excellent condition: all its feathers were growing in nicely, and it was fat and healthy.

Birds like macaws have a large dilatation of the esophagus called a crop at the base of their necks. The crop holds food until the stomach can process it, allowing the bird to eat a great deal quickly without overloading the digestive capacity of their two-compartment stomach. After the bird has eaten or, in the case of the chicks, after being fed, the crop is distended with food, which can be gently massaged back up the throat.

Jamie, the American graduate student who had come up on the boat with me, was there to study the diets of the macaws. He carefully squeezed the chick's full crop until some of the mixture of seeds and fruit and clay appeared in its mouth. With this small sample he would be able to identify which forest plants adult macaws use to feed their young. Jamie would also look at the clay material in the mixture to determine its chemical properties.

I took a blood sample from the jugular vein on the right side of the chick's neck. Most birds have a much larger right jugular vein, making blood collection easier and quicker and, therefore, less stressful to the bird.

By wetting the bird's feathers with a little alcohol, you can see the vein through the thin skin. In thick-skinned birds, or those with a lot of fat or darkly pigmented skin, however, this isn't possible. With proper training and experience, one learns where the vein runs and how it feels to the touch. Even without seeing the jugular vein, it's possible to obtain a blood sample with very little trauma for the bird. Many less experienced people prefer to use the veins under the wings because they are always close to the surface and are clearly visible, but easier for the collector does not mean better for the bird. These wing veins tend to bleed profusely after the needle is removed, leaving a large bruise, or hematoma, right at the elbow joint. I prefer the jugular vein method; the least we can do for these already endangered birds is disturb their quality of life as little as possible.

When I was finished, I put the chick back in our dumbwaiter bucket. Alvarro carefully pulled it up and placed the chick back in the nest. Before he had lowered himself twenty feet, one of the parents flew back and entered the nest cavity. Macaws are very attentive parents. While Alvarro was descending it began to pour. He quickly rappelled the remaining fifty feet and packed the climbing rope away. We made it to the lodge in twenty minutes. Back at camp, I showered with my clothes on under the thick stream of water pouring off the thatched roof and got ready for the labwork.

On the dining table at the lodge, we set up a small laboratory with the microscope and centrifuge I had brought along. For electricity I tapped into the twelve-volt car batteries the lodge used for running the egg incubators. It was still raining heavily, and the yearling macaws had flown into the lodge to stay dry. They entertained themselves by climbing on my lab table and chewing on the assortment of tubes and syringes I had laid out.

With the microscope I could count the number of red and white blood cells in the chick's blood and look for the presence of such parasites as avian malaria. The red blood cell evaluation told me that the chick was not anemic, another indicator of good health and nutrition. The white blood cells, which take an active role in the bird's immune system, also appeared normal. I centrifuged the remainder of the blood to separate the cells from the plasma, which I froze in liquid nitrogen for further laboratory analysis back in the United States.

While the rain continued, we took a short break for lunch. From the edge of the porch I spotted a drowning ten-inch-long earthworm. I went to find the trumpeter chick to see if he was interested. Trumpeters eat insects, worms, and small snakes rather than seeds or fruit. The little bird got extremely excited and made a trebling trumpet sound when I dangled the worm in front of him. He grabbed it from my hand and stomped on it. Although he didn't know how actually to eat the worm, he clutched it in his beak and enthusiastically ran up and down the center aisle of the lodge trilling. He would stop briefly, stamp his feet on the worm, and hit it with his beak as an adult trumpeter would to kill a small snake. Then he would warble excitedly and begin running with it again. Finally we all got him to settle down by petting him and talking to him. I held the long worm up for him so he could grab one end in his beak, and he swallowed repeatedly until the worm slid down his throat like a strand of spaghetti. Later that evening I was lying on my mattress, entering notes on my laptop, when my new friend came to visit. Clearly he had figured out that I was the guy with the worms. My reward was his company and his little gifts all over my bed.

Evening also brought the rain forest symphony. The insects, frogs, and birds called, chirped, and clicked in ever-changing patterns of rhythm and intensity. The sounds of falling leaves and water dropping from the trees provided a subtle background percussion, punctuated by an occasional branch breaking and crashing through the canopy. The volume seemed to rise and fall with changes in the wind, and any loud or sudden sound would cause the orchestra to pause briefly and then begin again, with members of the chorus joining in gradually. The music was perfect for falling asleep.

Rope of the Dead

Since the work with macaws could be done only during the day, I convinced everyone that it would be interesting and valuable to look for caiman on the river at night. Late night caiman hunting had become a habit. All the students and tourists said they wanted to go along to watch, but only four showed up. When I pointed out a caiman waiting in the water near the boat, everyone dashed down to get a closer look. They made so much noise in the process that the caiman disappeared immediately.

The staff insisted that we use the large boat in which we had come upriver—picture trying to fish from the *Queen Elizabeth II*. Since the boat was so long, we practically needed walkie-talkies for the person in the front of the boat to tell the driver in the back what to do. We floated down the Tambopata River a short way and then up a shallow tributary. Our boat was too big to get close to shore and too cumbersome to maneuver close to an animal without scaring it off. Plus, we had no paddles, so when we turned off the engine, we had to hope we would drift close enough to the caiman to catch it, but not too close to disturb it. Finally we ended up jumping into the river and wading to shore.

Our flashlights reflected the eyes of the caiman from a long way off. As we approached, they either heard or felt us walking on the loose rocks in the water and sank under the surface. I made a rope snare on a long pole that proved not long enough to catch the skittish caiman here. The Indian guides said they didn't hunt caiman (it's illegal), but if they did—just hypothetically, of course—

they would throw a round fishing net over the caiman. I got the point. I let Pedrito, the fourteen-year-old son of Fernando, try a few times, but he couldn't throw the net far enough. I didn't try the net, but eventually I caught one tiny caiman by sneaking up to him and grabbing him with my hand. Only a foot long, he was too small for me to obtain a large enough blood sample to run a meaningful number of health tests, so we measured him, made a little identifying notch in one of his tail scutes, and let him swim off into the night.

Farther up the river were five or six caiman perfect for examining and sampling. The water was far too shallow for the boat, however, so we couldn't get to them. Since we didn't have anything better to do besides sleep, we spent a couple of hours trying to approach them on foot. Walking up to caiman in muddy water over my knees, I would get about two yards away before they disappeared under the water. It was a bit disconcerting, especially after the Indians told us that a pet tapir at another tourist lodge had been eaten by a caiman. I found it hard to believe that a caiman could catch a four-hundred-pound tapir. Must have been a sixteen-foot caiman, or a young tapir, or a made-up story. The latter explanation was most likely but least exciting.

Our older Esheaja Indian guide, Augustin Mishaja, remained invisible most of the evening. I had seen him only when I'd caught the little caiman. Then Augustin had suddenly appeared next to me to help. Earlier in the day Alvarro had told me that Augustin rarely said anything and had five faces. So far I'd seen only his invisible one.

Augustin knew the medicinal and magical uses for all of the plants in the forest. The bark of one jungle vine contained a potent hallucinogen and supposedly was extremely dangerous if you didn't know exactly the time to harvest it and how to use it safely. Augustin said that the vine could be cut only during the afternoon and only while it was raining. Also, an experienced shaman had to guide you through the experience. If you proceeded properly, a virgin dressed in white flowing robes would appear and explain all of the plants in the forest and how they could be used. I assumed the reference had been taken from Catholicism. If you used the vine for bad reasons, such as getting high, a big man with a black beard wearing a metal suit appeared and you would have some type of horrible experience that I couldn't fully understand. The Spanish Conquistador as a symbol of evil was telling.

The name of the vine, ayahuasca, meant "rope of the dead." It was considered the mother of all the plants of the forest because of its power to educate people about the other plants during the hallucinogenic dream state it induced. Augustin would not approach or touch some of the other plants in the forest, such as the ayauma tree, which meant "head of the dead." Supposedly, if you touched it, you developed skin lesions, got sick, and died. I did not touch it. One modern botanical book cites two references to the ayauma. One reports the fruit to be delicious; the other states that eating the fruit can be fatal. I hate it when scientific references are inconsistent.

Augustin always used an animal analogy to describe situations. About our caiman hunt, he said later that the birds had come to the fig tree, but the butterflies flew away (many birds eat butterflies). I couldn't have described it more poetically, or obtusely. At any rate, by midnight we quit wading around in the river and quickly motored back upriver to camp. A dense fog moved in. As we came into the landing, I noticed Augustin sitting at the bow of the boat. As we crashed into the mudbank and overhanging tree limbs, I realized he had slept through everyone yelling at him to stop the boat. He must have been wearing his oblivious face.

REPTILE TRADE

The United States is the world's largest market for wildlife and wildlife products, a billion-dollar-a-year business. Illegal trafficking is believed to be even more lucrative. In 1997 the United States imported 1.8 million live reptiles worth more than $7 million and exported 9.7 million reptiles valued at more than $13.2 million.

It's a Buggy World out There

Between the intermittent rains, we continued hiking out into the forest every day to check on macaw nestlings. When I felt the air becoming heavy I predicted it would rain soon. The first few times I delivered my weather forecast no one believed me, being a gringo and all, but after the second or third time we were drenched by torrential storms, I gained more credibility.

On the other hand, I never did figure out the insect situation in that area of the jungle. Most of the time the mosquitoes were not a problem, but sometimes they bit furiously. They certainly had preferences about whom they would feed on. A few of us could wear shorts and tank tops when we were not working; everyone else had to wear long pants, long-sleeved shirts, and socks all the time. Everybody (even those of us the mosquitoes scorned) slept under a mosquito net to reduce the spread of malaria. The nets also let you sleep without mosquitoes humming near your ears all night.

During the day, the small biting blackflies or midges would attack for a while and then disappear. At day's end the tiny white mosquitoes known as sand flies, which transmit leishmaniasis, were most active. Some of the staff had contracted leishmaniasis, a parasitic disease that appears first as an extremely slow healing wound. Six months to years later the organisms attack cartilage. If the disease is not diagnosed properly and treated early, the most common outcome is loss of an ear or nose. Fortunately the sand flies tend to leave me alone.

Besides scratching yourself raw, the most common insect-related problem is fly bots—larvae of flies that infest animals around the world. Much bigger than a housefly maggot, these white bots grow to be three-quarters of an inch long and about a quarter of an inch fat. They penetrate your skin and maintain a little breathing hole that frequently drains pus while they grow up inside you.

The bot life cycle is fascinating. The fly does not deposit the egg directly on the host; instead, the eggs, which hatch to larvae, are deposited near the piercing proboscis of a mosquito. When the mosquito bites you, the egg or larvae is left behind. The minute larva then crawls in the puncture site and set up house for a couple of months, while it grows and eventually pupates into a fly. In the jungle almost everyone gets them, most often on the head, shoulders, or arms. Alvarro told me about one visitor who spent a great deal of time squatting over the lodge's latrine with terrible diarrhea. A few weeks later he was horrified by a number of new lumps down under.

When I work in tropical areas with bot flies, I always take an antiparasite medication that is effective against most larvae. It's the same drug with which I treated the maggot-infested okapi in Congo-Zaire. The drug allows the microscopic larvae to penetrate the skin initially, but it kills them as soon as they start feeding. So while I frequently see or hear the grotesque stories about bots in other people, I've yet to have one I could call my own.

Obviously insects come with the territory. I frequently have to watch a mosquito or two or three feed on some part of my body when I'm busy doing a procedure. For example, when I bled the macaw chicks, it was critical to keep absolutely still while I held the needle delicately in the jugular vein. Ironically, I had to observe the mosquitoes gorging themselves from the veins on the back of my hand while I was doing a similar procedure on the chicks, reminding me of when I collect blood samples from vampire bats.

Esheaja Indian with dugout canoe

A couple of the Indian staff picked up a fallen
tree and in two days had carved a small dugout canoe, twelve feet
long and two feet wide, which we could use to catch caiman. Apparently they had decided caiman hunting was pretty cool and
wanted to try again. We towed the canoe behind the *Queen Elizabeth III*, then two or three of us paddled into shallow areas to find
caiman. The sides of the canoe were only two or three inches high,
but the Indians could stand and pole along the rivers with amazing
balance. A heavy gringo like me had a very difficult time balancing
in the canoe even when sitting down. With three of us inside, at-
tempting to catch a six-to-ten-foot-long caiman was suicidal.
Luckily the animals were much too shy for us to snare, and we
didn't ever capsize the dugout. The students and tourists enjoyed
paddling in the canoe during the day.

One afternoon a Peruvian university student volunteering on

the project, Rosa Elena Zegarro, ran up to the lodge soaking wet. Unlike the other students on the project, Rosa Elena was trained in forestry and natural resource management rather than the more theoretical discipline of biology. When we went out caiman hunting, she was always the first to jump in the water.

Judging from her appearance, she had been in the water again—apparently she'd turned over the new canoe. Somehow she had been bitten on the shoulder by a wolf spider and was in a lot of pain. Rosa Elena had kept her wits about her and killed the spider with the canoe paddle and brought it back for us to see. The two-inch-long, brown hairy forest spider must have crawled into the canoe on shore or fallen from the overhanging vegetation and then gone boating with Rosa Elena. Her shoulder was already hot and swollen. I couldn't see the bite marks, so a venom extractor device was useless in sucking out any poison.

Some of the other Peruvian students ran to get their version of a snakebite electroshock device. What they actually had was an electric stun gun, but they had read about using a high-voltage, low-amperage electrical current to denature snake venom. The concept had been made famous by a scientific paper published in a British medical journal. Unfortunately, further studies showing that the treatment was truly ineffective had received far less publicity. The boys, being boys, really wanted to use the device on Rosa Elena's bare shoulder, so they chased her around the pavilion before she had time to change out of her wet T-shirt and shorts. I thought I was in a scene from a grade-B spring vacation movie.

I finally convinced them to either use it on themselves or put it away. They chose the latter. I gave Rosa Elena some antihistamines and ibuprofen and got her to lie down for a while. She was excited, partly from the bite, partly from being chased around by the boys, and partly because that was her normal, high-energy temperament. Just in case she had an allergic reaction and began asphyxiating, I rooted through my medical supplies and retrieved my emergency anaphylactic shock kit containing epinephrine (adrenaline).

In another fifteen minutes her arm was numb and her neck was hurting, but her vital signs were normal. She was in good spirits and was happy to lie on her mattress for a while. We were a day's boat ride from the nearest clinic, but I probably had a better selection of equipment and drugs. In another half hour Rosa Elena was starting to feel better. Most of the pain was gone, but her arm was still numb.

About an hour later a couple of the guys were trying to start a big chain saw to cut up a fallen tree. Suddenly I heard Rosa Elena yelling at them. She was standing out in the grass, barefoot, showing them how to start the chain saw and how to use it properly. Dumbfounded, I could only watch as this petite woman, with a numb arm and shoulder, cranked up a four-foot-long commercial chain saw and sank it into a log. She looked up at me and commented, "I'm a forester."

Life in the Canopy and Below

The students, tourists, and I all took turns learning and practicing free-rope climbing into the forest canopy. We used a platform 120 feet up in a massive tree lodge for climbing practice and as a pleasant place to view the surrounding forest and the Tambopata River flowing nearby. One of the Peruvian students, the young man who was studying hummingbirds, struggled up the rope ten feet and began to scream. When we got him down, he doubled over, clutching his groin in agony. He had just given himself an inguinal hernia by straining so hard. It wasn't too serious, but he was sore for a few days and was not allowed to climb anymore.

I fared better when I made my first practice climbs to the platform. Ascending the rope in the midday heat and humidity was difficult enough, but it grew even more complicated when the semitame macaws noticed the activity in the canopy and decided to investigate. I was hanging eighty feet above the ground when several of them landed above me on my climbing rope and began chewing on it. Shaking the rope and yelling didn't deter them at all. The only option was to climb as quickly as possible and push them away. They were the most demanding coaches I've ever had. The first time up, I almost didn't make it. I dangled near the top for a few minutes and tried to push away the rope-chewing macaw delinquents while my muscles slowly stopped trembling. Finally I swung myself up and over a limb and landed safely on the platform.

I was delighted to be up there in the canopy. The platform offers a spectacular view of the rain forest, the same view birds and monkeys have every day. The silvery Tambopata River stretched for miles in both directions. Looking east, I could see small rises— the beginning of the foothills that lead to the Andes. Small, colorful passerine birds were flying all around and landing at eye level in the treetops.

Ten or twelve of the tame macaws insisted on keeping me company and attempted to destroy everything they could get their beaks on. This included all of the climbing gear, my shoes, and even my hands. In all fairness, a couple of them were sweet; they wanted just to be scratched while they chewed on my climbing harness. The others screamed and tried to bite me when I reached out to touch them. Like very young children, the hand-reared macaws demanded constant attention and vigilance to keep them from mischief.

We continued checking the nests and examining the macaw chicks every day for the following two weeks. Some of the nests were within an hour's hike through the forest. Others were farther up the river, so we made day trips in the boat and then hiked in to the nest sites. I climbed up to get the birds, rappelled down to examine them, then climbed up again to take the bird back home. Except for the physical effort of making two ascensions, I enjoyed being so high up in the canopy. The light is brighter, and I caught some of the breeze blowing through the treetops. Many of the nests were high up in trees that stood out from the surrounding canopy like skyscrapers. In the architectural terms of the forest, these taller trees were called emergents. You actually look down on the treetops of the forest below.

I faced three challenges in removing the chick from the nest cavity—two physical and one mental. First, while dangling from a rope attached only to the hip harness near my body's center of gravity, I had to pull myself over to the trunk and somehow cling to the tree near the nest hole. If I let go, I would swing back out into the air. Once in place, I had to reach through the dark hole in the trunk and try to find the chick. The entry holes are only four or five inches in diameter, so once your hand is inside you cannot see anything. The macaws prefer to make their nests in cavities two to three feet deep—about arm's length.

In most cases, the hollow cavities have only a macaw chick at the bottom. However, other potential occupants included adult macaws that had decided not to leave, three-inch-long cockroaches, and bats. Luckily the bats hung from the top of the cavity, so my feeling around the lower part of the chamber did not disturb them, much. The cockroaches crawled on my hand and arm, but luckily I couldn't see them. I was also fortunate not to be bitten by an adult macaw. Macaw bites are extremely painful. I don't know the incidence of snakes in the nest cavities. I've never asked. If all went well, I'd find a chick at the bottom of the hole and get bitten a few times while trying carefully to restrain it with only one hand. Once I located the bird, I would have to maneuver my hand around its back to get a secure grip on its head and chest.

Because I was five to ten stories up in a tree, it was essential to have a good grip on the bird before working it out of the hole. Raising and releasing young birds since childhood has helped me find the delicate balance between holding the bird too snugly and injuring it, and holding it so loosely that it could wriggle free and fall to its death. Neither happened during our work. The last step in the procedure was to use my free hand to position the plastic bucket that hung from my harness securely between my legs, remove the lid, place the chick inside, seal the lid, and lower the bucket and chick to the ground.

By the time I rappelled down, Alvarro, Krista, and Jamie had already measured and weighed the bird. After a thorough examination and collection of a blood sample, one of us climbed back to the nest, raised the chick up in the bucket, and returned it to its home. We were then ready to find another nest site and start all over again.

Besides evaluating the wild birds, it was my task to evaluate the rearing techniques being used in the project. WCS considered this self-evaluation essential for continued refinement and improvement of our conservation efforts.

I examined the hand-reared chicks at the lodge when the heavy rains forced us under cover. In the brooder room were hatchling chicks ranging in age from a few weeks to two months; the youngest weighed only a few ounces and were sparsely covered with downy feathers. At that age they can stand up only for a second or two, but they can flap their little featherless wings and beg for food with their tiny beaks gaping open. By two or three weeks old the chicks are twice that size and covered with a thick coat of short, white down with emerging bright red or blue quills. By six to eight weeks of age they weigh two pounds and their down has been replaced with feathers that match their parents'.

We also caught the free-flying yearlings that had been raised and released the previous year. When they came to visit the lodge, we baited them with bananas or oranges and then grabbed them or threw a bath towel over their bodies. Although they like people, the illusion of tameness is quickly dispelled once you're holding one. They hate being restrained, and their crushing bites are tearfully painful. If you do get bitten, someone has to pry open the bird's beak to release your injured fingers. In the meantime you suffer and continue to control the bird.

When we finish with each bird, I would clip the tips of one or two feathers, thus identifying them without affecting their ability to fly. We didn't put leg bands on them because Eduardo and Kurt in the project office in Lima had told us that a BBC wildlife film-making team was coming. If the birds had bands on, viewers would realize that the crew had staged the close-up shots and were not really depicting wild birds. Staging shots is pretty much the norm for the television business. We hoped the film team wouldn't notice the clipped feathers, allowing us secretly to keep track of each bird.

Clipping lasts only a few months until new feathers grow in. Since we needed to be able to permanently match the individual birds with the results of their health exams, they would have to be caught again and banded once the BBC finished their "nature" documentary. A stainless-steel or aluminum ring above the foot or ankle is the best way to permanently mark most birds. Stainless steel must be used for parrots and macaws because of their powerful beaks. Banding the macaws would allow them to be identified for the next thirty or forty years of their lives.

Surprisingly, even after I finished examining them, taking blood samples and clipping a few feathers, they continued to amuse themselves at the lodge. Normally, when you handle parrots or macaws they are so agitated that they won't let you touch them, but this bunch didn't seem particularly disturbed. Even after this display of indifference, some of the staff worried that the birds might never return. I have to deal with these strange predictions about the impact of my work all too frequently. Rather than argue, I've learned the best response is, "I hope not." In this case, unfortunately, I was right. It would have been better for the birds if they'd become wild, but they didn't.

Owing to a miscommunication, no food supplies had come up on the boats from Puerto Maldonado since I'd arrived three weeks earlier. We ran out of coffee—a major problem for me. Anita, the cook, took pity on me and resorted to scavenging old cans of instant coffee from the trash pit. A dried paste forms on the sides and bottom of the can from the high humidity. She rinsed the cans with boiling water to make a coffee extract, which I diluted with hot water in my mug. She wouldn't let anybody else, even the tourists, have any—they were leaving earlier than I, and she told them they would have all the coffee they wanted when they reached Puerto Maldonado. I was touched. The reconstituted sludge was pretty awful, but it was coffee.

We were running out of food, too. We jokingly called it "a small food crisis" because the portions of food being served became smaller and smaller. We consumed all of the canned sardines, tuna fish, and dried beans. All we had left to eat was a small amount of rice and pasta. I think I lost five pounds in the last five days I was there. Some of the Indian staff tried unsuccessfully to catch fish. Anita ingeniously shifted to using small saucers so it looked as if we were getting a plate full of food. Someone did find a stalk of small bananas that were almost ripe, which Anita fried for one meal.

Instant *mazamorra* made from a packet of powder was served for dessert every evening. I only marginally like fresh *mazamorra*, made from purple corn, apples, cherries, and plums boiled all afternoon and cooled until it begins to thicken and becomes a pasty gel. The instant packages, though popular now in Peru, have a long way to go before they approach the real thing. Nevertheless, the sugar content is pretty high, so I finished my small bowl of the chunky purple spackling compound with no complaints.

When supplies finally arrived, the gang put a red bow (made from plastic tree flagging tape) around a can of instant coffee and stuck a lit candle on top. They all walked up to me holding the can like a cake and singing "Feliz Cumpleaños." I was moved, though it was not my birthday. They had also brought a fresh chicken, so we feasted at lunch and had a huge dinner that night.

Both the medical evaluations of the macaws in the field and the final results in the States showed that the wild birds were in excellent health. The data we had collected provided the first set of normal values for these three species, allowing us to compare these macaws with other wild macaw populations and to use the data for captive breeding programs worldwide. By encouraging and improving such programs and forcing the pet trade to obtain birds only from captive breeding operations, we can help protect the wild populations. The health information we obtained will help captive breeders do a better job by giving them normal blood, biochemistry, vitamin, and mineral values to compare with those of their own birds.

Our results showed that, in contrast with the wild birds, the hand-reared macaws had been exposed to the bacteria *Salmonella*, commonly found in chickens and rodents. *Salmonella* can cause a variety of diseases in many hosts, including humans. In birds it commonly causes infertility and poor egg hatchability—just the opposite of what the macaw project was trying to accomplish. None of the wild macaws showed any evidence of the organism, so the hand-reared birds must have been exposed to the bacteria around the lodge. Since they could fly in and out of the kitchen when they pleased and had access to the garbage, they could have easily picked up the bacteria while scrounging. The food for the hand-reared chicks was also prepared in the kitchen, another possible route of exposure. Mice and rats living around the lodge and foraging in the kitchen at night could have left contaminated feces that the birds came in contact with.

The lack of refrigeration at the project, as in most remote villages, research camps, and small tourist lodges, makes it necessary for animals such as chickens to be kept alive until they are cooked. Domestic chickens are a common source of *Salmonella* and can also carry other avian diseases that can spread to wild birds. The practice of keeping live chickens at camp had to stop immediately to prevent future contamination of the wild macaw population. The staff immediately agreed to be more diligent in cleaning the food preparation and storage areas and to prevent the macaws and other animals from gaining access to these areas. The staff also needed to burn, bury, or haul away the garbage. All of these recommendations were practical, and all were normal practice in an operation run by people trained in restaurant management or experienced in food hygiene, but ecotourism did not develop from the food service industry.

It would be ironic, and indeed tragic, if the macaw population was ultimately hurt by the newly popular approach of integrating tourism and research to provide financial and psychological incentives to prevent local people from poaching. It would not have been very surprising, though, since this approach was developed without input from people with an animal health background. Around the world, ecotourism and other multiple-use approaches are being touted as the answer to conservation problems. This macaw project is one of the few to be evaluated to ensure that the animals we are trying to protect are also being protected from us.

Up, Over, and
Down to the Coast

It's never easy to leave people I've become fond of. Leaving the animals, particularly when their future is uncertain, is equally difficult. At least when I left Tambopata, I knew the birds and their forest were being well tended to. After a day of boating downriver to Puerto Maldonado, I caught a flight back to Lima.

I left the macaws and the field team on the wet, eastern side of the country to head for the Pacific Ocean to work with Dr. Patricia Majluf, a well-known marine mammalogist who has worked for WCS for years. She picked me up at the airport and took me to her family home. Like Augustus's family, her grandparents had immigrated to Peru, and she was born and raised in Lima. Her combination of Middle Eastern and Asian genes blessed her with the shiny black hair, big brown eyes, warm smile, and tannable complexion of many Peruvians. At five-feet-nine she is taller than 80 percent of the population. Patricia's parents are both doctors, and Patricia was educated at Cambridge, England. She is smart, smart, smart. She returned to Peru in the mid-1980s to conduct her Ph.D. research on southern fur seals, and since then her work has become the most significant source of information on the ecology of the species.

Patricia's interests and invitation had originally gotten me involved in wildlife health work in Peru. Patricia was routinely handling mother and pup fur seals to mark and weigh them, but the males were too big to handle without anesthesia. Many biologists would have read up a little on anesthetic drugs and then begun to practice immediately on wildlife. Determined to take a more professional approach, Patricia decided to use the veterinary expertise available within our organization, WCS. She was also interested in learning about the health of the seals and how their health varied over time. I began working with Patricia in 1992 and have returned for almost every seal pupping season ever since. Because I bring my mobile medical lab, we also take the opportunity to evaluate the health of the seabirds living at the site. To get to her research site, we had to drive a few hundred miles down the coast.

THE DRIEST DESERT IN THE WORLD

Lima lies in the narrow strip of land between the Andes mountains and the Pacific Ocean. The Andes are so high that the moisture-laden air carried by the prevailing winds from the east across the Amazon basin is pushed skyward. Then the wet air is cooled to such an extent that it can no longer even hold water. The tips of the Andes are covered in snow year-round. As the air rolls down the western slopes and warms again, the moisture is gone.

The parched air and prevailing winds from the mountains keep even the ocean from contributing enough moisture for much rain. This desert belt that begins north of Lima and runs thousands of miles down the coast to the southern part of Chile is one of the driest places in the world. Some parts are said to get rain once every few hundred to a thousand years. Even a small amount of rain is immediately evaporated by the bone-dry, howling winds. You can walk for hours and not see a single piece of living vegetation.

The trip south provides spectacular natural vistas; it also reveals the amazing impact of humans over the centuries. As we drove south, every fifty miles or so we crossed narrow ribs of mountains that emanate from the Andes and run to the coast. Based on geology and the availability of water from the mountains, the valleys between each of these ribs have different characteristics. Some are vast, flat, sandy deserts that stretch beyond the horizon. Over the millennia the winds have created mountainous sand dunes.

Other valleys, their floors strewn with small pale rocks, look like the surface of the moon. One such valley, near the ancient but still populated city of Nazca, is the site of the famous figures drawn in the desert—the Nazca lines. A man named Erich Von Daniken saw the lines from an airplane and wrote a book that claimed the lines were proof of the existence of extraterrestrial visitors. He said that the drawings could have been designed and appreciated only by someone with a view from high above. The drawings depict hands and airplane runways, as well as animals such as monkeys, hummingbirds, and seabirds that do not live in the desert. This provided additional support for his theory.

The Nazca were a very advanced civilization that lived long before the time of the Incas. They built rock-lined aqueducts buried twenty feet underground to bring water from the Andes to irrigate crops. The aqueducts have survived the severe earthquakes in this region over the centuries and are still used for irrigation. The Nazca were also travelers and traders. Their city was the crossroads among the mountains, the forests, and the sea, making it a very important point of trade.

We stopped near Nazca to see the lines. The Peruvian government had built a fire lookout tower at the site so anyone could climb up the stairs and see the mysterious figures. The drawings were made by pushing aside the top inch or two of rocks to form marks in the desert. Some of these footwide lines were hundreds of yards long. The lack of rain has preserved them for over a thousand years.

The local explanation of the Nazca lines is far simpler than the interplanetary airport theory so popular in North America and Europe. If you do not have a spaceship or a plane, or don't want to climb the stairs of the new lookout tower to view the lines, you can always hike up to the nearest hilltop, just as the Nazca and other travelers did for thousands of years as they came through this crossroads of commerce and culture. The Nazca lines were welcoming signs—images of animals and objects from the places the travelers came from or were headed to. My theory, after living in Seattle and New York, home to such amazing structures as the Space Needle and the huge steel globe in Queens, is that the lines were left over from an ancient World's Fair hosted by the Nazca Indians in their heyday.

As we drove on and crossed other dividing ridges, bright green valleys began to appear before us. These were heavily irrigated, agricultural zones. Fruit orchards and row crops stretched as far as we could see. We drove past miles and miles of asparagus and cotton fields. Both crops thrive in the sandy soils and are grown for export. Some of the finest-quality cotton is grown in the deserts of southern Peru.

About three hundred miles south of Lima, we took a right turn off the two-lane Pan-American Highway and headed to the town of San Juan de Marcona. Marcona was the name of a former American-owned iron mine outside of town. Back in the 1950s, when Marcona Steel was operating, the company built most of the town. As a result, San Juan, unlike any other town in Peru, looks like a huge U.S. college campus or a housing project built of concrete cinder blocks. Although it is not particularly beautiful, unlike other towns in the region built with adobe, San Juan has not collapsed during the earthquakes that have occurred over the last few decades. At the end of the initial contract, in cooperation with the country's drive to nationalize private industry, the company turned over the mine to the federal government. Twenty years later the Peruvian government sold it to the Chinese government under their new policy of industrial privatization. With hundreds of Chinese people, streetlights, and a movie theater, San Juan is a strange little South American town, not quite an oasis, but certainly a cultural anomaly.

SLOTHS, UPSIDE-DOWN GARDENERS?

The diurnal three-toed sloth is often seen hanging from trees in the warm parts of Peru and Bolivia, while the nocturnal, two-toed sloth is rarely seen, as it is awake only at night. Three-toed sloths are popular tourist attractions in many of the central town plazas, where they live wild in the trees. Sloths are some of the most fastidious of wild animals in terms of their hygiene and bodily functions. They are known to climb down from their perch in a favorite tree (very slowly) for their weekly bowel movements. Scientists are puzzled by this habit.

Patricia's primary field site for over a decade is on a mile-long point of land on the edge of town, called Punta San Juan. This is the closest dry ground to the edge of the continental shelf of the Pacific Ocean, which runs along the entire coast of North and South America, ranging in width from a few dozen to hundreds of miles. Beyond the continental shelf, the ocean floor drops miles. At certain places along the edge of the shelf, a phenomenon called the Pacific upwelling occurs. Cold, nutrient-rich water rises up from the deep ocean to replace the warmer coastal water that is being blown westward by the prevailing winds from the Andes. The water

Punta San Juan

coming up from the deep at the edge of the shelf is teeming with
benthic organisms and organic detritis that provides a feast for
small fish. The small fish thrive in the waters of the upwelling and
in turn become food for larger fish. At the other end of this chain
of life are the seals and seabirds. Punta San Juan provides the perfect home for seals, sea lions, and a number of fish-eating birds
such as cormorants, pelicans, boobies, and penguins. The marine
mammals and birds can rest and reproduce on the point and have
to swim or fly only a mile or two to get to one of the best, all-you-
can-eat restaurants in the world—the Pacific upwelling.

Guano (dried bird droppings) was an extremely valuable
commodity before the advent of modern chemical fertilizers.
Rather than excreting their nitrogen wastes as urea dissolved in
urine, as humans and other mammals do, birds conserve water and
void their waste as uric acid. This is the white part of bird droppings. Nitrogen is the building block of proteins, and the dried uric

acids, or urates, are rich in nitrogen. With three or four million birds standing on a small area of land, tons of guano accumulated every year. The constant desert winds dried the guano perfectly. Once the guano accumulation was a foot or two deep, it was collected by dozens of shovel-wielding men, bagged, and loaded onto boats to be shipped overseas. Each harvest yielded hundreds of thousands of dollars' worth of fertilizer. The birds of Punta San Juan produced an extremely valuable resource.

To protect this money tree, the government built a wall across the point to keep people and predators such as dogs and foxes from disturbing the bird colonies. A team of harvesters arrived once a year when the birds were no longer nesting and collected all the guano from the point in a month or so. The rest of the year only a guard or two lived there. Over the next few decades, human disturbances, such as hunting and illegal egg collecting at similar but unprotected sites along the Peruvian coast, resulted in the disappearance of seals and seabirds from all areas that had not been established as guano reserves, or, as they are called in Spanish, *guaneras*.

This was one case in which commerce and conservation meshed nearly perfectly. While the *guaneras* in Peru were established only to protect the birds that produce guano, they also provide safe havens for the fur seals, sea lions, and Humboldt's penguins that live in the same spots. The penguins are not considered guano birds because their smaller population does not contribute significant quantities of this precious substance. Also, they nest in burrows or caves, so their droppings are not accessible. The guano harvesters actually considered them to be pests because their deep nest burrows along the cliffs would collapse when walked on. If they happened to catch a penguin, they would hit it with their shovel and then either eat it or throw it into the sea—a horrifying thought to us, but all in a day's work to the guano workers. In modern conservation and development jargon, the penguins were not paying for themselves.

Nature has a remarkable ability to strike back. Sometimes the guano harvesters became infected with a virus spread by the bite of ticks that normally live on penguins and other seabirds. The illness, Guano Harvesters Disease, causes a high fever. We do not know yet how or even if this virus affects the birds, but it is one of the many disease issues we are investigating. Most likely, like humans and the common cold, the virus and the birds have adapted to each other and the virus causes severe problems only under other stressful conditions. These complex interactions among environmental changes, pathogens, and the host species are what we hope to unravel by implementing a long-term health monitoring program for the birds and mammals living in this unique area.

The physical contrasts of Punta San Juan are startling. The starkness of the desert collides with the deep blue ocean. White-capped waves crash on the rocky point, providing one of the most dramatic and breathtaking natural landscapes in the world.

As you leave behind the almost sterile desert and enter the gates to the reserve, you are overwhelmed by the hundreds of thousands of seabirds. The birds form dark clouds as they take off on and return from fishing forays. The raucous cries of the birds, the waves pounding against the rocky cliffs, and the constant twenty-knot winds provide a continuous, if sometimes dissonant, musical background. In the evening, as the calls of the birds and the howl of the wind fade away, the barking of the sea lions and seals can be heard. The tremendous number of animals living on this thin interface of land and sea creates one of the most dynamic and unique wildlife spectacles left on our planet.

Over the decades the populations of sea mammals and birds living on Punta San Juan have fluctuated. Part of the reason is the natural cycles of the environment, and part, not surprisingly, is the impact of humans. When the wall that protects the site was built, the populations increased as animals reproduced more and other animals from neighboring, unprotected areas found it a safe haven. But a safe place to pup or nest is not enough; all of the animals in the reserve depend on the sea for their food.

Every seven or eight years a major El Niño will change wind and water temperatures, stifling the upwelling along the continental shelf. The resulting diminished flow of nutrients into the food web causes a dramatic decrease in the number of fish for the seals and birds to eat. Commercial fishing operations don't help by harvesting the few surviving fish. Without enough food, the females cannot maintain pregnancy or produce eggs. Even if they do, the food supply usually is not adequate to raise their young.

In the big El Niño of the early 1980s, fish numbers declined as expected. But commercial fishing operations were not restricted, and the fish population was severely depleted. So many fish were removed that not enough were left to ensure a breeding stock. What was once one of the richest marine fisheries in the world was left pauperized. Bird populations took a nosedive. The number of cormorants, boobies, and pelicans on tiny Punta San Juan dropped from well over three million—ten times the number we consider a spectacle today—down to several hundred thousand. The number of seals dropped to about three thousand, as did that of the highly endangered Humboldt's penguin.

The devastation of the fish stocks meant that populations would not be able to rebound quickly as they had after previous El Niños. Humans had amplified the effects of a normal cycle of nature, pushing once thriving populations of wildlife close to the edge of extinction. In over a decade the fish still have not returned in their former numbers. The seal, penguin, and other seabird numbers have slowly increased during good years and, luckily, the protection at the few *guaneras* has given them a safe place to breed. In unprotected areas of the immense Peruvian coast, however, wildlife no longer exists in significant numbers, if at all.

Punta San Juan, almost by default, has become one of the most valuable research sites for coastal wildlife in Peru. When Patricia began her studies, the guano harvesters were still coming once a year, but the dramatic decline of birds and, hence, guano quickly made the operation less profitable. The harvesters were now required to wait several years for enough guano to accumulate to make money from the harvest. Since the workers were going to show up only every few years, Patricia was allowed to take over the buildings at the site on a more permanent basis. Add "free lodging" to this well-protected wildlife area, and it became the perfect location for her work.

Immediately Patricia began to restore the run-down facilities. Using solar panels and car batteries, she generated enough electricity to switch on a few lights at night. She repaired the old water tank and pipes to get running water in the kitchen. Because the water has to be hauled in by a tanker truck, however, it's used sparingly. To flush the toilets, we carry seawater up the cliffs in buckets. Everyone is responsible for their own flush. She also convinced the nearby mining company to donate supplies so she could paint the buildings and replace the broken windows to keep out the windblown sand, dust, and dried bird guano. Simple but livable, the place has become a substantial research station.

To help with her research, Patricia rounded up Peruvian university students to participate during the field seasons. She taught them the practical side of doing scientific research and helped them design, conduct, and write up the results of their work. These projects would serve as their theses for school, and in return she had a dozen field assistants conducting a wide range of studies. The students documented various aspects of the reproductive biology of the fur seals. Some studied the penguins, others the pelicans and cormorants. Year after year her students graduated and have gotten positions with the federal wildlife authorities or taken the lead in other wildlife conservation projects around Peru.

MACHISMO Y SAPISMO

Both Patricia and Rosa Elena, the student working with the macaw research project, had bigger challenges to face than just the facts of conservation biology, challenges certainly not limited to working in Latin America. Their first challenge is related to sexism. For us to make progress in conservation, we still have to learn a great deal about the ecology of plants and animals. Unfortunately it's tough to find people willing to work long-term in the field. Although many students are excited to do a field project, their real goal is to get a good job in an air-conditioned building in a city and, like most scientists and university professors in developed countries, spend a couple of months a year in the bush almost as a vacation. Ironically, despite the shortage of dedicated field staff, it's hard for a woman to be accepted in this role. Too many men are uncomfortable having women from their own culture doing the same work males use to boost their *machismo* egos. For some reason, foreign women scientists fall in a different category and are exempt from local social mores. Luckily, that famous Latin blood runs in both sexes: women who refuse to be restricted by stereotypes are now doing some of the best field conservation work on the continent.

The other challenge, *sapismo*, is not limited to women or restricted to Latin America, but Spanish-speaking cultures seem to be the only ones open enough about the subject to give it a great name. The term comes from the Spanish word for frog, *sapo*, and refers to the concept of the big frog in a little pond. The big frog doesn't want the little frogs to grow up and claim its territory. He (or in recent years she) will offer only as much help to the next generation as is absolutely necessary. This lack of sincere support is all too common in both the university environment and in conservation work.

Rosa Elena, just starting her career, has both battles to fight. Patricia's dilemma is possibly more challenging: now well respected internationally, she must deal not only with the sexism around her, but also with the *sapo* that wants to grow in all of us.

The Annual Sex Festival

I come to Punta San Juan for the sex. Every November, 1,500 female fur seals claim a few rocks at the pounding surf's edge to give birth. The result is a seal colony. As if imitating the sardines they feed on, hundreds and hundreds of seals pack themselves tightly into a small area, each defending her own little spot. However, the location of this chosen spot varies, moving up and down the rocks according to the dictates of the tides. Remarkably, only a few days after giving birth the female seals breed with the males who have recently come to shore after spending most of the year at sea. The males may swim for nine months without ever setting a flipper on dry land. Once a year they come back to the rookery for sex.

The males fight with each other to claim a territory. Their territories are larger and encompass a number of females—their harems. Since all of the females do not arrive at the same time to give birth, the males stay very busy trying to maintain their territories for six weeks or more to breed with as many females as possible.

Because they are on such a tight schedule, the males cannot go to sea and eat. If they leave for too long, they lose their territory and the girls living in it. Some of them become too weak to keep their place for six weeks. Needless to say, the boys lose a lot of weight during breeding season.

It is crucial for us to understand each species' behavioral repertoire and quirks. Female fur seals, for instance, vigilantly keep their pups by their sides for the first three or four days. If a pup tries to wander off, its mother will grab it in her mouth and pull it back. Male fur seals try to rip out each other's throats with their huge canine teeth to establish and maintain their territories. Much of the males' fighting is ritualized, but they do gash each other seriously. These traits make working with them a bit dangerous. Patricia's kneecap was almost bitten off one year by a protective mother while we were trying to catch her neighbor.

Patricia's long-term studies require her to capture, measure, and mark the animals to determine their life histories, growth rates, and reproductive success, as well as other critical aspects of their ecology, such as how they adjust to variation in the amount of food available in different years. My job is to collect blood samples to determine what's happening inside the animals. Capitalizing on the especially strong maternal bonds that exist for the first few days after the pup is born, we examine both the moms and their brand-new offspring. This gives us a unique opportunity to see the effects the mothers' health and infectious disease status has on the pups' survival.

First Patricia gently lassos a pup using a twelve-foot-long wooden pole with a soft rope loop at one end. She pulls it away from its mother, who follows the pup out of her territory and up the beach. Unlike the males, females get preferential treatment in their territories and can wander away without losing them. When the female has been led well away from the harem, people from our team run out from behind the rocks and capture the female in a net. Several other team members then help to restrain the female while she is measured and weighed and has a numbered plastic tag attached to the web of her flipper. Like ear piercing, tagging a flipper takes less than a second and will allow Patricia to identify individuals for years and collect the information needed to protect them. While the team holds the female, I collect a blood sample

Three-day-old fur seal pup

from a vein in the hind flipper. I assume this is relatively painless since most do not react at all. Living on the sharp, rocky shoreline pounded by the surf and being bitten by aggressively amorous males makes them tough.

Meanwhile two other people in the team work on the pup. Like mom, the pup is measured, weighed, and tagged. The pups are pretty easy to handle, though their personalities vary tremendously. Even at two days old some will do anything to bite your hand with their needlelike teeth, while others seem almost to enjoy being cradled in your arms. With their thick soft fur and huge dark brown eyes, they look and feel like living plush toys. I give each pup a physical examination, checking its eyes, ears, and mouth. I listen to its heart and lungs and check its body for any abnormalities or deformities. Finally I collect a blood sample.

Both mom and pup are also marked with hair dye. A short name or number is first clipped in their hair with a pair of scissors, and then blond hair coloring is applied. Patricia found that Clairol Nice 'n Easy works best. As soon as the work on both animals is finished, the pup is returned to its mom. The female grabs the pup by the scruff of its neck and carries it back to her territory on the rocks. The mothers are amazingly rough with their pups. You would think they would be more careful. In some seal-breeding colonies, the most common cause of pup mortality is being squashed by an adult.

With the blond names on the animals' brown hair, Patricia can monitor them from the cliffs overhead and record how each one is doing. She and the students check every day for the next few months to see if the pups are surviving and growing, if the moms stay in the same territory, what day and with which territorial male they breed.

After a few months pups and mothers both molt their hair coats, and the hair coloring identification is lost. The plastic flipper tags are their permanent identification. Tagging has allowed Patricia to determine how long fur seals live and reproduce and how many pups survive their first year of life, essential information for sensible conservation planning.

SEALS VS. SEA LIONS

Seals and sea lions are classified scientifically within an order of mammals called pinnipeds—meaning they have wings or flippers for feet. Anatomically, pinnipeds are subdivided into two groups, otarids and phocids. The common names we use in English—seals and sea lions—conform only loosely to the scientific division and make the descriptive names a bit confusing.

Sea lions have external ears and are therefore put in the scientific family Otaridae, meaning "eared." On land they can use their front flippers to stand up or raise the front half of their bodies. They "walk" using both their front and rear flippers. Their flippers are fairly dexterous and work well for scratching their coats or rubbing their faces. In aquariums they can be trained to use their front flippers to clap.

On the other flipper, true seals, or the Phocidae, can hear well and still have middle and inner ear components like other animals, but they have no external ear flap sticking out from their heads like sea lions. The most dramatic difference is that seals' front flippers are not built to support their weight on land, although they are very effective for quick maneuvering underwater. On land seals bounce along the ground on their bellies like people with their hands tied behind their backs. Harbor seals, gray seals, and elephant seals typify this group of "true" seals, or phocids. Phocid seals never clap during a show at Sea World.

Male sea lions have long, thick fur around their necks that resembles the mane of a lion. They also have long, stiff whiskers not unlike those of a cat or dog. In Spanish they are called *lobos marinos*, or sea wolves, and they do indeed have a vocalization that sounds more like barking than roaring lion. The South American sea lion is a huge animal—the males easily weigh eight hundred pounds.

Confusion occurs because, in English, what we call fur seals are technically otarids, or sea lions. Northern fur seals and South American fur seals are really sea lions. Like all otarids, they have little ear pinna and can move around on land using their front flippers. In South America the fur seals are called *lobos marinos con dos pelos*, or sea wolves with two furs. Fur seals have an external layer of thick guard hairs and an extremely fine undercoat. Newborn pups start out life with only the fine undercoat of hair and later grow the longer guard hair layer. The pelt of newborn pups is soft and dense, providing the highly prized skins that have been used for fur coats for thousands of years.

Until the early twentieth century, sealing or harvesting pinnipeds in South America was the greatest threat to their survival. For example, almost all the fur seals and sea lions in Argentina were killed during the eighteenth and nineteenth centuries to make lamp oil for European consumption. Skins were a by-product. The development of petroleum production coupled with the disappearance of seals put an end to the southern sealing industry. In modern times the biggest threats to the surviving populations of these species are the overharvesting of fish by commercial fleets, marine pollution, and outbreaks of disease. Nonetheless, the concept of economic utilization, a euphemism for harvesting, is now being proposed in Chile and Peru.

Okay, Take a Deep Breath

Unlike the adult female fur seals, which weigh only 120 pounds and can be physically restrained by a few people, the 250-pound males require anesthesia to be handled safely. They are too strong to restrain and are behaviorally programmed not to give up without fighting. Anesthetics make the procedure safer for the researchers and much less stressful on the males. For ten years Patricia had worked only on the females and pups. Once she had access to my services through the WCS Field Veterinary Program, she was able to include the males in her studies. Our combined knowledge of marine mammal biology and veterinary medicine was just what was needed. As with the females, understanding the males' behavior made the procedures we performed safer, both for us and for the fur seals. Unlike working with the females, however, handling the males requires more finesse than strength.

Territorial males refuse to leave their claimed spot, which, peculiarly enough, makes them better suited for our work. Males who do not have territories will run to the water and swim away if they feel threatened. If I were to dart one of these animals, he would jump in the sea before becoming unconscious and then drown when the drug took effect. By watching the males' behavior carefully, we can identify which ones have established territories. Just to be sure, Patricia or I slowly approach a male and touch him with a twelve-foot-long wooden pole. Territorial males will not give ground and bite the pole instead. A few minutes later I quietly approach the male again and dart him with an anesthetic. My

Darting a male fur seal

lightweight plastic darts and air gun make almost no noise. When the dart hits the male in the rump, he usually turns around quickly to see what happened. Unfazed by the dart protruding from his backside, he then goes on about his normal business—looking tough or resting. (I dart sea lions in the rump or hip because those are the only places they do not have a thick layer of blubber. If the drug injects into fat, it is poorly absorbed into the bloodstream and the animal is only partially sedated.) In three to five minutes the male is sleeping in the same spot he was darted.

Once the male is asleep, we slowly move into his territory, check his vital signs, put him on a stretcher, and carry him twenty or thirty feet from the colony. The females waddle ten or fifteen feet away with their pups and wait indifferently until we finish.

Marine mammals are some of the most difficult anesthesia patients. They have two very different circulatory and respiratory modalities. One is for land and is similar to that of all other animals. The other enables them to spend ten to sixty minutes deep in the sea, where their heart rates change and the blood flow to various parts of their bodies shifts to conserve oxygen and body heat. This second modality renders the effects of anesthesia very complex.

During anesthesia the animal's control mechanisms do not work properly. The dive reflex—what we observe as an animal holding its breath—commonly occurs with marine mammals during anesthesia. The animal may stop breathing as if it just took a deep dive, but the other body functions, such as shunting crucial oxygen-rich blood to the brain and heart, may not occur. Traditionally this resulted in a high incidence of death. Recently, however, veterinarians familiar with the idiosyncrasies of anesthetizing pinnipeds have begun to use new drug combinations to lessen the risks of immobilization.

Two items in particular have made the procedure much less risky for the animals. One is a palm-size device called a pulse oximeter (or "pulseox"), which determines how much oxygen is being carried by the red blood cells. A normal, awake person or animal should be at close to 100 percent capacity. If the heart or lungs are not working properly, the percentage of oxygen carried drops quickly. The pulseox provides me with the continuous reading of how the animal is functioning internally, regardless of how often it is breathing.

The other key item is related to the development of an antidote for people who overdose on Valium. The best injectable agent for immobilizing seals and sea lions has a component that is in the same class of drugs as Valium. One of its negative side effects, however, is that it can slow or stop breathing, exactly what we do not want when working with marine mammals—their breathing patterns are confusing enough as it is. By using a small dose of this new antidote, I can reverse the drug's depressant effects on breathing but still keep the animal under anesthesia. When we are finished with our procedure I administer an additional dose to speed recovery, and the animal is quickly back to normal, further lowering the risk of complications.

Compared to administering and monitoring the anesthesia, all the other work with the males is easy. It takes only four people to lift them or turn them from side to side. I listen to their hearts and lungs, examine their eyes and mouths. The males have inch-and-a-half-long canine teeth. All of their teeth are conical and pointed rather than flat surfaced for chewing their food. A good grip is important if you are trying to catch slippery fish three hundred feet underwater.

The physical exam also includes checking their bodies for scars and wounds. During breeding season the males always have numerous lacerations from brutal fighting. Their massive, maned necks commonly have three-to-four-inch-long gashes draining pus, and they typically have a large tear in their cheek or at the corner of their eye. The females will also bite their suitors when they don't want to be bothered. The toughest males hold their ground and seem undisturbed by their battle scars.

Next I take a blood sample, which can sometimes be tricky because the blood is shunted away from their flippers as part of their diving reflex to conserve oxygen and body heat. Since they don't have much in the way of arms and legs, the flippers are about the only place to take blood. Actually, seals and seal lions do have the same arm and leg bones we have, but they are extremely short and hidden in their torsos. Their wrists and finger bones form the framework for flippers. Like our hands and feet, the flippers have arteries and veins, which is where I collect blood samples.

Drawing blood sample

After all the procedures are completed, we move the male back to his territory and I give him the drug antidote. Most of the team backs away. Two of us stand close by to help defend the male's territory while he is waking up. Using the long wooden poles, we prod any male that tries to invade or claim the territory of the anesthetized male. Within an hour of having administered the original anesthetic injection, my patient is fully conscious again. That's the moment I look forward to the most. As soon as we move away, he resumes his role as king of his hill, and his entourage of females returns.

The Big Picture

Thousands of years ago millions of seabirds and marine mammals colonized coastlines around the world. Thanks to centuries of hunting, overfishing, and coastal development, only a small number of colonies remain today. Coastal areas like Peru may have only a handful of species, but their concentrations are so dense that the introduction of a disease or the effects of an oil spill on one or two crowded colonies can wipe out a fourth of the entire world's population of a species.

The situation in these isolated colonies of wildlife is critical, which is why we must assess the threats to their well-being as rapidly as possible. Monitoring the health of these marine mammals plays a vital role. The samples we collect will reveal the diseases they have been exposed to and the strength of the animals' immune systems. In addition, we can monitor the degree of contamination in the water and in the fish they eat.

These factors have complex interactions, necessitating a broad battery of tests and analyses on the samples. For example, some pollutants such as polychlorinated biphenyls (PCBs) interfere with the use of vitamin A. Vitamin A is essential for proper cell function for the body's immune system. With depressed cell function, the animals will become more susceptible to serious infections.

Another example is the pesticides that mimic the action of reproductive hormones such as estrogens. At very low levels during pregnancy, or egg production in the case of birds, the developing fetus senses these pseudohormones in addition to those of its mother. To compensate for the perceived higher levels, the fetus develops fewer hormone receptors. When the offspring become adults and begin producing their own reproductive hormones at normal levels, they lack the proper number of receptors to trigger appropriate behaviors. Birds have been observed abandoning their chicks because they have lost their hormone-regulated parental drive before the young are ready to be independent.

To unravel the cause of these mysterious events, the original parents and two generations of offspring need to be examined. Years of observation and analysis will be necessary to begin to understand these more complex and indirect interactions between wildlife and humankind. Much of our work has truly just begun.

Our health monitoring program for rare species of wild animals around the world is in its infancy. The baseline data we are collecting will be compared with changes over the years and correlated with the reproductive information collected by our field biologists. This combination of scientific capabilities and established study sites is rare for any conservation organization. We are in a unique position to monitor environmental situations and evaluate their impact on wildlife because we take the science to where the wildlife is. Most important, we focus our attention on working with local people and government authorities to develop solutions that mitigate negative effects on animals, plants, and ultimately, humans.

This long-term approach to ensuring the health of wildlife means that when I leave Peru, it's only a temporary departure. I'll take back samples that will be analyzed by a number of laboratories over the following months. The results will be compiled and evaluated, and reports will be prepared for government agencies. Scientific papers will be written about the findings, so wildlife managers in other parts of the world have access to the data. Finally, I or one of my colleagues will return to Peru to continue monitoring the health of its rare and spectacular animals. If we are successful in our conservation work, I will be watching many more sunsets over the Pacific Ocean from the cliffs at El Parque de Amor.

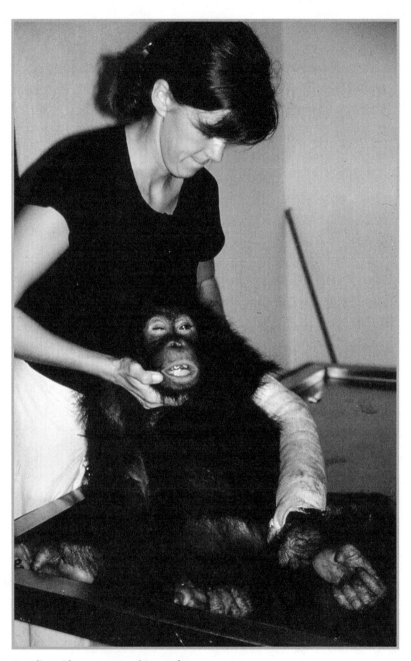

Annelisa with orangutan waking up from surgery

Part Six

Borneo

Hanging Out with Orangutans

On one of the largest but least-known islands in the world, I capture—and am captivated by—the extraordinary orangutans.

Hanging Out with Orangutans

If you want to work with wild orangutans, you have to go deep into the jungle. The name alone will tell you this. In the Indonesian or Malaysian languages, *orang* means "man" or "human" and *utan* or *hutan* means "forest." When in these countries, therefore, it's inappropriate to use the English nickname "orang." Most people—and especially the local Muslims, who make up the majority of the citizens in Indonesia and Malaysia—do not appreciate being confused with apes because the Islamic code considers them dirty. These were two of the first things I learned when I began my work on the immense island of Borneo.

Orangutans, one of the three great ape families left on our planet, are considered by wildlife professionals to be the neglected species. Most people are more familiar with Africa's gorillas and chimpanzees, thanks to a general European bias in science caused by Africa's relative proximity to Europe and the less arduous working conditions there. In contrast, the animals of the jungles of South America and Asia have attained little fame.

Those who have had the pleasure of working with orangutans know they are the smartest of the apes. I realize that chimpanzees test better on intelligence evaluations designed by people. Chimps have developed excellent communication skills to exist in large groups; even in captivity, chimpanzees seem to enjoy their interactions with their keepers and researchers. Chimps learn the skills that will include them in a social group, whether that group is composed of other chimps or humans.

Orangutans, on the other hand, live solitary lives and have never developed complex communication or social skills. Members of each sex defend their own territory and occasionally come together to mate. If food is abundant, they may tolerate others in the same fruit tree. Mothers must be skilled at teaching their offspring, but complex group cohesion techniques are not necessary. When given a test by humans, orangutans are not driven to perform for the researcher. The comparison between chimps and orangutans is similar to many people's view of dogs and cats. Dogs will learn to do almost anything to be accepted into their owner's pack, while most cats stare at you in disgust if you try to teach them a trick.

Given a sensible challenge, orangutans often excel beyond their cousins. A colleague working at a German zoo told me a story about putting an artificial termite mound in their chimp exhibit to entertain the animals and to educate the public about chimps' tool use. The artificial hill had small holes leading to cups of honey, which could be accessed only by using thin sticks. After a few days the chimps figured out how to use the system, so the staff decided to install the same devices in the gorilla and orangutan cages. The gorillas never discovered how to reach the honey; the orangutans required only fifteen minutes.

If anything, orangutans seem to delight in being contrary and doing things people do not want them to do. In northern Borneo, at the government-run rehabilitation center for orangutans, the young animals are constantly finding ways to disassemble machines and even entire buildings. They tear off tin roofing to gain access to storerooms. They pull electrical conduits and water pipes off the sides of buildings to see what's inside the tubing. They are the ultimate escape artists. After breaking a leg, one young orangutan was supposed to rest for a month in a cage. Within twenty-four hours he had torn off his fiberglass cast, removed the metal pin stabilizing the bone in his leg, and used it to pick the lock on the cage. Then he opened the door of the infirmary ward and scaled the building to sit, triumphantly, on the roof.

An old male orangutan in a zoo in the Midwest became famous for sneaking out of his exhibit at night and ransacking the kitchen and storage area of the building. In the morning the staff would find him locked securely in his cage. They checked the entire exhibit and found no route for his escape, but his nighttime adventures continued. When he was finally immobilized by the zoo vet for a physical examination, a short length of wire was found hidden in his cheek. He had been using the wire to pick the lock on his cage to get out at night. When he got tired of his exploits (or eaten his fill) and was ready to go to sleep, he would lock himself back inside.

Humans would be sorely mistaken to judge orangutans' problem-solving skills by their poor test scores. Wild orangutans spend their days and nights living in a complex three-dimensional world: they must travel, eat, sleep, and breed in the multiple levels of the rain forest canopy. Simply to move from one place to another, an orangutan must possess the evaluative skills to assess from a distance the strength and stability of branches and limbs. As orangutans grow older and larger, they must change the criteria they use to evaluate the safety of their routes. The only human I know of with these skills was Tarzan.

Orangutan conservation is mired in a number of conflicting issues. Not surprisingly, the biggest threat to their survival comes from humans. Their homelands on the islands of Sumatra and Borneo contain the commercially prized resources of tropical hardwoods and agricultural land. The islands are divided between two countries—Indonesia and Malaysia—which leads to jurisdiction and policy complications.

The orangutan once numbered in the hundreds of thousands. Over the last few decades the clearing of the forests combined with the hunting of adults and the collection of young animals for the pet trade had created an extraordinary population decline. Our best estimates suggest that there may be only twenty thousand to thirty thousand orangutans scattered in isolated pockets of remaining forests on the two islands.

I've worked on a number of projects with orangutans over the years. Each has led to new approaches and improved techniques in the conservation of orangutans and the other rare animals of Borneo and Sumatra. Working closely with government agencies, we have assisted in providing critical information about orangutans and trained their staff to do the same.

My relationship with orangutans began when I was working as a veterinarian at the Woodland Park Zoo in Seattle. At that time a committee of curators from zoos in North America and Europe, called the Species Survival Plan committee, realized that orangutans from Sumatra and Borneo might differ genetically. In truth there are some physical differences. Sumatran apes are typically a brighter orange, and the males have a short, fine coat of blond hair on their wide cheek pads. Bornean orangutans are darker red, and the males have hairless cheek pads that curve forward like a dish antenna when they get to be in their thirties. This is a broad generalization—some orangutans from Sumatra are dark red and look like their Bornean counterparts. Early studies of orangutans in zoos had demonstrated significant differences in the structure of their chromosomes. The zoos wanted captive collections to accurately represent wild populations, but housing was limited and many exhibits were already filled with the hybrid offspring of one Bornean and one Sumatran parent or grandparent. To ensure room for future generations, the zoos decided to stop breeding hybrids until the exact nature of wild populations could be determined.

To further complicate the picture, some of the old scientific literature suggests that there may be not just two, but several subgroups or subspecies of orangutans. The two islands have been separated since the ocean last rose fifteen thousand to twenty thousand years ago. In addition, old mountain ranges and wild rivers on the island of Borneo have been present for over two hundred thousand years. These physical barriers between populations might have caused different subspecies to evolve. The basic problem was that nobody knew. Believe it or not, when I first went to Borneo no one had ever looked at the actual genetic patterns of the various populations of wild orangutans. Thus no one knew what group or groupings we were supposed to be trying to conserve, either in zoos or in the wild.

The breeding moratorium made sense but also created conflict. Because many zoos had only a mixture of orangutans from the two islands, or their hybrid offspring, they were not allowed to breed them. Much to the disappointment of zoo visitors, this meant no more babies. Mixed couples were separated or given birth control medication. Some animal rights activists protested to keep established couples together. The fact that orangutans in the wild do not pair bond and are naturally promiscuous was irrelevant to the activists. Birute Galdikas, the famous orangutan behavioral researcher, went on the speaking and fund-raising circuit to announce to great ape groupies and anyone who would listen that all orangutans were one and the same. She also made it clear she would happily take all the hybrids and release them in Borneo. That the Indonesian government did not agree with her seemed not to matter. The emotionally charged situation that evolved was almost completely devoid of objective information on which to base decisions. Resolution seemed distant.

Harmony Frazier, a veterinary technician at the Woodland Park Zoo in Seattle, suggested that we should try to resolve the issue by actually examining wild populations. We found a geneticist from the National Institutes of Health who would perform the laboratory procedures on samples we collected. Unfortunately, at that time the only methods available required us to collect blood samples and get them back to the lab in the United States for analysis while they were still fresh. Since orangutans lived a hundred feet up in the remote jungles of Borneo, this posed two great challenges.

Reluctant to anesthetize orangutans and have them fall a hundred feet out of a tree just to answer a genetics question, we had to figure out an alternative approach. We knew that skin cells also contained DNA, so we figured out a method to collect skin biopsies from orangutans without having to catch them. This was done by modifying a drug dart to take a tiny cut of skin without immobilizing the animal. Next we developed a method to freeze the skin cells in liquid nitrogen so we could store the samples in the field for long periods of time. When they were thawed out, they could be grown in laboratory cell cultures and the DNA harvested for analysis. None of these procedures had ever been tried before. It took only a year to work out all the preliminary techniques between the zoo and the lab. Then came the time to put the plan into action.

I had spent more than two years writing letters and proposals to different agencies in Indonesia and Malaysia without getting a single reply. Fortunately, when Harmony and I arrived in Jakarta, the Indonesian capital, the appropriate offices actually did have files containing all the letters and forms we had submitted.

The first order of business was to get written approval from

POSTCARD FROM BORNEO

Borneo is the third largest island in the world, after Greenland and New Guinea. The northern third of the island is Malaysian and is divided into two states—Sarawak and Sabah. On the coast between Sarawak and Sabah is a tiny wedge of land that makes up the entire country of Brunei. The other two-thirds of the island is Indonesian and called Kalimantan, which means "River of Diamonds" in Indonesian. Depending on what book you read or what atlas you consult, you will become either more or less confused.

Borneo's rain forest is the second largest in the world (after the Amazon). Much of the timber shipped from the interior is floated down to the coast on the island's rivers. The immense network of rivers is the island's highway system. The rivers are essential for transportation within the island and, therefore, indispensable to the island's commerce and prosperity.

Because the equator runs across Borneo, the climate is extremely hot and humid. To say it rains a lot is an understatement. Coastal areas receive an average of 120 inches of rain per year, while inland areas may receive even more. Such conditions may not make many vacationers happy, but the climate does foster an extraordinary array of vegetation and tremendously lush carpets of greenery.

There are fig trees and ebony trees, ironwood trees and *upah* trees, which produce a deadly poison. Orchids in abundant varieties climb and drape among many of the trees, while the stunning, gigantic *tapang* trees tower over the forest canopy. The *tapang* has a majestic white branchless trunk and may grow to more than two hundred feet. The *tapang* trees look like white spires rising out of the greenery. In all, there are approximately 780 species of trees on the island. (To put this in perspective, compare this number to the number of species of trees in England—35.)

In addition to an abundance of exotic trees, flowers are also well represented. Borneo is home to 11,000 species of flowering plants, including the rafflesia. The largest and one of the ugliest flowers in the world, the rafflesia is known for its fleshy blossom, which can grow to over a yard in diameter and weigh up to eighteen pounds.

The inland tribes of Borneo are generally referred to as Dayaks, though many different groups fall under this general name, from the nomads in central Borneo to the Iban groups in the northwest. When the first Dutch and British colonialists arrived on Borneo in the early 1800s, they were most fascinated by the Dayak tradition of head-hunting but soon came to appreciate the architectural sophistication of their huge longhouses built on stilts and their beautiful art, including exotically decorated headdresses and shields. The Dayak or Orang Ulu (river people) group are still Borneo's predominant population.

When the Japanese invaded in 1940, Dutch Borneo (now Indonesian Kalimantan) had a population of about 2.4 million, and the British protectorates on the island had a total population of approximately 800,000. By the time the United States dropped the atomic bombs on Japan, many indigenous tribes had been organized into efficient guerrilla forces to fight the Japanese. When the Allies arrived in Borneo, Japanese forces posed little threat and surrendered almost immediately. After the Allied victory, Borneo and the rest of Indonesia was returned to Dutch rule. After intense fighting, particularly in Java, Indonesia declared independence in 1945 and kept the Kalimantan two-thirds of Borneo. Sarawak and Sabah chose to become part of Malaysia after giving up their British colonial status, and Brunei became completely independent.

the Ministry of Science. Similar to the National Science Foundation in the United States, this Indonesian ministry also reviews proposals to determine their scientific merit. Then the forestry department and the wildlife division of Indonesia had to approve our project and give us permission letters for the regional offices during our travel. The police and internal security services had to

Floating the forest away

grant approval for our travel to remote areas and provide us with *surat jalan*, or letters of travel. This required background checks, and I had to supply them with official letters from my local police in the United States, certifying that I had no criminal record. This all took several days, but then we were ready to fly to Borneo.

Our first stop after leaving Jakarta was the regional capital, Pontianak, a port city on the west coast of Borneo just a degree or two south of the equator. We showed our documents immediately to the police and obtained another *surat jalan* to travel into the interior of Borneo. We obtained a second letter of permission to work in a national park at the local forestry and wildlife office. With these regional permits we continued by boat to the next smaller town, Teluk Melano.

I had arranged for a water taxi to take us in the morning to Teluk Melano. Borneo's water taxis are huge speedboats, packed with people, goats, chickens, dried fish, fruits, vegetables, and assorted heavier cargo. If the boat is fast, you can get to the next town before dark. The trip took us inland on rivers draining the interior of Borneo, past mangroves, and occasionally along the coast in the open sea. All along the way we saw logs floating down the rivers. Near the coast, the logs are loaded on barges and shipped to the more developed world. The huge logs, some as big around as a small car, literally represented the forest being dismantled piece by piece.

The Voyage from Hell

Teluk Melano is a village surrounded by a mangrove swamp and built almost entirely on wooden pilings along a widening in a river near the coast. The village had a few dirt roads and two vehicles that had been brought there by boat. The only hotel and the public market were built on none-too-steady docks. The wooden structure constantly rocked and creaked as people pushed small cargo carts through the maze of wood-planked alleyways.

We arrived in the month of Ramadan, the annual Muslim religious celebration. People fasted all day, eating only after sunset. During daylight we could eat only if we hid in a restaurant's kitchen. The mornings began at three A.M. with banging and clanging in the kitchens; food had to be prepared and eaten before the sun came up. Praying, celebrations, and more eating began again after sunset and lasted until well after midnight. Sleeping is not an important part of this religious celebration. All the buildings shared walls, like a huge wooden beehive, so my bedroom window opened into the bathroom/kitchen/washing area of the family next door. Needless to say, I didn't sleep much.

Every day the town baked in the equatorial sun; a breeze was rare. My shared window did not make my room any cooler. The oppressive heat, rotting fish, and human waste trapped under the docks created an overwhelming stench, but this was not a vacation and we had no choices on how we traveled or where we stayed. We only had to decide how to cope. As if the environment in Teluk

Giant fruit bat

Melano were not hellish enough, once again we had to spend two additional days checking in with the local police, forestry, and wildlife authorities.

Traveling with Harmony and me was Seti, our Indonesian counterpart, a veterinarian from the university near Jakarta. He had joined us during our initial days in Jakarta. At about five feet ten, he is tall for an Indonesian. He was born and raised in western Java. Like most of the people from that area, he is a practicing Muslim and was making a significant sacrifice to accompany us during the month-long Ramadan festival. In Teluk Melano he told me he had never been in the field before; I tried not to worry.

We connected with the local staff from the Gunung Palung National Park, who had come to pick us up and restock camp supplies. The next morning before dawn we loaded our gear and supplies in a small motorboat and left. The sound of pots and pans banging in town eventually faded into the distance. As the sky grew lighter, long, streaming flocks of giant fruit bats returning to their roost sites flew past us. Known as flying foxes because of their foxlike heads, prominent canine teeth, and brown furry bodies, these bats develop wingspans four feet across—hence giant. Every evening they fly vast distances to find the fruit trees they feed on and then return to the same roost site every morning to sleep through the day.

HORNBILLS

The three dozen species of hornbills make up one of the strangest groups of birds in the avian universe. They are notable both for their large and sometimes brightly colored beaks and their strange nesting routine: The male entombs the female in the nest cavity and feeds her through a small hole until their eggs hatch. The largest hornbills of Indonesia can reach up to five feet in length from beak to tail tip. The rhinoceros hornbill has a spectacular red, black, and yellow-orange arched horn rising from its beak. This bird's "ivory" was traditionally prized for carving and led to extensive hunting throughout its range. Only in recent times has the sale of hornbill beaks and the huge black and white feathers been banned to help protect the birds from extinction.

With the incoming tide, we made good time going upriver—two and a half hours to the first stop, the village of Simanja. There we hired a small boat and two guides to work with us once we got to the research camp. As we moved farther inland away from the sea, the river narrowed. After another four hours of motoring upriver in a small boat with an eight-horsepower motor, we had to stop at a logging site to transfer over to even smaller boats. These wooden sampans, or canoes, held three or four people and most of the gear. With only one motor we towed the second sampan loaded with gear and one man to steer it with a long oar.

By this time the river had shrunk into a moderately flowing

stream, ranging in width from six to fifteen feet. The banks were lined with overhanging thorny rattan, which made for slow going and, at times, extreme pain. The long, whiplike shoots of rattan, covered with curved thorns, look like instruments of torture. In fact, they are the canes used in corporal punishment in Southeast Asia. If one so much as rubs against you in the boat, it will tear through both your shirt and your skin.

By late afternoon Seti had slumped onto the floor of the boat. Because of his Ramadan fast, he'd had neither a sip of water nor a bite of food all day, and the extreme heat and effort required to keep the boat from crashing into the heavy jungle overgrowth had dehydrated him. The anxiety of being in the wild did not help him, either. He was starting to mumble incoherently, and his eyes were beginning to roll up into his head. We laid him down on the wet floor of the little boat to cool him off; he still did not want to drink.

The stream got narrower and shallower; often we had to drag the boats over the sand, rocks, and fallen trees. As darkness approached, a torrential downpour began. Our small stream rose dramatically, and the little motor could no longer cope with the current. We left one boat and two guides to spend the night at another logging site while five of us continued on in the pitch black. Pelting rain made it hard for us to keep our eyes open. Lightning bolts cracked in the jungle all around us as the stream flooded its banks to become a raging river. The water was rushing through the jungle, and there was no way we could follow it to camp. Trees blew over, crashing into the water around us.

Every few minutes the boat got stuck, forcing us to jump into the water, now over our heads. Clinging to branches and small tree trunks to keep from being swept away, we pushed, pulled, and lifted to free the heavily loaded boat. The noise of the rain, thunder, and rushing water was so loud that we had to scream to keep track of each other in the water.

To add to our predicament, and contribute to its already ludicrous aspect, throughout the entire trip the little outboard motor kept breaking down. Each time it did, the boat was swept away through the jungle until we could grab hold of something solid, like a tree trunk, and regain control. At least ten times we had to stop and clean the spark plug. Several times the propeller's shear pin was broken by submerged tree limbs. Changing the shear pin was an adventure. One of us would have to jump into the pitch black water and hold on to the back of the boat to make sure the propeller did not fall into the water as it was removed. In the pouring rain, we made replacement shear pins by cutting up rusted nails with a pair of pliers. The situation sounds horrifying in retrospect, but other than being exhausted at the time, I thought of it more as a great adventure. Death didn't seem likely.

After three hours of this, yet another fallen tree limb blocked our way. Physically and mentally spent, we were ready to give up. We could lash the boat to a tree and wait for dawn. Suddenly one of the guides jumped off the front of the boat, dragged himself against the current, and climbed on top of the tree. With his machete he chopped the trunk between his bare feet. It cracked open, and he fell into the water. Three seconds later he popped up next to the boat, laughing. We all cheered. The current forced the freshly cut gap to spread wide enough that four of us could push the boat through the opening. Seti was still lying in the bottom of the boat.

By ten-thirty that night we finally made camp, then had to hike another half mile through the flooding forest with our gear to get to the cabins. This gave us an excellent opportunity to collect a tremendous number of leeches on our wet clothes and bare skin. During the rainy season in most of the lowland jungles of Borneo, leeches are a constant presence. Cabang Panti, our research camp, seemed to have more than its share.

Cabin at Cabang Panti

Cabin interior

The matchsticklike leeches in this part of the world live on land. They hide in the leaf litter or on low bushes and wait for warm-blooded animals to walk by. The leeches find their way onto your shoes or clothing, then inch up your pants or down your shirt in search of a tender spot to feed on. Some species hurt a little when they bite; others are painless.

At first, you notice them only after they are fat and full or after they let go and you see your blood soaking into your clothes. After a few days of living with leeches, however, you become sensitized to how they feel on your body and sometimes can grab them before they bite you. In the early stages of life with leeches, most people become obsessed, hardly able to walk through the forest without staring continually at their boots and legs, checking over and over again to see whether they have picked up a hitchhiker. Such obsessive-compulsive behavior doesn't leave much time for enjoying the scenery. During the next phase, when you can discriminate the feel of a leech from other irritants in the forest, you spend a lot more time seeing the forest and less time looking at your feet. If you stay long enough, you finally reach the point where you stop paying attention to the leeches, letting them feed if you don't notice and nonchalantly rubbing them off if you do.

Finally, after hiking in the rain through the dark, leech-infested jungle, we arrived at the cabins. The initial introductions to staff members and the requisite salutations completed, we each found dry places on the floor of a wooden hut, shed our dripping clothes, checked for leeches, and dried off as best we could. After saying his prayers, Seti finally ate some food and drank some water. It felt great to be out of the flood—simply to be still—and sleep came easily. Soon enough morning would come and we'd be busy unpacking our equipment and planning our strategy to find the elusive orangutans.

The sounds of the jungle and the equatorial heat woke us early every morning. Right after dawn Bornean gibbons start their booming calls to claim their territory. A similar species in Sumatra, the Siamang gibbon, is named "wah-wah" because of its loud call, which gradually rises to a crescendo of wahs followed by a rapid staccato of hollow whoops. Gibbons have an inflatable throat sac that connects to the sides of their larynxes and provides the boom-

ORANGUTAN CONSERVATION

For more than three decades now the plight of orangutans has been brought to the attention of the world. As the years have passed, the public has recognized that orangutans are in trouble but has also been relieved to know that the situation is being addressed. Some well-intentioned and devoted people have even become famous through their association with the charismatic orangutan: Birute Galdikas, for example, has campaigned in the name of her orangutans for over twenty years.

However, the sad reality is that orangutan populations have continued to decline drastically, and no one is sure how many actually are left. Between 1960 and 1990 estimates of the number of orangutans ranged widely from 4,000 to 160,000. Now we hope that 30,000 orangutans remain living in scattered populations of questionable viability. Politics, economics, development, cultural differences, and even clashes among personalities have led us to today's complicated orangutan conservation dilemma.

Forest clearing for agricultural development has eliminated much of the lowland habitat in which orangutans thrive. As a result, animals who are isolated and displaced become locally extinct. Occasionally some become agricultural pests and are captured or killed. Although the timber industry may cause less damage to the forests than does agriculture, it affects orangutans and other animals by increasing access for humans and a demand for meat to feed workers, their families, and others who move into these areas.

Centuries of traditional orangutan hunting by peoples living in remote areas have always taken a toll on wild populations. But modern times contribute other threats to wildlife populations, including roads, motorboats, and guns, all of which make hunting much easier. Television and advertising have created awareness and a demand for consumer products that require cash to purchase. Subsistence hunting is now easily expanded to market hunting to earn cash, thus further tip-ping the balance against the orangutan and other wildlife species.

As conservationists we face enormous challenges. Rather than thinking we have all the answers, we must acknowledge that one of the most important keys to success is working closely with local people and agencies to develop strategies and implement programs to help their fast-disappearing great ape and its neighbors.

ing resonance that carries their calls for miles through the jungle. They are also one of the few groups of primates that are monogamous. An adult male and female maintain an exclusive territory, and only the last two or three offspring are allowed to live with them. Taxonomically they are considered a lesser ape, which places them somewhere between monkeys and the great apes.

Besides the sounds of whooping gibbons, singing birds, and buzzing insects, the rising sun quickly heats up the jungle, and within an hour of sunrise it's too hot to sleep. We took turns bathing in the stream that flowed by camp. Most local people bathe twice a day. Cleanliness is a highly regarded virtue, which makes sense in the heat and humidity. Indonesians and Malaysians would skip dinner at night if they had not had time to bathe. This Asian custom does not seem to be prevalent in Africa or South America, and certainly not in places influenced by Europeans. Even in the dirtiest places, like Teluk Melano, the people are fastidious about bathing.

A biologist had set up Cabang Panti as a research station in the Gunung Palung National Park. He was not there during our time but sent a letter to the staff and the students, informing them of our plans. The camp consisted of seven or eight buildings separated by thick forest stretching along the stream. All of the buildings were on wooden platforms, raised three to four feet above the ground for protection from flooding during the heavy rains. The bottom half of the walls was thatched with palm fronds, and the top half was normally left open. Rolled-up plastic tarps suspended around the edge of the corrugated tin roof could be lowered during storms to keep out the rain.

Four small huts, about twenty by twenty-five feet, were built for visiting scientists. There were no beds or furniture, so we slept on the wood floor, not bad compared with other places I've slept. Mosquito nets were an absolute must. A large thatch house had also been built for the students and another for the head researcher. The huge, open-sided main building housed the cooking and dining area, a library of scientific literature, two computers for data entry, shelves and shelves of data sheets, and fruit specimens pickled in alcohol. The computers ran on truck batteries charged by solar panels during the day and by a generator that ran for a few hours each night. Some rattan chairs along the stream side of the pavilion provided a fairly comfortable lounge area.

CICADAS

Cicadas are probably the best-known noisy bug in the world. One type in North America spends seventeen years as a grub in the ground before emerging as an adult to make its evening courtship call. Thousands of years ago the Chinese buried their dead with cicadas carved of jade to inspire resurrection. The giant, three-inch-long cicadas in Borneo are so loud, they sound like a chain saw or an outboard motorboat engine.

I was impressed with the incredible job Mark Leighton, the chief scientist from Harvard and funded by WCS, had done in setting up a research camp at this remote site in the rain forest. The place ran smoothly, and an amazing volume of rain forest research was being conducted. During our stay, the research team tagged their twenty thousandth tree. This meant that the tree had been observed flowering, a leaf and flower specimen had been collected, dried, and pressed for a permanent museum specimen, and a small aluminum number tag had been attached to the trunk. Then the tree was marked on a map of the research site. With this detailed documentation, the natural cycles of the forest might, over time, be unraveled. Few if any forest research stations have been this productive in such a short period of time.

Gunung Palung National Park was wisely planned. It stretched from the coastal mangrove swamps through virgin Bornean lowland rain forest and peat swamps up into the inland mountains. This allowed a single park to protect a contiguous expanse of land with a complete diversity of habitat types. In many countries parks have been established to protect a particular habitat type, resulting in a disconnected patchwork of parks and reserves. In some situations such islands of protection may work, but in complex ecosystems, and especially for those that are still poorly understood, a great deal may vanish when interdependent ecosystems are separated from each other.

Dr. Leighton's work has shown, for example, that orangutans occupy different habitat types as fruiting seasons change among the various areas of the region. They may spend part of the year in the peat swamps, while during other seasons they may move into the hill forests. If only one habitat type were protected, far fewer orangutans would be supported in the area.

The Hunt Begins

Unfortunately for us, this was not the season in which the orangutans stayed in the flatter forests with dry land. They were in the steep hill forest and the flooded peat swamps, where the trees with ripening fruits such as figs grew. Using a hand-drawn map of the narrow trails carved through the jungle,

Harmony wading through swamp

Harmony, Seti, one of the guides, and I spent days hiking through jungles, wading through swamps and across rivers, climbing ridge after ridge, just to find a single orangutan. The heat and humidity were debilitating; it was crucial to carry drinking water and not forget to drink it. The weather was too hot for us to be interested in food, at least during the daytime. Then, after a week in the steamy jungle, my body adjusted to the heat—even when it was eighty degrees at night I wanted to sleep with a blanket.

Without the help of local guides—Ibans, Kadazans, or Dyaks in this part of Borneo—we would have had little hope of finding the orangutans. Members of these indigenous tribal groups have the forest skills necessary to recognize the signs of nearby orangutans. The problem is that orangutans live basically solitary lives high in the thick forest canopy and sit so quietly that people may walk through the forest without even knowing these huge animals are right above them.

We needed to listen for clues, such as the sound of fruit falling in the distance or the creak of a bending branch—sounds that easily may be confused with the wind or the movements of monkeys and birds in the trees. The sounds of small objects falling through the leaves was always worthy of further investigation, because when orangutans are eating they drop bits of fruit, nuts, or seeds. Sometimes we smelled fresh urine or feces that had splashed among the understory bushes and realized an orangutan was close by. On very rare occasions we would even hear one urinating from a hundred feet up in the canopy.

Orangutans will sometimes descend to ground level to feed on the succulent stems of low herbaceous plants or to cross a distance when there is no aerial alternative. Otherwise wild orangutans spend almost all their lives in the forest canopy. Their travel

THE DAYAKS OF BORNEO

The name *Dayak* means Inland or Upriver People and is the generic name used to refer to all of the inland tribes of Borneo, although many disparate tribes such as the *Iban* and *Kayan* fall under this heading. In northern Borneo the name *Orang Ulu*, or River People, is commonly used to refer to these groups.

Having moved from western Kalimantan to Sarawak in the north, the Iban now number approximately 350,000. They are famous for their communal longhouses, which may house over a hundred community members. They practice slash-and-burn rice cultivation, rotating growing areas and allowing fields to go fallow and return to forest between cycles. The Iban are renowned for their extraordinary enthusiasm for head-hunting (although they no longer engage in this practice).

The Punan are the only Dayaks who are nomadic hunter-gatherers. For centuries they wandered deep in the remotest jungles, completely self-sufficient, obtaining large amounts of almost pure starch from the wild sago palm and developing the state-of-the-art blowgun, or *sumpitan*, for catching wild prey. Their game of choice was the wild bearded pig, but everything in the forest, from rhinos and monkeys to birds, was fair game. Though few Punan still maintain this ancient lifestyle—nomads being frowned on by both colonial and modern governments—you may still find them leaving their now permanent huts for long, long treks in their forests.

through the trees is completely planned, like the moves of a champion chess player. They recognize a tree with the elasticity to bend far enough under their weight to let them reach the branch tips of another. While hanging from a hand or foot—their big toes are apposable, like our thumbs—they carefully pull the leaves of the next branch toward them until they can get hold of the stem. Then they pull it a little harder to get a grip on a thicker portion. Finally, when grasping a section that will support them, they let go and catapult across to the next tree in their path.

When they're in a hurry, all this intricate hand-and-foot-work can be done with amazing speed. Listening for the sounds they make while traveling is one of the best ways to find them. With practice we learned to distinguish the sound of an orangutan weighing 30 to 150 pounds swinging from branch to branch from the noise made by smaller monkeys leaping between trees.

When we finally did encounter an orangutan, I spent the next few hours or days trying to dart the animal, waiting to get a safe shot. My goal was to hit them in a place on their bodies with a lot of muscle—for example, their shoulders or upper legs—which would then protect them from injury. So we tracked them, then waited until they were still and not looking down at us. When they turned away from me, it was safe to shoot. Their awareness of our presence and their curiosity made it a time-consuming affair.

All of this toil was done in the hope of obtaining a tiny piece of skin for genetic analysis. For this we used the biopsy dart that we had designed and tested back home at the zoo. The dart cut out an eighth-inch piece of skin and then fell to the ground, thus avoiding the risk of anesthetizing an orangutan a hundred feet up in the trees.

The females and younger animals squeak-called at us after being darted. This high-pitched sound, made by pursing their lips and sucking in air, is used as a warning or threat. The dart probably felt like the sting of a wasp. They reached around with their hands and touched the place where the dart had hit. Then they would smell and taste their finger in an attempt to understand what had happened. After this routine, many of them, and almost all the males, would climb down lower in the trees to get a better look at us. They probably wondered what we were doing crawling around in the bushes and mud.

Finding an orangutan was difficult: finding a four-inch-long dart in the jungle was close to impossible. The inside of the dart was packed with closed-cell foam, to keep it afloat if it fell in the swamp. We often spent an hour or two wading through the muddy water, combing the bushes, and turning the leaf litter in search of the dart.

If we were successful, the biopsy dart contained a tiny but extremely valuable piece of skin. We carefully removed the sample with forceps so we would not contaminate it with our own DNA. We also carefully removed dirt and organic matter from the tiny piece of tissue and washed it in antibiotic and antifungal solutions to prevent any other possible contamination. We placed the tissue in a cell culture growth medium to keep it alive until it could be frozen in the portable liquid nitrogen tank we kept at the research station. On successful days, we hiked back to camp with our "trophy" or, as Harmony noted, like proud primitive hunters returning with dinner.

After a few weeks of work at Gunung Palung we got enough orangutan skin biopsies to provide a genetic picture of the population. The camp staff and students had been great to work with and had taken good care of us. Seti needed to get back to the university to teach, and Harmony and I had to go to a new site on the opposite side of Borneo to collect more samples.

Two years previously, Harmony and I had sampled wild orangutans on the island of Sumatra. Since that first trip I had left my job in Seattle and gone to work for WCS. Harmony and I continued to collaborate on the genetics project we had begun together.

THE BIOPSY DART

Samples of DNA are required to study the genetics of a species. Traditionally, cells containing complete strands of DNA were obtained by collecting a blood sample, and the genetic material of the white blood cells was purified for research. Modern laboratory methods now allow for small segments of DNA to be copied repeatedly in order to obtain enough material to analyze. This explains how a single strand of hair or a few cells under a criminal's fingernail can be used to help determine innocence or guilt, but this works well only if you know which segment of DNA to amplify in order to distinguish individuals.

For many species, the critical piece of DNA to compare is still not known. For orangutans, a complete set of genes was needed for the key segment to be identified. To begin a study for orangutans, we needed whole cells containing the complete complement of their DNA. This left us two choices. The first was to immobilize the animals with a drug dart. Once they fell from their perch high up in the trees, a blood sample could be collected. Hopefully they would recover from the fall and go back to their normal lives. A second, much safer option required the development of a dart that would cut a small piece of skin without having to take the risk of anesthetizing the animal in order to catch it and collect a sample.

Working with Felner Smith, a biomechanical engineer at the University of Washington, we modified a standard drug dart to act like a tiny cookie cutter that would take a piece of skin from an orangutan. The front end of the dart was made from a small piece of stainless-steel tubing sharpened on the edge like a hole punch. Inside this quarter-inch-long tubing we placed three dental broaches. The broaches are thin strands of wire covered with hairlike barbules used by dentists to extract the dead nerve material during a root canal procedure. In the biopsy dart, they would hold the tiny punch of skin inside the tip when it bounced off the animal and fell to the ground. If the darting was successful, the recovered dart would contain a small sample of skin, which, like all skin, contained hundreds of thousands of DNA rich cells.

We tested the dart on leather objects first, then on dead animals, and finally on animals at the zoo in Seattle. When it was clear that the technique was safe for the animals and effective, we took it to Sumatra and Borneo to begin our studies on the genetics of orangutans. Since that time, the dart has been used on dozens of other species around the world, including elephants and rhinos, sea lions, and even crocodiles.

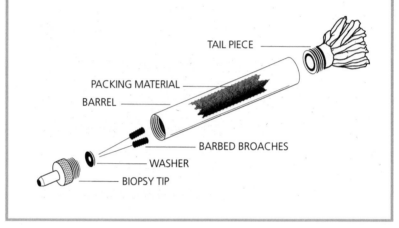

TAIL PIECE

PACKING MATERIAL

BARREL

BARBED BROACHES

WASHER

BIOPSY TIP

With this trip to Borneo we were closer to collecting samples from enough geographically separated populations of orangutans to develop a profile for the species as a whole.

On the trip back to Teluk Melano the stream was flowing smoothly enough to take us downriver without any wild adventures. At one point some of the spiny rattan vines grabbed the liquid nitrogen tank and pulled it out of the boat. Before the rest of us could react, Harmony dove headfirst into the water and swam upstream to the tank. Luckily the rattan kept the top of the tank above the surface, and our precious samples were not ruined. Nonetheless her quick reactions and fearlessness were impressive.

BODY ADORNMENT

Tattoos were traditional among most Dayak tribes. Men and women were tattooed all over, particularly members of the aristocracy. They used tattoos to commemorate success in warfare and to protect against disease. Patterns were made by a needle in a wooden handle, the tip of which was dipped in soot and natural dye. A Dayak might spend as many as six hundred hours enduring this painful process.

Today's youth could learn a thing or two about body piercing from the many Dayak tribes of Borneo. Traditionally, Dayak women and men distended their earlobes and pierced them many times to display large hoop earrings. Some tribal groups preferred large brass weights resembling pendulums. Successful head-hunters wore not only heavy earrings, but also carvings from the casque of the hornbill bird or the claws and fangs of bears and leopards.

Perhaps most unusual (and painful) of the Dayak adornments was the *palang*. Bluntly put, the *palang* is a penis pin. The glans and urethra are transpierced, and a piece of brass wire or carved bone is inserted. The resulting flare resembles the penis of a rhino or tapir. Men willingly submitted to this painful procedure in adulthood to help them pleasure their women.

She was cut up and bleeding from the rattan, but those were minor injuries compared with how battered we were from the previous month in the jungle.

We retraced our steps, visiting the proper authorities in Teluk Melano, Pontianak, and Jakarta. A few days later we flew to the eastern side of Indonesian Borneo to repeat our sample collecting for another four weeks. A month later we returned to the United States briefly, with liquid nitrogen tanks full of frozen but still living samples from the orangutans. That same year we made our third sample-collecting trip, in the two Malaysian states in the northern part of Borneo—Sabah and Sarawak. Once again we worked closely with the wildlife authorities to track down orangutans, and we sampled dozens of animals from each state.

The field component of the project was finally finished. Harmony returned to work at the zoo in Seattle, I went to New York to prepare for my next WCS project in some other part of the world, and the frozen orangutan skin samples went to the genetics lab.

The Genes

After three years we had collected enough skin biopsies from five geographically isolated populations of orangutans to evaluate the differences and similarities among them. Back in the United States at the National Institutes of Health's genetics laboratory, the frozen samples were carefully thawed, chopped up into microscopic pieces, and grown by tissue culture. This method produced an almost unlimited amount of cells, each with the identical genetic material of the original sample. The DNA could then be harvested from the cells and studied. The cultured cells could also be frozen again for future studies by other scientists, and, in fact, we returned these live cultures to Indonesians investigating genetic questions.

The results uncovered for the first time the historical relationship among the various populations that now exist. Even though land connected the two islands and the mainland of Malaysian peninsula as recently as fifteen thousand years ago, the lab work showed that the Sumatran and Bornean orangutans have been separated genetically for over a million years. Moreover, the genetic differences are as significant as those between distinctly separate species such as common chimpanzees and pygmy chimpanzees. This finding strongly supported the earlier concerns about not mixing Sumatran and Bornean orangutans either in captive breeding or in reintroduction programs in Indonesia and Malaysia. The data suggest that genetically the two subspecies could actually be considered two separate species.

The genetic makeup among the various orangutan populations on the island of Borneo were also different. The mountain ranges and rivers of Borneo have effectively isolated these populations. The analysis showed that populations in different parts of the island have not mixed for 250,000 years. While this seems like a long period of time, in evolutionary terms it's fairly short. Therefore, the genetic differences we found among the populations in Borneo did not warrant separating them into distinct subspecies.

Besides being academically and theoretically interesting, the results of the project have a very practical use. We found that each of the individual populations has a high degree of genetic variation. These individual differences indicate they are not all susceptible to the same risks, such as the introduction or mutation of a new disease. The findings also showed that risk of inbreeding was not a concern within any population.

The distance separating the various populations has now been permanently widened by the clearing of forests. If little genetic variation had been found to exist within a population, wildlife managers would have had to consider introducing unrelated animals to increase genetic diversity. This type of intervention would be expensive as well as politically and scientifically controversial. Not everyone agrees with managing populations.

Many scientists feel that our job is to observe the course of events as journalists would, but not to participate. Ironically, humans already have dramatically altered the course of events. Observing rather than managing is not an acceptable approach for those responsible for conservation. In the past, game managers ensured a plentiful supply of wild animals, which is why, for example, there are so many white-tailed deer in the United States. Their lack of attention to nongame species in the sixties and seventies allowed academic ecologists to take the lead in dictating conservation policy.

While the scientists have contributed some brilliant insights, they lack the practical animal management skills of the old-time game biologists. As we enter the new millennium, I hope the pendulum will swing back to a middle ground where expertise in both these disciplines will be utilized to help manage and conserve wildlife.

While government wildlife agencies traditionally have been good at the practical aspects of natural resource management, planning, policy, and law enforcement, often they still are poorly equipped or trained to handle the care of individual animals, an infrequent part of their work. In developing countries, the cost of medical care and behavioral rehabilitation is extremely high. The lack of both capabilities and funds have been stumbling blocks for progress in protecting endangered species.

The results of our genetics project had immediate applications toward solving this problem. The differences between the Bornean and Sumatran populations confirmed that animals should always be returned to their islands of origin or, if kept in captivity, not be allowed to breed with each other. The similarities among the Bornean populations granted authorities greater flexibility in choosing homes for these animals.

However, one of the most important results of the orangutan genetics project was less tangible. Our willingness to take on such a challenging task in so many areas and actually accomplish our goals impressed the local authorities in both Indonesia and Malaysia because it demonstrated our sincerity and commitment. The project required the establishment of trusting, working relationships with the staff of numerous ministries, agencies, and universities in Borneo and Sumatra. Good relationships like these are highly valued.

One of the obvious questions for all of us was, "What's next?" As it happened, there was an area that my program could help with: the medical problems and captive care needs for confiscated and displaced wildlife. Wildlife authorities in both countries had become inundated with orangutans, bears, gibbons, and an assortment of other threatened species that had either been confiscated from the pet trade, surrendered by owners who had grown tired of them, or found injured. Training local veterinarians, staff, and students in caring for wildlife was one way I could contribute.

Since doing the original fieldwork for the orangutan genetics project, I have been returning to Indonesia or Malaysia every year to conduct training courses and help with conservation efforts. My involvement with orangutans has not ended. Probably, my getting involved again with rehabilitation work as I did as a child was unavoidable. I guess we continually return to childhood dreams throughout our lives.

Let's Not Throw the
Baby out with the Bathwater

Throughout the developing world, government
agencies are increasingly faced with receiving and caring for orphaned or injured animals. In North America and Europe the situation is different because many private individuals are financially
able and have the facilities to care for small wild animals. In most
developing nations the animals in question are often endangered
species that grow to be dangerous, are susceptible to diseases of
people and domestic animals, and become too expensive to care for.

Sometimes government agencies confiscate these animals
from illegal traders or from individual owners, and sometimes an
injured wild animal is found and brought to the nearest wildlife
department office. Occasionally owners surrender the animals
themselves. Baby sun bears and gibbons are cute but soon grow to
be terrible pets. In Malaysia and Indonesia baby orangutans are
frequently kept as pets until they become unmanageable.

On my last trip to Borneo one young animal had just been
turned in by its owners, who were extremely wealthy and had provided the orangutan with everything they thought it needed for
the first five years of life. They had dressed the young orangutan
like a little girl and shaved and powdered her entire body. Since
they did not have children of their own, they had raised the young
orangutan as a daughter.

She was a sweet kid but unfortunately had little training in be-

Orphaned orangutan

ing an orangutan. Animals raised so closely to humans are severely handicapped. They have not learned the proper language to communicate with their own kind and have not developed physically as they would have in the wild. One baby orangutan I know of had been carried so much by its owners that it did not have the muscle strength or knowledge to walk or climb. When coaxed to do so, it curled up in a fetal position and cried in fear. Government agencies find themselves with hundreds of these animals and must make sure the animals are properly cared for as well as decide their fate.

If you chart out the age and sex distributions for a given population of plants or animals, you get a picture of the structure of any group. Population biologists use these demographic models and add mathematical formulas to take into account factors such as longevity, age of puberty, and number of offspring born and surviving to different ages. But by using computers to speed calculations, they can provide precise information regarding one population of a species and play with various scenarios to make predictions regarding long-term population growth and decline.

Orangutans have unusual natural life patterns. They live in low densities—very few animals per acre of land. Like humans, orangutans are long lived and do not reach puberty at an early age. A female invests much of her energy in raising one offspring and will not give birth again for eight years, so she can be close to twenty years old before her first offspring successfully raises her own first infant.

The implications of this type of "life history" is that population stability or persistence is extremely dependent on the survival of adult females. To replace a successful female takes decades. This is why it is so critical to protect wild adult females. On the other hand, the loss of an infant has little effect on the population as a whole. If an infant dies, another one is born very soon. Adding young orangutans that were previously pets to an existing population has little beneficial effect. In fact, it can be detrimental to wild populations because young animals previously exposed to people can carry human diseases back to the wild population. Also, the rehabilitation process is expensive and may consume resources that could otherwise be used for habitat protection.

Ironically, one of the reasons orangutans are known around the world has to do with the magazine and television stories about rehabilitation centers. This publicity has resulted in financial donations to support private orangutan rehabilitation centers. As the cycle of publicity and investment continues, rehabilitation centers tend to become more self-serving, since they need more baby orangutans to keep operating. Wealthy adventure travelers spend thousands of dollars to visit, and in some situations help care for, young animals at rehabilitation centers. This is the scenario that developed at Birute Galdikas's rehabilitation center in the southern Indonesian part of Borneo. It is a sad truth that such high-profile visitors and the income they provide *reduce* motivation to change conservation programs, try new approaches, or aggressively protect other areas of valuable orangutan habitat that have yet to be plundered.

Birute first went to Borneo to study wild orangutans for her Ph.D. She became enthralled with their lives and concerned over their plight. During the next two decades her research site became a refugee camp for over a hundred confiscated or surrendered young orangutans and also the mecca for any tourist willing to pay to volunteer as caretaker-researcher. She, her Indonesian husband, and a few private investors built the only hotel close to the center, and volunteers and tourists had little choice but to stay there. What began as her student research project developed into a private enterprise with typical high-stakes politics and cutthroat business practices.

Indonesians I know began to call Birute "the White Rajah," a disparaging reference to the colonial governors who seized power from traditional local leaders. Her struggle to amass power, cloaked in the righteousness of protecting orangutans, has resulted in far too much conflict among conservation professionals and has led many government agencies and conservationists to focus a tremendous amount of valuable time and effort on her rather than orangutan conservation. Meanwhile, baby orangutans keep showing up on the doorstep.

There is a true need for places to care for young orangutans. Law enforcement officials cannot do their jobs if there is no place to send the confiscated animals. Without good law enforcement, there will be no disincentive for killing adult females to collect the infants. And if rehabilitation centers are going to exist, they need to be operated professionally rather than staffed by inexperienced foreign volunteers. I was once told by a friend who heads the Orangutan Foundation in the United Kingdom, which mainly supports Birute Galdikas's rehabilitation center, that physicians are much better qualified than veterinarians to treat sick orangutans. We do not always agree.

It is true that the great apes share many anatomical features with humans. At Galdikas's center, physician tourists from the Northern Hemisphere work on the animals. Inexperienced veterinarians or student volunteers do the same. I don't know which of these groups can better handle a case of primate malaria, but I do know that neither is a substitute for medical care provided by individuals trained or experienced in treating and caring for great apes. The welfare of these young animals is important. There is no need to justify their care by saying that rescuing the infants is significant for conservation. The work of caring for animals displaced or abused by humans stands on its own merits. Misleading wealthy or influential people into focusing only on rehabilitation distracts them from helping to effect changes that could protect wild populations of orangutans and the thousands of species that share their natural habitat.

Besides serving an essential role in law enforcement capabilities, well-run rehabilitation centers can contribute significantly to conservation in nontraditional ways. One way to deal with the large number of young orangutans being obtained by authorities is to use them to establish new populations. Rather than continually releasing young animals into viable wild populations where they do not contribute significantly and also pose the threat of introducing new diseases, a group of forty or fifty young orangutans could potentially be used to repopulate an area where they formerly ranged but no longer exist. This type of rehabilitation center could operate for three to four years and then be moved to a new location to repeat the operation with a new batch of young orangutans.

This concept was developed in Indonesia with the help of two Dutch scientists. While it is still too soon to evaluate the success of the first attempt, the potential application for this approach is great, and with modification it may also be of value for other species such as sun bears and wild cats. There are many areas where orangutans have been "hunted out," and there are hundreds of young orangutans that could be rehabilitated and released. The risk in this approach lies in the realities of human tendencies. Any type of project creates jobs, a new local economy, and curiosity. Staff and visitors turn into customers for kiosks selling food and drinks. This is not so much a problem in itself, but closing down the operation will meet with opposition from those seeking to maintain their jobs and businesses. Nonetheless, the concept of short-term rehabilitation facilities is sensible, and most likely the final results will depend more on how the project is implemented than on whether or not the approach can work.

Another area where orangutan rehabilitation centers can have major conservation impact is local public education. The abundance of young animals provides a unique opportunity for people to learn and become excited about orangutans. Even in the countries where orangutans live, the vast majority of citizens never have the chance to see them. An environment where children and adults can watch orangutans climb through the trees provides the perfect setting for conservation education programs. The orangutans can serve as ambassadors from the forest. I believe that seeing them in their natural habitats instills a far greater fascination than seeing them in photographs. The Sepilok Orangutan Rehabilitation Center in Malaysian Borneo is visited by over 150,000 people a year; a few thousand of these are foreign tourists, and all the rest are Malaysian. There is hardly a person in the region now who does not understand that orangutans are endangered, something to be protected. Influencing local people, and especially children, is truly our only hope for the future.

In Malaysia and Indonesia, finding opportunities to get experience in taking care of dogs and cats or cows and horses is easy. But students are often hard-pressed to get practical experience with exotic animals or wild species. One reason is that wildlife rehabilitation programs, a common training ground in the United States, are not very common in developing countries, and if they exist, they lack good facilities, professional resources, and affiliations with universities. The other reason is that wildlife medicine is still almost unheard of, even though the quality of veterinary training in many countries is now excellent.

The result is a field fertile with dedicated, credentialed, but inexperienced people with an abundance of wild animals needing skilled attention. Capitalizing on this, I and my colleagues invest our energy into building capacity among locals to be able to do the same work we do. Wildlife rehabilitation centers provide a unique venue for teaching local biologists, veterinarians, and wildlife managers how to handle and care for unusual but native species.

THE LONE RANGER SYNDROME

In my travels, I too often meet expatriates, usually from developed countries, who are working in developing countries and exhibit peculiar social skills. I don't know if these traits predispose people to working in strange places or are the result. Almost by definition, people wanting to spend their lives in a culture different from their own fall outside the norm. Within this subset, you find a wide range of personalities. Many are delightful people, while some become particularly unbearable. Greg Thompson, a sometimes wise friend with whom I worked years ago at Woodland Park Zoo in Seattle, classified one group as suffering from the "Lone Ranger syndrome."

Lone Rangers believe they are the only ones with the knowledge and motivation to do things "right." After spending time in the bush with less educated people who don't have the same value systems, a Lone Ranger easily falls into the trap of thinking of himself or herself as superior, almost godlike. Lone Rangers frequently are uncomfortable when they return to their former cultures, where they are no longer comparatively rich, influential, or special, and therefore they tend to remain in foreign countries.

Living in a different culture allows all personality quirks to be passed off as foreign and forgiven. Unfortunately, the citizens of many developing countries meet only the most unrepresentative ambassadors from North America and Europe. Sometimes they start out fairly normal and succumb to the Lone Ranger syndrome later. After a while, they manage to offend so many locals and government officials that they become a hindrance to conservation efforts and therefore a problem for everyone. Local people may associate conservation with the Lone Ranger and work against the efforts to protect the animals. On extremely rare occasions they have even been killed, like Dian Fossey, by local people or fellow scientists. They are not bad people; on the contrary, most started out just trying to do the right thing.

As it happens, Lone Rangers are rare and most conservation field-workers adapt well to local cultures. They may sacrifice the comfortable lifestyles of their home countries, but they gain a new family of people, plants, and animals to care about. One shift in the approach to conservation has also helped reduce the number of Lone Rangers: supporting the professional development of locals so they can assume responsibilities formerly held by foreigners. Since this is the appropriate route for achieving long-term conservation goals anyway, Lone Rangers should fade slowly into history.

Field School

To take advantage of the goodwill we had built, we began to run training workshops for veterinarians in Indonesia and Malaysia. In Indonesia veterinarians already working in zoos and at the university's primate center were logical choices to participate. They had the interest, but their experience and exposure to wildlife medicine were limited. My boss, Bob Cook, the chief vet at the Bronx Zoo, and I conducted the first workshop at a safari park in the highlands near Jakarta.

We focused our training on the native wild species. Bob and I demonstrated modern darting equipment and techniques for immobilizing hoofstock such as deer and antelope. We anesthetized orangutans and tigers and demonstrated the proper methods of conducting complete physical examinations. We conducted sessions on working with cockatoos and birds of paradise and even Komodo dragons. All of these species are common in Indonesian zoos, and more important, they were species with which wildlife authorities needed the most help.

During each session the Indonesians had to do the procedures themselves. They practiced taking blood samples, ear tagging, tattooing animals for identification, and taking X-rays. None of these procedures were unusual for the Indonesian vets, but they had never realized they could perform these techniques on nondomestic species with just slight modifications.

Mornings were spent in lectures, and afternoons were devoted to practice sessions. With our laptop computers and a portable

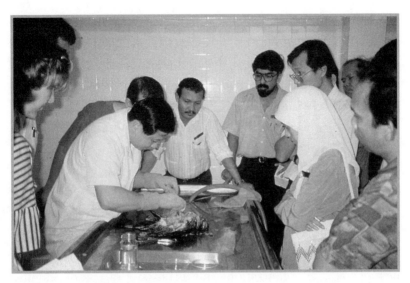

Training course for Malaysian vets

printer, Bob and I would stay up past midnight each night, putting together additional materials for the next day. The Indonesians' biggest concern was making a mistake while trying a procedure for the first time on an endangered species. Their ethics mandated that medical procedures be conducted by qualified individuals, and they previously had not felt qualified professionally. By having each workshop participant perform all of the medical and handling procedures, we helped them feel more confident. Something that seems so easy, such as putting a plastic ear tag in a deer, still requires knowledge of the anatomy of the blood vessels and the supporting cartilaginous ridges. If placed too high, the tag could be torn out by heavy brush or the extra weight might cause the ear itself to flop over. Too low a placement makes the tag difficult to see from a distance and also bothers the deer. But once the vets had the information they needed and saw a procedure performed, they felt comfortable doing it themselves. This was the goal of our training workshops.

Bob and I did not anticipate the other significant result of our workshops. Most of the vets we asked to participate knew of each other or had met before, but they did not regularly collaborate or share information. Many had knowledge and experience in one area but were weak in others. Bob and I fostered discussions by having participants describe their experiences with a given species or problem, making it clear that they could learn from each other.

The role that professional organizations play in encouraging the dissemination of information is often taken for granted. In North America and in Europe, associations of wildlife and zoo veterinarians have been active for decades. They serve as conduits for sharing information, and their meetings allow colleagues to network. These organizations and forums are rare in developing countries because so few people are involved in the field of wildlife medicine or conservation. One of my main themes in our training workshops is to demonstrate how comfortable I am with saying, "I don't know." I've learned how to say it in the language of every country I've worked in! I try to show that it's okay not to know everything. Certainly I don't, and I'm always learning.

Both of these concepts were successfully transferred in Indonesia. The group of vets who participated in our first workshop went on to form the Indonesian Association of Wildlife Veterinarians. Several times a year Bob and I get a fax or e-mail from them requesting information or suggestions on handling a medical problem. They are on firm footing and making great strides.

Compared with Indonesia, Malaysian veterinary universities have been better funded and therefore have been teaching more advanced levels of medicine. As a result, veterinary training there is similar to that in most developed countries of the world. The Malaysian Veterinary Association publishes a scientific journal that reports on subjects such as embryo transfer techniques and the newest treatments for livestock diseases.

An interesting situation has evolved in Malaysian Borneo that I have not seen elsewhere. Because most of the vets have been interconnected by government service and common goals, they have all assumed responsibility for the health of the animals in their states. They have eradicated Foot and Mouth Disease, African swine fever, and rabies from the Malaysian part of Borneo. None of them act as if a problem is some other vet's worry. No one points fingers to lay blame. Quite the opposite—they are quick to consult with each other. Moreover, their sense of responsibility extends to wildlife, and they were also quick to say that they wanted more training.

Similar to the veterinary programs, the wildlife agencies in the two Malaysian states on Borneo are made up of relatively small groups of people with good education levels. I had already worked with both of these wildlife departments during the orangutan genetics project, and we all agreed that the opportunity was perfect for developing training programs in these two states. Some of the biologists working for WCS implemented a long-term training program for the wildlife departments that identified the specific needs of wildlife rangers, officers, and managers and then helped provide that training. The wildlife medicine training component brought together vets working for the agriculture department and those in private practice with some of the wildlife department staff.

Linking the two groups was perhaps one of the program's most significant achievements. In our modern world of modified habitats and easy access to once remote areas, building working relationships between the wildlife authorities and animal health specialists is crucial.

Sepilok

In the Malaysian state of Sabah, the wildlife department has evolved rapidly since its creation in the 1980s. During our first training sessions in Sabah, we targeted the ranger and officer levels to provide the basic knowledge of caring for wild species. The department was actively involved in law enforcement and confiscating animals from the pet trade. Rangers around the state needed skills in handling and transporting these animals, and the staff at the rehabilitation center needed to be updated on current techniques.

By the end of the eighties a veterinarian from the veterinary services section of the agriculture department had been assigned permanently to the Sabah Wildlife Department. Over the years the individuals filling this post have changed, and I've gotten to work with three of them. Dr. Edwin Bosi is currently the sole veterinarian for the state's wildlife department. Edwin is of Kadazan ancestry, one of the largest indigenous groups in that part of Borneo. He had excellent veterinary training in Malaysia and later obtained a master's degree in New Zealand. Since joining the wildlife team, he has worked hard in training his staff members and upgrading the facilities.

For over thirty years now Sepilok has been operating as a center for orphaned orangutans. Located in the Sepilok Forest Reserve, this large chunk of virgin jungle was set aside during colonial days. It has massive tropical hardwoods towering 150 feet into the air. Other areas are seasonally flooded peat forests, and the coastal edge of the reserve is tidal mangrove swamp. At only twelve thousand acres, the Sepilok Reserve is a small representative of what once existed. On the other hand, someone's foresight resulted in a valuable resource today.

The Sepilok Rehabilitation Center has grown into a facility that receives thirty or forty injured or orphaned orangutans a year. The center's staffing levels and funding have fluctuated over the years, but in recent times the government has made a sincere commitment to improving the facilities and upgrading the quality of the programs. They have built a new public education center and are constructing a huge new clinic to better care for the number of animals arriving at the center—and just in time.

In 1998 the drought from El Niño and the clearing and burning of land for agriculture resulted in uncontrolled forest fires and dense smoke that blanketed much of the region. The smoke and fires drove orangutans to the edges of forests, where they encountered villages and crops, which led to a surge of arrivals at Sepilok.

In Sabah, where the wildlife department is organized and trained in moving and caring for orangutans, at least something could be done for some of the animals. Local people either caught them or called the wildlife department to collect them. Many of the animals could be released in other areas of forest, but some were too weak or dehydrated to be released immediately. Fortunately the Sepilok staff was prepared for the crisis, if not emotionally, at least professionally.

At this time we had another collaborative project running with the Sabah Wildlife Department. One component was to help with the medical care of animals at Sepilok and provide more advanced training of the technical staff. I hired a young veterinarian, Dr. Annelisa Kilbourn, to work on the project for a year and a half. Annelisa had grown up in Europe and spoke French and English.

Her mother is Dutch, so she also speaks that language well. Because of her father she has British citizenship, but she went to high school, college, and veterinary school in the States. She has also worked in southern, eastern, and northern Africa and Madagascar. The moving around may have given her the diplomatic skills that this job required. She has the typical overachieving qualities of a veterinarian: while she was in school she trained for a pilot's license, got a black belt in karate, worked in a veterinary clinic, and pursued her skill as an artist. In addition, she is amazingly gentle and kind. When I asked Annelisa if she could handle a year of being away from home and living in Borneo, she answered, "Where's home?"

That was the answer I needed to hear, so we packed her off to the tropics. I spent the first month with her. One of her assignments was to assist Dr. Bosi. Edwin has many responsibilities in addition to being the veterinarian at Sepilok; Annelisa could help him at the center by working with his staff on the increasing number of cases.

The Sepilok center cares for over a hundred orangutans. Many are old enough to live in the surrounding forests, but they occasionally return to the feeding platforms where tourists can see them. Another thirty to forty live at the clinic because they are too young to fend for themselves. The ones under a year or two are still bottle-fed and monitored closely every day. Just like human babies, they are weighed often to ensure proper growth. As they get a little older, they are allowed playtime in the forest under supervision from a caretaker. This time is essential for them to develop good motor skills and hand-eye coordination and to learn about the forest.

As with any orphanage with 150 kids ranging in age from six months to twelve years, illnesses and injuries are common. When something as simple as a flu virus hits, dozens of them succumb to fevers, coughing, or stomach upset. They don't want to eat or

Young orangutan with Sarawak wildlife officials

drink, and in the tropical heat they quickly become dehydrated and can easily die. The tiny orange babies just lie on their backs, staring up at you with huge sunken eyes. Annelisa and the staff would then spend the next week or two trying to keep a dozen or two young orangutans alive by giving them intravenous fluids and encouraging them to eat and drink electrolyte solutions. No one sleeps much during these crises.

On normal days she would be helping with the more routine cases: broken arms and legs needing surgery and casting, suturing up a cut, vaccinating the youngsters for the same childhood ill-

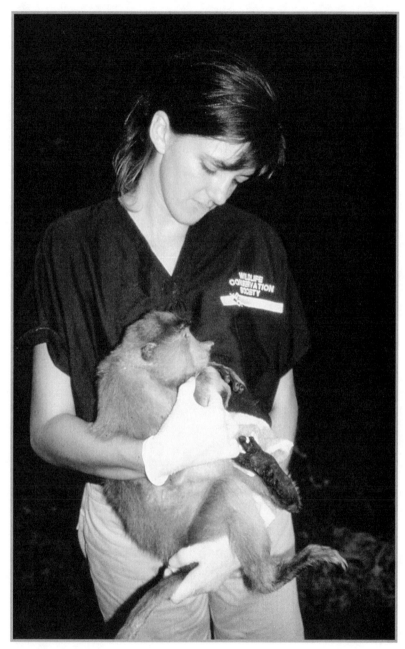

Annelisa holding confiscated proboscis monkey

nesses that affect humans, or providing intensive care for a baby with malaria. Many other animals also arrive at Sepilok. Young sun bears, gibbons, leaf monkeys, owls and eagles, and pythons and cobras are dropped off by the public or by law enforcement agents who confiscated them from private individuals. Mistreated by their former owners or injured during forest clearing, these animals need medical care. All new animals, even the healthy ones, require quarantine examinations, vaccinations, and parasite treatment. Under Dr. Bosi's supervision, Annelisa treated eye problems in venomous snakes and fixed broken wings on endangered species of birds. The days were long: she arrived before eight in the morning and would go home at midnight or not at all. And this was just the work at Sepilok.

The other component of our project was actually the primary reason for sending Annelisa to Borneo. A rare opportunity to learn about the health of wild orangutans existed in Sabah. The wildlife department had been translocating wild orangutans from small forest remnants to protected areas in the state. Translocation means moving free-ranging animals directly from one area to another. The approach is used to restock depleted areas and sometimes, as in the case of the orangutans, to provide protection.

A COMPLEX DILEMMA

Logging and agriculture go hand in hand in much of the tropics. Tropical hardwoods are worth tremendous sums of money on the international market. Both Indonesia and Malaysia have been trying to develop their economies as rapidly as possible. The Malaysian states of Sabah and Sarawak on Borneo have large petroleum reserves, but most of the revenues from oil and gas go to the federal government on the mainland rather than to the two states—something of a modern-day colonial system. As a result, the two states have turned to their forests to provide revenues.

Huge tracts of forest, ranging from a hundred to several hundred thousand acres, are auctioned off as logging and agricultural concessions. The most precious hardwoods are worth thousands of dollars per tree, and three to six of these can be harvested from each acre; thus a concession can be worth millions of dollars.

Selective logging, if done carefully, can be performed without completely destroying the wildlife if hunting is prohibited. But generally the concession holder is interested only in making a profit, not in reducing the impact on wildlife. Governments are becoming more aware of the issues, and in a few places better controls are being implemented.

In other areas, harvesting several trees per acre is not enough; governments want to make the land more "productive." In Malaysia and Indonesia, there has been a shift to agricultural use, requiring the clear-cutting of forests. Most of mainland Malaysia has been converted from tropical forests to vast plantations of rubber trees and oil palms. Oil palms thrive in the tropical climate, are virtually disease-free, and produce huge clusters of orange red palm fruits or nuts that are cooked and pressed for vegetable oil. The yield per acre of land is as high as that for sunflower or safflower oil but has the advantage of not having to be replanted every year. Each palm tree will produce for thirty to forty years. In the two Malaysian states in Borneo, conversion of forests to agriculture has been implemented at an amazingly rapid rate. Indonesia is trying to follow as quickly as possible.

Unlike selective logging, the clear-cutting of forests and burning of the less valuable wood and underbrush to prepare for agriculture is the activity that resulted in the out-of-control fires during the El Niño droughts of 1997 and 1998. But even without the fires, clear-cutting such large tracts of land is devastating to wildlife. As is common in many countries, laws protect endangered species but not their homes. Concession holders cannot legally kill an orangutan, but they can cut down a hundred thousand acres of forest. In many places around the world this destruction is subsidized by loans from international development and banking agencies—our tax dollars.

However, efforts to clear the large tracts of land leave little pockets of forest protected by deep ravines or steep hillsides. Too small to be significant as reserves, these little pockets provide temporary refuge. The birds fly away with the hope of finding a patch of forest they can move into. Some animals can flee on the ground, but tree dwellers such as orangutans become trapped. The Sabah Wildlife Department began capturing orangutans stuck in these small forest patches and moving them to a reserve in another area of the state where orangutans formerly ranged.

These were adult, reproducing orangutans. Many females were accompanied by their four- and five-year-old kids. These successful adults were the key to maintaining sustainable populations—and the most difficult to work with. They live high in the trees, which makes them hard to catch. Being four or five times stronger than humans and having four hands, powerful jaws, and good brains also makes them dangerous to handle.

For the original genetics project, we had developed the biopsy dart to avoid subjecting the orangutans to the risks of capture. Now, however, to save these animals from starvation or from being killed by the oil palm plantation workers, we had to accept certain risks both to the animals and to ourselves. Fortunately the wildlife department has dedicated staff, many of them indigenous Kadazans, who have few fears of the forest or the animals. They had participated in our training programs, practiced more on their own, and were willing to take on the challenge.

Forest cleared for palm oil plantation

Never before has anyone had the opportunity to handle wild orangutans, and we needed to learn about their health. Twenty-five years of behavioral observations by researchers had told us if they used their left hand or right hand more, but we didn't have a clue about what diseases played a role in their lives in the wild. The only orangutans previously handled by scientists were youngsters that had lived with humans. This unique opportunity to study wild orangutans brought us together again.

Since my only responsibility on this translocation and health study project was to get it started and make sure everything went smoothly until it was over, I had it easy. After a month in Sabah making sure Annelisa could handle the work, the environment, and the people, I was free to leave. Annelisa would stay for eighteen months to work with the Malaysian team. I came back for a one-month visit about halfway through her time there. She fit into the program as if she had been designed for it.

Like so many of my assignments, the routine required days of walking through steaming hot forest patches in search of our quarry. When one is found, the team assembles at the spot and makes a plan. First the animal has to be isolated in a few trees from which it cannot escape. This is done by forcing it to move from tree to tree until it reaches a dead end in the patch. Sometimes we use a chain saw to cut down a tree or two to block its retreat. Cutting down trees to save orangutans is a bit ironic, but the little patches are doomed anyway.

Using lightweight plastic darts, we eventually inject the animal with an anesthetic. I say eventually because it's not particularly easy to hit a moving target a hundred feet overhead. Moreover, anesthetic dosages are based on body weight. While the animal is high in the trees, we have to accurately estimate its weight and make up a dart specifically for each individual. Then we have to wait until the orangutan is low enough in the trees to be within range of the dart gun—seventy to a hundred feet. It also has to be standing still and presenting a part of its body with a lot of muscle, like an arm, leg, or shoulder. This can take hours, but for the safety of the animal it's essential to be patient.

Once the animal is isolated in a single tree, the team members use their parangs—locally made, traditional versions of a machete also used historically for head-hunting—to clear the surrounding undergrowth and make a huge brush pile around the tree. If the orangutan falls, the ten-foot-high pile of leafy branches cushions the impact. More often the darted orangutan falls asleep in the tree and someone climbs up to retrieve it.

Once under control, the animals are given a complete physical examination. A great ape's anatomy is very similar to that of a human. Looking in their eyes with an ophthalmoscope provides a view of an iris, lens, and retina almost indistinguishable from our own. Their mouths, lips, and teeth are bigger, well adapted to tearing off tree bark to get to the tender inner cambium layer and breaking open the hardest nuts and fruits. A coconut still in its husk poses no more challenge to an orangutan than a piece of candy in a paper wrapper to a child.

Their hands are long and huge in proportion to their bodies— a male's is about three times bigger than mine. The length of the bones in their arms and legs combined with the points of muscle attachment provide the fulcrums and leverage that make them so strong. A forty-pound adolescent is as strong as or stronger than I am. Since orangutans can use their feet as a second set of hands and splinter giant bamboo with powerful jaws, they have a definite advantage in a wrestling match.

For all their toughness, an orangutan's skin is soft and pliable, much like ours. As they get older, their dark red hair gets longer and forms a thick coat. As in humans, there is a range of hair color, length, and density among individuals. In general, by the time the males reach thirty, they have long capes of curly dark red hair draped from their shoulders and back.

In orangutans there is a great size difference between the sexes. The adult males can weigh 120 pounds and the females about half that. They are all lean and muscular from living in the trees. Zoo orangutans misrepresent the species by frequently being obese—sometimes two to three times the weight of their wild cousins who work for a living. Zoo orangutans suffer from high cholesterol levels, diabetes, and heart disease. Not surprisingly, we have found no evidence of these lifestyle diseases in wild orangutans. The free-ranging animals occasionally show the scars of a rough life, but they are in excellent physical condition.

We needed to tattoo them so their success after the translocations could be determined. The only place on their bodies a tattoo would show was the inside of their almost hairless thighs. Using an electric tattooer made for people, we gave each one a large black or dark green number that could be read with binoculars when they were hanging from the trees. Identification photos were also taken because, like people, almost every orangutan has a distinct face, though family resemblances do occur.

Before the anesthetized orangutans woke up, we carried them from the forest patch and secured them in a transport cage loaded onto the back of a pickup truck. The cage was covered with palm fronds or other tree branches to provide shade from the relentless sun and to provide some privacy for the animal during the next leg of the process. Sabah is a small state with fairly good roads. Within half a day's drive the team and the orangutan arrived at one of the department's wildlife reserves. The animal, who had by that time fully recovered from anesthesia, was immediately released back into the forest; it wasted no time climbing the nearest tree and disappearing in the jungle canopy. The reward for a few days' hard work was immediate—a big adult male or a mother with a youngster swung off into the rain forest.

The feelings at that moment are almost overwhelming. Everyone is sweaty and tired, and at the same time we're immediately relieved by the success. Every step of the translocation procedure is risky for the animals. For the first time in days we have the opportunity to look at each other and recognize what we've done as a team. Finally, as we turn again for a last glimpse of the orangutan traveling off into the forest, I think we all are struck by the same realization: Maybe we've just compensated, ever so slightly, for the horrible things our species has done to theirs.

The wild orangutans' pretrip physicals included the collection of fecal samples to check for parasites, and blood

Releasing translocated orangutan

samples to determine their history of exposure to infectious diseases. The blood samples were processed initially in the field and stored away in a small liquid nitrogen tank. Then laboratory testing identified which diseases existed in wild orangutan populations. This had never been determined before, and the results have had several practical and immediate applications.

The first is that we now have baseline information to compare against an individual animal. Before this work, we could say only that the test results from an orangutan were similar to or different from the "normals" compiled from orangutans living in zoos.

Another pressing issue had been the inability to properly evaluate the health of confiscated young orangutans. We were able to test them and find that they had been infected with this virus or that disease, but we did not know if they would be a threat to wild populations if they were released.

A third component of the project was based on collaboration with Malaysian public heath officials and a graduate student from

Harvard. Since great apes and humans can become infected with similar diseases, we wanted to know if this was happening where humans have moved into proximity with the animals. Recent outbreaks of "new" and deadly diseases in other parts of the world, such as the Ebola virus in Africa, have made emerging diseases an important topic. It is frequently assumed that wildlife is at fault. Even if the diseases did originate from animals, the problem is that humans are now encroaching on previously uninhabited wild places and killing the natural hosts or reservoirs of these diseases, so the viruses and bacteria then transfer to humans. This human encroachment rarely is identified as the issue to be confronted; instead the animals are blamed.

Working with Malaysian health officials, who were keen to participate in such an innovative approach to health, we were able to gather objective data. We already were collecting the appropriate samples from the orangutans; for the human side of the equation, plantation workers and some of the wildlife department staff from Sepilok volunteered themselves.

Our preliminary findings show that the wild orangutans are almost completely free of infectious diseases that affect people, and the incidence of the few bacteria they do carry is lower than in mice and squirrels and even cows. The malaria we found in the wild orangutans does not infect humans.

On the other hand, the former pet and captive orangutans have been exposed to human diseases not found in the wild. Flu viruses, the hepatitis virus, and tuberculosis have all been found in young orangutans cared for by humans. Birute Galdikas once told me that if we set the orangutans free, nature would heal them. That is a wonderful dream, but it is a dream. We all know nature doesn't play favorites. Infectious diseases are caused by tiny living organisms that are trying to survive and reproduce just as vigorously as the host organism. Releasing animals with diseases back into the wild threatens the health of the individual as well as that of the entire wild population.

The Malaysian approach to helping wildlife offers a good example of how agencies are struggling to do the best they can for wildlife while faced with seemingly insurmountable obstacles. Despite limited resources and overwhelming pressures altering the landscape of Borneo, dedicated individuals have come up with creative ways to try to at least mitigate the impact on endangered species. They have also acted responsibly by seeking out training for their staff, consulting with experts within their country and from other parts of the world, and gathering scientific data on the animals upon which they can base management decisions.

After the Malaysians in Sabah became proficient at translocating orangutans, they expanded their activities to include elephants—a huge and dangerous undertaking. Will they save all the wildlife of Borneo? Of course not. But rather than counting down the number of animals until they reach extinction, the Sabah officials are taking an active approach to protecting what they can.

As outsiders, we can take two approaches to the dilemma Borneo faces. The easiest and safest is to criticize them for what they are doing to their land and what they are not doing for their wildlife. This way we can be self-righteous and at the same time not risk being associated with governments that have environmentally destructive policies. The alternative approach—the one we at WCS have chosen—is much more difficult and frequently messier. It calls for continual engagement and hard work, mutual respect and long-term commitment. Working with the people who are ultimately responsible for their country's native species and trying to find ways to help will produce real results, in the field, for the animals. In the end, this is the only way.

OUTRAGEOUS NUMBERS

By the late 1980s poaching reduced the number of African elephants to half a million. Public outrage around the world resulted in a ban on international trade in ivory. Few people know that the situation for Asian elephants is ten times worse; they are believed to number no more than forty thousand.

Orphaned Asian elephant calf

Friends around the world

Part Seven

A Quick Trip
Around the World

Catching up with old friends,
feathered, furred, and human.

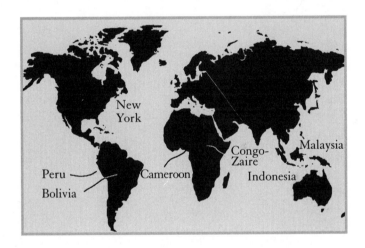

Congo-Zaire—
Back to the Heart of Africa

Staying abreast of developments in all the countries where I work and the people and projects I've become attached to has become almost a full-time job in itself. News reports, letters, and e-mail help, but I feel best when I can see everyone myself.

In Zaire President Mobutu continued to lead the country into despair, finally paving the way for Laurent Kabila's takeover in 1998. For most Zaïroïs, life could only get better. The rebellion took an immediate toll on all the conservation efforts in the region by temporarily closing down all projects. The Zairian army ransacked villages as they retreated. Ironically, the arrival of the rebels generally brought a return to stability, at least if you were Zaïroïs.

Before the rebels arrived, however, government forces had already managed to steal vehicles, radios, and other essentials to a normal, daily life. Karl and Rosie, the Harts, and Kes and Fraser all returned to Zaire after the fighting. They found that their homes had been plundered—every dish, fork, knife, pot, pan, mattress, sheet, and pillow was gone. Ten to twenty years' worth of personal household items had disappeared. Their short-wave radios and vehicles had been taken. Handmade gifts such as bowls and cups were gone, and nothing could replace those items filled with memories.

As Terese Hart remarked optimistically, "The really important things were still there." None of the staff, foreign or Zaïroïs, had been killed directly by soldiers on either side, although old Basi Senoco, who had worked for the Harts for fifteen years, had died of a simple infection during the uprising. Because the medical dispensary had been plundered, he was unable to obtain the antibiotics that could have saved his life.

All the okapi at the station had survived, despite fears that the army would kill them for food. Jean Nlamba had convinced both the Zaire army and the rebels to leave the okapi alone and allow the local staff to continue to care for them. When things settled down, the new government appointed Jean acting conservator of the Okapi Forest Reserve. The okapi I'd treated in Epulu has grown big and healthy.

The jungle camps where the Harts conducted field research were so far from the road that no rebel or army soldier had the time or interest to venture in that direction. When John and Terry returned to their *parcelle* in Epulu, they found that at least their extensive library and collection of botanical specimens were not damaged. In addition, the staff had gathered the Harts' most valuable possessions and buried them in a footlocker. When the Zairian army arrived in Epulu, local "informants" relayed the information about the buried treasure. Since this was an easy trip for the marauding army, involving no jungle terrain, the treasure chest was dug up almost immediately. Lo and behold, the Harts' most valuable possessions turned out to be notebooks filled with years and years of research data. Needless to say, the soldiers were dismayed, but they left the notes for the staff to bury again.

Garamba's remoteness from the original uprising and its well-maintained airstrip at park headquarters made it the perfect staging area for European mercenaries who had come to support President Mobutu. When Fraser first flew in from Nairobi during the middle of the rebellion, the base had been occupied by mercenaries who had brought in thousands of gallons of fuel and several months' supplies of food rations. But even the outside help could not stop Kabila's forces. Shortly after the Zairian army retreated to Garamba and the mercenaries' protection, they were all forced to abandon the park because of the advancing rebels.

We all hoped that the fuel and supplies they had left behind could be used to help restore the park, but the local people had other priorities. Before order was completely restored, villagers took what they needed. They poured out all the fuel from the fifty-five-gallon drums and absconded with the precious empty barrels to store water for their huts.

Despite the occupation by mercenaries at the base camp at Garamba, and some poaching during the interim period, the white rhinos, hippos, elephants, and buffalo seemed to be thriving. In fact, three more rhino calves were born this past year. As it happens, a bigger threat to the future of the park comes from Switzerland. Kes and Fraser have been terminated because the World Wildlife Fund, their employer, has a policy stating no one can work on a project for more than ten years. They are now struggling to find funding so they can stay and continue their amazing work.

What impresses me the most is how my friends, John and Terese, Kes and Fraser, Karl and Rosie, all so different in nature and background, have one trait in common—perseverance. None have been dissuaded from continuing the research and conservation work they have dedicated their lives to. All of my friends—my extended family—in what is now called the Democratic Republic of the Congo have returned to their homes. The houses and huts have been emptied of beloved objects, but their inhabitants are back at work. They refuse to give up.

Bolivia—
Back in the Land of
Butch and Sundance

Political Life in Bolivia is much the same as previous years. Ironically, one of the last generals of the military dictatorship that governed the country twenty years ago was recently elected president. The Bolivian public has either a short memory or a great gift for forgiveness. We'll see where this president leads them.

Rob and Lil have returned to England to write up the results of their peccary and spider monkey research for their Ph.D.'s. When they return to Bolivia next year, Lil will be only the third or fourth Bolivian ever to receive a doctoral degree in ecology. Rob almost became the first British man to become pregnant in Bolivia, but it turned out to be a huge bot larva wiggling under the skin of his normally lean abdomen.

Our work with the peccaries has provided many insights into the infectious diseases that occur in their populations and has given us a better handle on their natural reproductive capabilities. The research camp at Lago Caiman, thanks to Rob and Lil's hard work and commitment, will continue as an important site for studies that examine the dynamics of tropical forest and wildlife and also for training Bolivian students to assume the role of managing and protecting their country's natural heritage.

Andrew's years of studying peccaries, deer, tapirs, and other wildlife in Bolivia made him invaluable to the environmental planners in Bolivia. His dedicated efforts have recently led to the establishment of a new national park in the southern dry Chaco region of the Santa Cruz Department, to be managed by the indigenous Indians living around its borders. Combined with the adjacent protected areas in Paraguay and Argentina, this newly created reserve helps to form the largest protected natural area in South America. Andrew was recently appointed to head WCS's Latin America programs and is now using his skills in biology and with people to help guide our projects on the entire continent.

Cameroon—
Two Steps Forward,
One Step Back

Before leaving Cameroon, Buddy and Maureen continued the struggle to develop protection strategies and research efforts for the northern part of Korup National Park. The park project did not evolve as well as we had hoped because of the political conflicts that often occur when too many organizations with different agendas try to solve one problem together. We recognized the difficulties going into the project and worked hard not to let the differences among the organizations get in the way of accomplishing the basics. Most of us in the field are driven to make the most impact with the little we have to work with. Thus, political infighting can be particularly frustrating. However, despite the lack of cooperation, Buddy, Maureen, and the team of Cameroonians did accomplish a hell of a lot at Korup. Unfortunately, the villagers living in the park accomplished a great deal also: over the last few years they have hunted out most of the mammals.

The results of our radio-tracking studies revealed for the first time the true land requirements of the endangered forest elephant: Each animal uses about two hundred square miles of jungle. We tracked the radio-collared elephants to a rich forested area outside of the park. Working closely with local Cameroonians and government officials, WCS has now been able to establish the new

Banyang-Mbo Forest Reserve. The area was chosen not from studying a map, but by looking at the forest that elephants were using heavily and people were not. People living near the reserve helped develop the management plan, integrating the needs of surrounding villagers and the objectives of wildlife conservation. While this project has been more successful, overexploitation is still a real threat. The next few years will reveal whether progress in protecting wildlife is truly achieved there.

Peru—
On a Wing and a Prayer

Ecotourism is booming in the Amazon forests of Peru, Brazil, Bolivia, and Ecuador. Is it good or bad? Like most things in life, it can be both, depending on how it's managed. One thing is certain, we have to keep trying innovative approaches to advance conservation efforts worldwide.

On the macaw project, our self-evaluation led to improvements in how the facility was managed and maintained. These new procedures will help protect the local wildlife from any potential adverse effects of tourists, students, and even visiting researchers.

The young macaws I examined have all grown up and flown away. The team in residence at the lodge, including Alvarro, the regular staff, and new students, have continued to learn about wild macaws, which in turn helps them successfully raise additional chicks at the lodge. I still get e-mails from them with questions and requests for scientific literature to help them design new research projects.

On the coast, Patricia has negotiated an agreement with the Peruvian government to allow WCS to assume the management of the reserve at Punta San Juan. The guano market no longer generates enough revenue of the reserve to maintain the basic infrastructure of the reserve. Since we do not need to make a profit, we are willing to maintain the facilities in exchange for the protection of the wildlife that live in the reserve. With Patricia's continued help, we will be able to monitor the health of the fur seal and sea lion populations there and possibly elsewhere in Peru.

The 1997–1998 El Niño had disastrous effects on coastal Peru. The absence of fish, a result of warmer ocean temperatures, left little food for the sea lions and marine birds. The hundreds of thousands of cormorants, pelicans, and boobies that normally nest at Punta San Juan vacated the site in search of food. Penguin nest burrows were flooded by once-in-a-lifetime rains. Fewer fur seal pups were born, and because the mothers were so malnourished, they could not nurse, and most of the pups starved to death. A similar but more severe fate befell the sea lions. Not one sea lion pup survived this breeding season, and many of the adult females died as well.

To some degree these deaths are a natural occurrence. El Niños happen every seven or eight years. Many of the adult animals left the area in search of food. Most of the female fur seals survived and will breed next year. In past El Niños the coastal area was simultaneously overfished, which compounded the effect on wildlife. This time the damage to the animals was caused primarily by natural phenomena, although more severe than normal. No matter how creative our conservation efforts become, we still can neither control the weather nor predict the future. We won't know for a year or two how the animals will recover from this El Niño's effects. We do know that at least the mammals and birds at Punta San Juan have a safe place to return to.

Borneo—
People of the Forest

The economic crash in Southeast Asia put a damper on the efforts of government agencies to advance wildlife conservation. The droughts caused by El Niño and the resulting fires have further complicated the situation. Nonetheless, everyone I work with in Borneo has continued to give their all.

Dr. Bosi and his staff continue to rescue orangutans and other wildlife from the remaining forest patches in the state of Sabah. The wildlife department is developing new programs for other species and has already moved dozens of highly endangered Asian elephants to protected forest areas. The vets in both Indonesia and Malaysia are taking a more active role in protecting the health of wildlife in their countries. Annelisa finished her work as a part of our team and is now participating in a postdoctoral residency program at a zoo in Chicago to learn more about wildlife medicine.

Our long term study of orangutans in Indonesia and Malaysia is a paradigm for how wildlife conservation efforts can grow from simple, though challenging, beginnings to long-term partnerships. The ultimate goal of the Field Veterinary Program is to become obsolete. I hope that much of the work WCS does becomes unnecessary and our overseas counterparts develop the capabilities to do the work we do. Will we really run out of projects? I don't think so. But it's a great goal to strive for.

And Briefly in
New York

In all of the countries where I work, I'm blessed with colleagues who share my goals. Headquarters in New York is no different. Culturally it may be a slightly more intense environment than those I find in most tropical countries. But there is something to be said for the fast pace. I always have a lot of correspondence to catch up on and projects to plan. Besides the orangutans, elephants, buffalo, and peccaries, I've got other ongoing projects that need attention—flamingos in Chile and Bolivia, elephant seals, guanaco, and pampas deer in Argentina, penguins in Peru and Argentina, rhinos in the new Congo, forest elephants in the old Congo, mandrills in Gabon, and crocodiles in Belize.

I need to prepare presentations for scientific meetings, and I try to give at least a few university lectures every year. I look up at the six-foot-wide marking board in my office and see the list of projects around the world, a reminder of all the tasks I must still accomplish. Another wall has two Year at a Glance calendars. Tentative schedules are already being set.

I also have to accept the reality that conservation advances slowly. Sometimes we take two steps forward and one step back. All of our best efforts cannot prevent an El Niño.

A television reporter once asked me, "Is there really any hope for this planet?" "Absolutely," I replied.

We can't stop the world from changing, and much will be lost.

Clearly our planet will be a different place twenty years from now. But we can make a significant impact in protecting vast, wild areas if we act now rather than throwing in the towel. We still have time to make a difference.

We are inundated with news of our planet's demise, but giving in to pessimism will get us nowhere. In truth, progress is being made. I've seen it all around the world. A newly established protected area in the Brazilian Amazon is the size of the whole country of Costa Rica. Coastal wildlife reserves in Patagonia are now getting more protection than they have had in thirty years. More now than ever before, people living in cities are taking active roles in improving their urban environments, reducing their consumption of disposable products, and recycling refuse. More people are volunteering their time and contributing money to environmental organizations.

Out in the wilds I've seen the results of dedicated people pushing to make the planet a better place for all of us, plants and animals included. I know these people, and they won't give up. Their photographs are on the huge bulletin board in my office in New York. They are ordinary human beings, like you and me, who have found their own way to contribute. They also know a secret: Each one of us can make a difference.